Technological L
and the Curric

Technological Literacy and the Curriculum

Edited by

John Beynon and Hughie Mackay

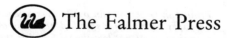 The Falmer Press

(A member of the Taylor & Francis Group)
London • New York • Philadelphia

UK   The Falmer Press, 4 John Street, London WC1N 2ET
USA   The Falmer Press, Taylor & Francis Inc., 1900 Frost Road,
Suite 101, Bristol, PA 19007

First published 1992

British Library Cataloguing in Publication Data

A catalogue record for this book is available from the British
Library

**Library of Congress Cataloging-in-Publication Data are
available on request**

ISBN 1 85000 985 6 Cased
ISBN 1 85000 986 4 Paperback

Typeset in 10/12 Garamond by
Graphicraft Typesetters Ltd, Hong Kong

Jacket design by Caroline Archer

*Printed in Great Britain by Burgess Science Press, Basingstoke
on paper which has a specified pH value on final paper
manufacture of not less than 7.5 and is therefore 'acid free'.*

Contents

Preface and Acknowledgments

This is one in a series of three books published simultaneously by Falmer Press, one edited by Mackay, Young and Beynon, and the other two by Beynon and Mackay. Each addresses the question: 'Of what should technological literacy consist?' Our view of technological literacy is very different from a narrow, skills-based, technical perspective. We see the cultural and social as central to the technology curriculum, not marginal. This book and its companions, taken together, push forward and explore the possibilities of a new, expanded, cultural definition of technological literacy, one that can inform National Curriculum Technology and IT across the curriculum.

In this enterprise our greatest debt is to Michael Young of the London University Institute of Education and our co-editor in the opening volume, *Understanding Technology in Education* [1991]. For him technology is, above all, a *cultural* matter not only because it is tied up with questions of rights and democracy, but also because it is 'the most human of phenomena and is intimately involved in all spheres of social life'. The problem is that technology, for all sorts of reasons to do with how both technology and the curriculum have been historically conceived and defined, is not usually treated as cultural,

> although Technology is no longer only associated with specialist engineering it is far less clear what a broad notion of Technological Literacy might mean. [Michael Young in Understanding Technology in Education, p. 236]

The advent of the National Curriculum allows for the first time the opportunity for a systematic understanding of technology's significance in our lives. The danger is that, separated from the social sciences and humanities, technology is reduced to no more than a combination of artefacts and specialized knowledge:

> What will be needed will be knowledge about how technological choices are enmeshed organisational, economic and political choices

... a concept of Technology as a social phenomenon ... we have to find ways of making explicit how different purposes are involved in its design, its implementation and its use, and how at each stage there are potential choices and decisions to be made. This means a technologically literate population and an increasingly wide debate about the content and meaning of Technological Literacy. [Michael Young in Understanding Technology in Education, p. 243]

It is our hope that this book and its companion volumes will contribute towards these debates. We also extend our debt to Malcolm Clarkson (Managing Director) and Carol Saumarez (Editor) of the Falmer Press for their patience and unfailing courtesy; to Routledge and Kegan Paul and to Michael Apple for permission to reprint Chapter VII of *Teachers And Texts: a Political Economy of Class and Gender Relations in Education* (1986); all of our contributors who stuck with us through what turned out to be a protracted project; to Steve Lee of the Polytechnic of Wales' Learning Resources Centre for his help with bibliographical matters; to Joyce Fox, whose word-processing skills and good humour even when under pressure ensured that the final stages of manuscript preparation were relatively trouble-free; and last, but not least, to our respective partners and families for their immense forbearance.

John Beynon and Hughie Mackay
The Polytechnic of Wales

Chapter 1

Introduction: Learning to Read Technology

John Beynon

Introduction

In *Understanding Technology in Education*, a companion volume to this (Falmer Press, 1991), we brought together a range of important and provocative statements on technology which, taken together, constitute a 'tool-kit' to help take apart and thereby understand technology in ways relevant to teachers (and, through them, to their pupils). The benefits of this analytical interrogation of something which, on the surface at least, seems so solid and indisputably 'given' would be — we hoped — not only intellectual and personal, but pragmatic at a time when teachers were in the early stages of putting the National Curriculum into operation. This second collection continues that enterprise by providing additional tools for the kit, tools which are more directly educationally oriented. The aim is, unashamedly, to 'educationalize' an educational technology which has hitherto, I maintain, been predominantly concerned with technology rather than with education. The tone for the whole project is set by the papers in this volume by the distinguished American sociologist Michael Apple who argues that we must treat technology as a 'text' to be 'read'. But first we must learn how to 'read' technology. Hence the usefulness, I hope, of the tool-kit mentioned above.

There are at least two reasons for us editing these books at this time. The first is that what is proposed as the Technology National Curriculum is, in many ways, radical and progressive (but not in all ways, as the essays by Barnett, Capel and Medway make clear). It has been wedded to Design and is to take place across the curriculum, with the additional brief that social aspects be given a prominent role. We comment in our introductory paper to *Understanding Technology in Education* that this opens up tremendous innovative possibilities for teachers:

> Going are the days of Information Technology being a part of the mathematics or business studies departments; of traditional gender divisions in technological subjects; and of Technology being a subject

only for the least able pupils. Teaching may come to be *about* Technology — about Technology in its social context as opposed to abstracted machines.

We wish to inform that 'aboutness' given that computers-across-the-National Curriculum certainly does not mean that all teachers are suddenly required to engage in teaching basic keyboard skills. What it could result in is the generating of a coherent series of subject-led 'shafts of light' on the whole issue of IT/Education, with technological literacy as the key unifying concept, as well as a more subject-sensitive and varied use of computers as teaching and learning tools across the full span of the National Curriculum.

A second reason for producing this and the companion volume is that computers were introduced into schools in ill-considered haste and with little planning and little debate (Beynon and Mackay, 1989). As it stands the educational rationale is largely being produced after the event! We wished to contribute to the debate by advocating a revitalized and much-widened 'cultural' definition of technological literacy. Our intention in the companion book is to challenge dominant assumptions and prevalent definitions of technology and to extend it to include socio-economic, political and cultural dimensions. That intention is maintained here but given a specifically educational focus and momentum.

In this opening paper I set the scene for what follows by doing three things. Firstly, I attempt to provide an overview (admittedly selective and, in place, oversimplistic) of the complex debates surrounding IT/Education. It is a literature which includes a very mixed bag of writers and constitutes a broad church of theoretical perspectives between which there is, often, little or no common ground. Indeed, as we said in our introduction to *Understanding Technology in Education*, it was this lack of common ground between what might broadly be described as the technological and social perspectives which led us to edit these books in the first place. Here I try to make some sense of the literature by identifying four different starting-points, four different discourses or 'voices', although they clearly overlap. Secondly, in the process of exploring the four voices I relate them to those in *Understanding Technology in Education*. I illustrate how some of the themes which appear there are both complemented and sharpened by reference to educational practices. I also show that to understand technology in the context of education demands not restricting oneself to the literature on educational technology (as it has been constructed and established) per se. Moreover, even within the present focus on education the lens has to be widened to include a consideration of topics as disparate as hidden debates informing the emergence of the Technology National Curriculum (Barnett's paper, for example) through to ethnographies of micro usage. Finally, I highlight the term technology literacy (in Mackay's paper) and the need, in my view, to learn to 'read' technology that takes into account social and cultural aspects. This volume and its companion publication will, I hope, result in an increased awareness of the usefulness of an essentially critical, 'cultural' definition of technological literacy and how this might (both directly and indirectly) inform teachers in their planning and implementing of Technology in the National Curriculum.

Technology: Voices and Arenas

In an earlier paper (Beynon, 1991), I attempted what turned out to be and overambitious topographical exercise, namely the mapping out of a series of 'paradigms' of technology which summarized the very different concerns of authors who, nevertheless, share a strong interest in future developments. A paradigm in Kuhn's (1970) sense is a clearly articulated and relatively coherent explanatory model, supported by an underlying body of theory. It is, perhaps, too strong a term to use in the fractured and contested world of IT/Education. To be more cautious it is best, rather, to identify distinctive ways (or 'voices') of approaching (and talking about) technology. In what follows I attempt this topographical sense-making by identifying two principal arenas of disagreement (rather than debate, since there appears to be relatively little common ground), namely:

Accolatory as opposed to Dismissive Voices
(that is, those who promote IT/Education with great, but often uncritical, zeal and those who are, conversely, rigid and dismissive).
Technological Determinists and Social Determinists
(that is, those who lean towards technological determinism as against those who adopt an equally authoritarian social determinism).

It must be said at the outset that these two arenas and the respective voices within are not unconnected. Indeed, one reflects the other: the voices of AI have much in common, translated into the context of schooling, with those of the accolatory. Similarly, the dismissive voices in education inevitably draw strongly upon the social critique. What we are dealing with then are pro- and anti-technology lobbies (to dichotomize it crudely), one operating at the pragmatist level in schools and the other at the political and philosophical outside schools.

Before turning to the four 'voices' and the ways in which they talk about technology it must be made clear that I use the umbrella term of 'IT/Education' to cover technology and education and the impact between them as it operates on a number of fronts. I do this to signal that the 'technologizing' of education cannot be reduced to one aspect (such as 'hands-on' skills or the employment of computers). It is, rather, a multi-faceted process, and IT/Education bridges debates that are currently taking place within and around both education and technology. To focus, as some writers have, on technicist aspects to the exclusion of cultural, contexual and implementational ones is not only reductionist, but also ducks the question which it seems to us must now be placed at the very head of the agenda, for both researchers and teachers, namely: 'what do we mean when we talk of Computer (or is it Technological?) Literacy?'

This book and its companions aim to stimulate ideas with that central issue held firmly in mind.

The Accolatory v. the Dismissive

The Accolatory
By this I mean an uncritical, almost evangelical advocacy based on general, unresearched assumption, an advocacy which, at its most strident, urges a lemming-like acceptance of the benefits of micros. Most papers delivered to the recent International Conferences on Technology and Education adopted this line (for example, those by Bork *et al.* in 1989). The literature of advocacy is overwhelmingly written by either technologists or the recently coverted and predominantly focuses on the particular technologies as opposed to educational processes or outcomes. The rhetoric of the principal UK journals ('*Computer and Education*', '*Educational Technology*', etc.) is an addressing of the initiated in the metalanguage of High Tech. Typical head-lines include 'Instantaneous feedback in the teaching/learning lab'; 'Computer Education: should Pascal come first?'; and 'Everyone is a programmer now'. In comparison few articles broach social issues relating to IT. The same subtext runs through the Open University course *Educational Computing* (EH221).

The claims which have been advocated for micro usage have not always been either modest or realistic. Retrospectively some sound quite absurd:

> One can predict that in a few more years millions of school children will have access to what Philip of Macedon's son Alexander enjoyed a royal prerogative: the personal services of a tutor as well-informed and responsive as Aristotle. (Suppes, 1966 cited in Open University course EH221, 1985)

> By the year 2000 the major way of learning at all levels, and in all subject areas, will be through interactive use of computers (Bork, 1979, cited by O'Shea & Self, 1983).

In general, the claims made for microcomputers in education can be summarized as follows:
They:

- teach better what is already taught;
- teach what otherwise could not be taught;

- facilitate creative interaction between student and program;
- involve users in high-level intellectual activity (for example, logical thought through problem solving);
- offer more varied or interesting presentations than conventional pedagogies or other educational technologies;
- allow pupils to work at levels appropriate to their (varying) ability and understanding;
- facilitate a variety of functions across age and ability ranges.

Undoubtedly the most strident indirect advocacy of IT/Education is that by Stonier and Conlin (1985), who regard microcomputers as nothing less than an evolutionary bench-mark in human history, namely the emergence of 'Homo Sapiens Cerebus', beings whose brain powers have been increased by computers and are accessed to incredible amounts of 'instant information'. They argue that computers will

> help solve problems by extending our brain power outside our heads and they will also vastly improve the information handling processes going on inside.

Heady stuff! Moreover,

> new behavioural patterns rather than new anatomical features [will] set the stage for a revolution as profound as the hominid revolution of half a dozen, or so, million years ago . . . .

In similar vein, Golden (1985) sees technology leading to the emergence of a new generation of super-intelligent, super-informed 'micro kids', whilst Evans (1979) predicts that it will transform the teaching and learning processes by rendering books redundant. For Dede (1985) its emergence is every bit as profound as the advent of the printing press, a view shared by some literacy theorists. Computer advocates argue that we are irreversibly heading towards what Dordick (1986) has aptly termed the 'Wired Society' in which 'a network of electronic highways ... allow instant access to, and communication of, information to everyone'.

Perhaps the most respected and certainly best known educationalist advocacy of computer has been that by Seymour Papert (1980). Inspired by Piagetian developmental psychology, Papert argues that his programming language LOGO allows independent learning and the development of general problem-solving skills, creativity and self-confidence. Others have subsequently pointed to its capacity to engender cooperative learning. LOGO, it is claimed, is a language with no thresholds and no ceilings, used by 4-year-old pupils and to teach physics to MIT undergraduates alike. Papert's principal aim is to put pupils in control of their own learning and he claims that LOGO, and Turtle Geometry in particular, allows them to test their theories about both the physical and the abstract. It employs fantasy, curiosity and challenge as motivating factors, and enables participants to engage in educationally useful tasks hitherto beyond possibility for all but the most able, articulate and literate. It highlights understanding problems before working them out; thinking through solutions; and pupil programming to test their speculations. There has, however, been little research into LOGO in practice, leaving most of Papert's challenging claims unsubstantiated. Pea's (1987) conclusion to his discussion of LOGO is, for example, hardly enthusiastic, He comments that

> these studies do raise serious doubts about the sweeping claims for
> the cognitive benefits of learning to program, particularly in LOGO.

A central element of Papert's philosophy, the autonomy of the pupil over the learning process, is to a significant extent only possible with the provision of a micro per pupil, the scenario Papert had in mind at the design stage. Resource reality has, in fact, been rather different: there is an average of approximately fourteen microcomputers per secondary school (one per sixty pupils) and two per primary school (one per hundred pupils) in the UK at present.

It is a relief to see a more restrained and carefully considered advocacy at last beginning to emerge both in the UK and internationally (see Vitale, 1987, for a summary) concerning the use of microcomputers across the curriculum. Two recent publications in the UK well illustrate this, namely the statement by the National Association for the Teaching of English (NATE, 1988) on using computers; and essays by Ennals (on computing in the humanities), Adman (history), Corns and Smith (literature teaching), Pearce (music), and Dyer, Howard and Richards (art/design) deserve to be noted (all in the book edited by Rahtz, 1987). They each point to the real possibilities of microcomputers as a useful pedagogical tool that can enrich the curriculum whilst, at the same time, safeguarding more traditional subject values and identities. The tone of these articles is exemplified by Ennals who argues that

> there is a need to attract the energies and enthusiasms of humanities
> specialisms who have so far resisted the attractions of the computer
> and who have remained faithful to the principles of their specialisms
> . . . computers could offer a whole new lease of life for humanities
> specialists. If left in the hands of scientists they could contribute to
> the ending of Humanity as we know it.

The Dismissive
There is an irony in the fact that critics of microcomputers in classrooms are frequently as sweeping and extravagant in their criticism as are proponents in their advocacy! Both parties consistently fail to acknowledge the absence of hard evidence in terms of well-conducted research. Moreover, they share a

tendency to make huge suppositions based on precious little real data. As a result a dangerous circularity is set in motion in that critics quote other critics, advocates fellow advocates, with little chance of even minimal dialogue between the two.

One of the most comprehensive critiques of microcomputers in education in the UK is one of the earliest and is by Baker (1983; 1985), who raises a number of provocative allegations:

1 *The marginalization of teachers*
    Teachers have little influence when decisions about software design are taken and are rarely involved in field testing. They have neither been able to state the problems nor suggest solutions, a process which has been left to software experts whose understanding of educational issues is generally inadequate. Indeed, teachers are being seduced into inappropriate practices by little more than clever programming, attractive graphics and visual gimmicks.

2 *IT as an intrusion into education*
    Computers are an intrusion into the curriculum, both insensitive to the agreed aims of a liberal education and opposed to proven practices and, in secondary schools, subject values (see Tomlinson and Quinton, 1986). Educational progress is not an inevitable consequence of technological advances, as is often the case presented; on the contrary, microcomputing can disrupt teachers' established classroom practices.

3 *Format*
    The basic games format still persists and is preventing the emergence of a more flexible, educationally challenging deployment of the micro. Amusement and attractiveness are taken-for-granted ends in themselves, and the mystique still surrounding computers can blind some teachers to their own skills. Is software really the springboard to learning that the manufacturers claim, given that large numbers of programs are basically banal, allowing only stereotyped feedback? Too often they reduce tasks to sequential structures which result, in Baker's words, to 'an emaciation of typical teacher-pupil learning situations'. Too often software narrowly prescribes what is to be learnt, controls levels, provides rigid feedback, and judges correctness in a narrow and mechanistic way, whereas a teacher can react to the individual needs of pupils with regard to ability, attitudes, sex, cognitive development, cognitive style, motivation and mood.

4 *Reification of computer*
    Baker argues that there is a distinct danger of (some) pupils reifying the computer into a 'superbrain'. The computer as a source of 'knowledge' could thus attain an unjustified centrality in the curriculum. Furthermore, the microcomputer can isolate individuals and render students passive and controlled rather than support them as initiators. Indeed, he argues that the general state of software still dictates that

responses be predictable, sequential and logical, rather than divergent, idiosyncratic and exploratory.

Advocates point to 'discovery learning' through sophisticated databases and simulated experiments hard to reproduce in the laboratory and the field. Their picture is of enthusiastic pupils actively interacting and controlling the speed and level of their responses. Baker contests this and argues that we do not yet know what kinds (and quality) of interaction actually take place. Computers could so easily produce quiet, dependent, 'hooked on machines' (Turkle, 1984) pupils and, indeed, set back the beneficial deployment of a far wider range of linked, multi-media technologies in classrooms.

5 *Unintended consequences*
Baker reports that in micro usage in a Welsh-speaking school only academic pupils were granted access. There is evidence that more boys than girls use micros, in both the secondary and primary sectors, along with more male teachers. Baker's implication is not only that micro technology may well be reinforcing gender and ability differences, but that software content excludes the concerns of 'minority' cultures and languages.

Just as Baker has raised provocative criticisms unsubstantiated by data, so does Karger (1988), but from a North American standpoint. He makes the following points:

(i) Interaction between children and computers is overwhelmingly a mechanistic one in spite of increasingly sophisticated hardware and varied, 'user-friendly' software. An illusion of warmth and concern is created but this is no substitute for genuine cognitive and emotional feedback. He argues that 'for many young children, confused about the line between fantasy and reality, this misrepresentation only obfuscates what is real and true'.

(ii) Computers shift the arrangement of time by their rapid task performance. Brod's (1984) study alleged that time accelerated for video game players with the result that their patience was easily exhausted. Karger argues that, in a developmental sense, young people need to suppress the desire for instant gratification because

> while the intensity of the electronics provides constant stimulation at an almost relentless cadence, it also helps shorten the already brief attention span of children. As the sensory threshold for stimulation increases, every day life events become more monotonous.

(iii) Child-computer encounters may become 'solitary endeavours whilst opportunities for socialising with others are curtailed'. Karger refers to the study by the Schneiders (1984) which suggested that socially inept children may actually come to enjoy the lack of interpersonal complications offered by the computer. For Karger there is even a risk of an escape *into* a machine that then becomes more human-like. Indeed, at its worst the computer can hinder the social skills development of young children, especially the shy and introverted, who may even personalize their relationship with the machine. Karger quotes writers who have voiced similar disquiet, namely that computers can lead to social isolation, even psychosis, in young children (Abt, 1980), so that some may grow up choosing to interact with machines rather than people (Heller and Martin, 1982). The result is that excessive access to micros could lead to immediate and long-term problems in social interaction (Barnes and Hill, 1983). Each assertion points to our huge ignorance of either the positive or negative effects of placing the very young in contact with computers.

(iv) Karger is particularly critical of the way in which parents have pushed them in front of their children, so that they may be 'creating a child who experiences the world not through their own eyes, but through the eyes of a software programme designed by adults'. He talks of the 'commodification of play', by which he means the transformation of unstructured play (as a learning activity in both social and cognitive terms) into producer-related activities.

(v)   Another concern is that excessive exposure to computers will provide the young with an overtly technocratic perspective on life, with information reified in importance. Postman (1984), in asking 'Information for what and whom?', makes the same point in his declaration that children are in danger of becoming 'information junkies who believe that access to informational is an end in itself'. For Postman, indeed, the computer has become 'a distracting technology' because it encourages the mistaken belief that lack of information is a problem, one which only the machine can remedy. Furthermore, Karger attacks the myth that information is value-free, a myth which presupposes that computers merely give 'pure' information rather than information heavily impregnated by values and beliefs. These are, indeed, part and parcel of the 'technocratic mentality' Karger seeks to dispel.

(vi) Another aspect of this he terms 'mind pacification', in which the computer begins to be viewed as an undisputed source of authority. In an earlier article (Seltzer and Karger, 1974) Karger went as far as to argue that computerized education operates to prevent genuine learning in that it provides 'no context in which ideas can be conceptualised and tested and talked about'.

Or, as Apple (1987) would have it, they will be locked into the technical aspects rather than exploring the social and ethical implications. The computer curriculum must confront the moral and social issues occasioned by the advent of new technology, a view with which I (and all the authors in his volume) wholeheartedly agree.

In conclusion, Karger acknowledges the potential of computers to alter social relationships and their power to shape social consciousness. But, he concludes in

> the frenzied rush to introduce children to computer technology the question of 'Why?' is often overlooked. Even though we have unquestionably entered the Computer Age, is it desirable to introduce young children to computers?

Baker and Karger may, at first, appear to be grossly overstating the case and overtly dismissive and uncompromising, but they do raise important issues that deserve to be treated seriously and taken further. In recent years in the UK a steady flow of critical statements has emerged mostly based upon teacher-researchers' experiences of using computers: many of the most insightful appear in the volume edited by Garland (1982), especially the contributions by Davies, Golby, Lane and Walton. Further probing assessments (notably by Larsen and Hebenstreet) are included in Blagovest and Stenchev (1986), and Giannelli (1985) focuses on teacher powerlessness in the formulation and implementation of IT/Education policies. Other questioning voices are those of Walker (1982), Howe (1983), and Dede (1985). Many build on the 'uses and abuses' approach toward IT/Education adopted by Obrist (1983) when evaluating computers in the primary sector, and by Morrison (1989) in the Secondary School.

In summary, although the accolatory and dismissive critics undoubtedly raise important issues which should inform research, they too readily adopt a factual tone and are no substitute for a wealth of data collected on a broad front across all aspects of IT/Education.

Technological Determinists and the Social Critique

Technological Determinists

The dominant discourse to date in IT/Education debates has been a derivative of the cognitive psychology/Artificial Intelligence one, with an emphasis upon AI development and cognitive psychology. Many, but not all, workers in this field can be described as technological determinists and focus upon the relationships between AI and development issues and how these might inform and generate theories of cognitive development. They have constructed an interdisciplinary framework of computational and developmental research, one that points to a new and revitalized developmental cognitive science.

Only then, it is argued, will the full instructional potential of IT/Education be realized in terms of more effective teaching and learning. Amongst the major questions are:

- what is the contribution of new computational models of the learning process to education?
- more specifically, how can insights that arise from AI help define new computer-based environments for learning?
- how might new technology restructure and enhance the power of education?

At the heart of the discussion of one school of AI is the computational metaphor of the human brain; the strengths and shortcomings of computational models of learning; and the constructing of models of mental processes. The AI community, for example, has debated at length in the past whether representatives which underline human knowledge should be considered 'imperatively' (that is, primarily databases of information, together with logical rules for sorting, ordering therein). A good example of the scope of the CP/AI paradigm is the collection of papers brought together by Julie Rutkowska and Charles Crook (1987). It is in three sections.

The first part focuses upon computers as practical tools and how they are restructuring children's experience of both education and leisure. It includes research into children's attitudes towards computer; computers' influence on social interaction and communication; and their potential to extend learning environments for the handicapped.

The second part explores the application of AI so that computers may go some way to perform our naturally intelligent abilities like perceiving, reasoning and remembering.

The third part explores the influence of computers on cognitive psychology and how this may be extended to developmental cognition.

In summary the CP/AI model is, the authors claim, promoting important conceptual advances on three fronts:

- the way in which computational metaphors are contributing to the advance of theory in cognitive development (including ongoing debates between Piaget and Vygotsky — derived theses);
- the way in which the achievements of AI are defining exciting new computer environments to foster intellectual development;
- the way in which technology is encountered in everyday life and its influence on young people's psychological development and subjectivity.

One has only to flick through the annual volumes of papers of the International Conferences on Technology and Education (for example, 1988) to appreciate the dominance of the CP/AI paradigm, one which too readily focuses on the technological and cognitive at the expense of the social and cultural. However, like all paradigms (Ball, 1982) it is far from unified, and certainly some workers are beginning to research the pupil/cultural end of the Machine/Technology-Pupil/Cognition continuum (witness Hughes *et al.*, 1987) and even attempt to contextualize and define a 'social context' for IT/Education within classrooms (Crook, 1989; Chandra *et al.*, 1988).

The CP/AI movement is fuelled by simplistic approaches both to human thought and culture and rips technology from its social context. It stands accused of fostering a technological determinism that equates technology with being inevitable, beneficial and autonomous, somehow existing 'outside' its society. As such we can easily accept that we have no way of influencing either it or the way in which technical change fuels social change. As Lyon points out in *Understanding Technology in Education*, technological determinism (that is, that new technology is inevitable and inevitably good for you) is as pernicious as the counter view of social determinism (that new technology is necessarily aggressive and exploitative). In our opening chapter in *Understanding Technology In Education* we wrote:

> Technological determinism diverts attention from such questions as the relationship of technology to human need. Implicit in technological determinism is that there is no choice about the technology we have.

However, in numerous publications the CP/AI thesis has been directly employed to advocate the use of microcomputers in classrooms. Some educationalists and teachers have been converted into computer zealots, rarely standing back to question the long-term wisdom of what they are doing and locked inside what has been aptly termed 'Technoromancy', or 'the inclination of those involved in New Technology to see into the future with blinkers which exclude both those aspects of Education which are successful without microcomputers and also the potential pitfalls of New Technology' (Beveridge, 1987). Even an apparently critical voice such as Heaford (1983), who challenges many current ideas in educational technology and calls for the development of computer formats which genuinely cater for the idiosyncratic capabilities of learners and student access to a genuine 'freedom of learning' experience, is trapped inside the CP/AI paradigm. One has to move far outside education to figures such as Athanasiou (1985) to find a genuinely alternative voice. He attacks what he regards as AI's imperialism in seeking 'to expand the kingdom of the machine . . . the rationalisation of our sloppy universe into piles of little microworlds amenable to knowledge-based computerisation'. He traces AI's long-term quest for formal theories of intelligence and how these, in turn, lend themselves to codification as computer programs. The outcome has been that information processing has assumed an unjustified prominence. It is, however, in his view 'Tayloristic' in its bedrock belief that human skill can be 'extracted by knowledge engineers and codified into rules and heuristics, and immortalised on magnetic discs...'. However, Athanasiou himself might justifiably be accused of 'superheated rhetoric' when he dismisses the whole of AI as nothing more than 'the dangerous fantasy of powerful men overcome by their own mythologies, mythologies which flourish in the superheated rhetoric of the AI culture'. In the process of accusing AI of producing over-designed and unreliable technologies, he makes a more important point; in order to counter the way AI is shrouded in myth and ideology, he calls for a new and critical 'Politics of Technology'. At its most ambitious AI seeks to create a 'superbrain', one capable of intelligent response and decision-making. Many regard this as an insult to human dignity, wisdom and uniqueness. Athanasiou asks:

> What should be automated or rather, who should decide? This is not a question about technology, but about political power.... We must develop a more coherent and nuanced Politics of Technology. This Politics must be based not on dreams of class reconciliation, but rather on a recognition of the degree to which social antagonisms are mediated by technology.

AI's claims are yet to be matched by real achievements and its critics naturally play upon the weaknesses rather than the strengths. Many restate the Dreyfus thesis of the 1970s, namely that human intelligence is unique and cannot be recaptured. This is the line taken by Albury and Schwartz (1982) for whom a computer is

> nothing more than a glorified adding machine. It can store numerically coded data internally. It can do arithmetic rapidly according to a pre-programmed sequence of instructions. And it can branch on zero. But that is all it can do!

But perhaps the most telling criticisms of AI have, ironically, come from within the AI community itself, notably those working on the reproduction of natural language. For the philosopher John Searle (1985) machines will never have 'intelligence', but — at best — only simulate it. Moreover, Terry Winograd (1985) argues that responsibility and accountability have too readily been brushed aside by AI scientists. Furthermore, reality has turned out to be far more complex and elusive than their vision, so that Turing's 1940s prediction of computers with human cognitive capacities by AD 2000 now reads like science fiction. Meanwhile, connectionism — the study of simulated neural networks — is again strengthening the belief that intelligence cannot simply be programmed, but must be grown. On this score alone, in spite of the rhetoric, progress is slow, although public expectation, fuelled by media fantasies, runs ahead of actual achievement.

Books about educational technology which apply the AI stance are thick on the ground, both in the USA and the UK. Examples include White (1983), which investigates the nature of learning and the 'psychology of electronic learning'. The O'Shea and Self (1983) volume also considers the educational application of computers from the standpoint of AI which is defined as the science 'of developing computers to carry out functions associated with human intelligence'. Computers, they argue, properly used, will 'enhance the educational process and equip each learner with an exciting medium for problem-solving and individual tuition'. A major contemporary UK application to education of CP/AI is the work of the London Mental Models Group (1988), although it must be stressed that they also contain a broad spectrum of researchers, not all of whom can be so categorized. The Mental Models Group addresses two main questions, namely:

- in what ways can interaction with tools containing representations of a domain facilitate learning of that domain?
- are learners helped by representing and exploring the consequences of their own mental models of a domain?

The project is to study pupils from about 10 to 16 years and raise issues concerning:

- the nature and functions of mental models;
- the distinction between tools which represent a domain and ones which allow learners to express their representations of a domain;
- a clarification of the nature of tools required for different domains.

The main emphasis of this research is clearly upon the 'mental model' which, whilst it need not be a precise replica of the phenomena to be understood, must be functional; must provide some sort of explanation; and must facilitate predictions. This is challenging and clearly pedagogically-pertinent research, but it is clear that its concerns differ greatly from those of other parties which are outlined in this paper and who also have a heavy investment in IT/Education.

Social Determinists

The sociology of technology has determinedly attempted to counter technological determinism as many of the papers in one of the companion publications, *Understanding Technology in Education*, clearly show. Much of the impetus for this approach arises from the work of the American David Noble (for example, 1977) and the 'culturalist' critique associated with Raymond Williams (1974). For Noble, technology is part of the mental machinery of dominance, with a massive potential to lock masses of people into alienating ways of life. Far from being an innocent, neutral force, it is a political weapon shaped by dominant groups for their own ends, namely to support the workings of capital. The fact that we do not recognize technology as such, but rather as progress, is addressed by Albury and Schwartz (1982):

Because Science and Technology were mythologised by the Victorians as intrinsically progressive we have been accultured into not interrogating them as to their moral justification and actual social usefulness.

This interrogation I regard as central to technological literacy.

Behind this facade, the computer revolution is, in reality, Capital renewing and reinvigorating itself, so as to

ensure its continued domination over social and economic developments during a period of crisis and change. The myth of technological progress serves to disguise the class interest at work behind the introduction of these machines. We live with the illusion that Science and Technology happens by itself: it is not true (Albury and Schwartz in *Partial Progress*, 1982).

Two influential writers in the UK, Webster and Robins (1986; 1989), also question whether technology necessarily equates with progress: they argue that 'silicon utopianism', embedded in glitzy futurology, is the central mechanism in the switch from one mode of Capital accumulation in the West (namely Fordism to another (neo-Fordism). This is accompanied by a transformation of the social relations necessary to sustain and reproduce this. The move is from a monopolistic regime of mass production to one in which the accent is on flexibility of production, Capital investment, and disinvestment of consumer markets, production and labour practices. The essay by Murray in the companion volume *Understanding Technology in Education* represents an extensive platform of work exploring this shift (for example, by David Harvey, Christel Lane, Eileen Giles and Ken Starkey). Webster and Robins advance a Luddite analysis of technology, arguing that Luddism was a resistance not to machines but to the social relations represented by them. It can, therefore, constitute a way of viewing technologies which, because they are presented as mere matters of technical change, appear unstoppable and unobjectionable. A Luddite analysis, however, refuses to extract specific technologies from their social relations and insists that they be regarded as the outcomes of values and choices. Technologies are explained, therefore, not in terms of machines per se, but as expressions of social relations, processes and values. They do no start their analysis with technology and then ask what will be the results, but commence with an examination of the social relations within which individual technologies have and are being developed. Indeed, for Webster and Robins the new communications and information technology approximates to an electronic version of Jeremy Bentham's Panopticon, upon which design Victorian prisons and penal workhouses were modelled so as to maximize the surveillance and control of inmates. All this clearly has very profound implications for how technology is to be handled in the National Curriculum. Indeed, employers are increasingly demanding an 'understanding' of technology and calling for a wide range of transferable, flexible skills rather than narrow technological ones.

Webster and Robins (an extract from whose work is included in *Understanding Technology in Education*) see computer literacy as a means of inculcating people into 'passive flexibility', a key element in the vocationalizing of education. (There is a parallel: early print literacy a century ago was predicated on the principle on preparing a workforce which was increasingly required to read simple instructions and machine guides. See Shayer, 1972.)

Their Luddite analysis, whilst being stimulating and provocative, can alternatively be seen as ideologically rigid and overtly rejectionist of the possibilities of technology. This is what Young and Capel (1987) argue when they restate the importance of Noble's (1984) work on the social choices behind machine tool design and the relevance of such an analysis to IT/Education. For them technology, properly employed, can be a liberatory force and they are critical of Webster and Robins's case that it is a direct attack on education. They comment that the thesis

> heaps all current social and educational ills on to Capitalism ... IT developments across the curriculum have to be seen not just as an example of the successful duping of teachers but as, in part, a progressive development which can lead to the breaking down of barriers between academic disciplines and vocationally related courses and to the possibilities of a broader understanding of the significance of technological change for the majority who are *not* going to be IT specialists.

Some writers argue that 'male' technology controls and imprisons women most of all. For example, Cockburn's (1985) influential work takes as its starting point the idea, attributed to Simone de Beauvoir, that technology is an inspired act of transcendence by men. Cockburn views it as irreversibly masculine and to dismantle gender would mean dismantling it since it equates with production and power as the principal devices whereby men keep women in their place. She argues that gender is inextricably entwined with technology:

> It is there, in partnership with class, behind fast cars and fast breeders, behind nuclear war heads and their phallic delivery systems....
> It is often proposed that Technology today, like Frankenstein's monster, is 'out of control': it is not Technology that is out of control, but Capitalism and Men.

She documents how, over the past five centuries, access to technological competence has been a major factor in sex-segregation as women have been actively excluded from technological knowledge, acted upon by technology and not interactive with it. What is particularly disturbing is that in the second half of the twentieth century 'liberated' women's relationship with technology has not changed. They are

> to be found in great numbers operating machinery ... but continue to be rarities in those occupations that involve knowing about what goes on inside the machine.... Women may push the buttons but they may not meddle with the works.

One of the most powerful calls for a social analysis of technology, one that focuses upon the interplay between the social shaping and its shaping of society, is that by Lyon (1988), a paper by whom appears in *Understanding Technology in Education*. He argues that since technical development and innovations are never self-explanatory they have to be placed in a social, cultural context in order to be understood. He comments that

> just as social factors helped to fashion the kinds of technologies now available — and even their 'convergence' — so their impacts may also be understood in terms of those factors. This calls in question the notion that new technologies *themselves* being about new kinds of social relationships or a whole new 'information society' of a particular sort. Without doubt, social change is related to technological innovation. But the eventual outcomes are the result not of mere 'technological impacts' but of a subtle and complex interplay between Technology and Society.

To understand technology demands an ability to 'read' this interplay. Later Lyon highlights the need also to raise ethical issues concerning technology, issues which are generally granted low priority and hidden from view:

> Within today's political climate, overshadowed as it is by technology policy (whether to remain economically competitive or militarily secure), strenuous attempts are made to co-opt social science for technological ends.... To question social goals, to explore the possibilities for emancipatory, appropriate Technology, to examine the ethics or cultural dimensions of New Technology, these are not perceived to be priorities.... Social analysis has unavoidable moral dimensions, and is concerned in profound ways with the 'human condition'. This is why issues of the magnitude of the social shaping and social consequences of Information Technology may not be siphoned into mere social engineering.

The possibility of an 'emancipatory, appropriate technology' has been taken up and advanced in the UK by the socially useful production (SUP) debate, contributors to which argue that we should collectively produce those things that we need, rather than produce commodities and services for profit. Emphasis upon the latter has resulted in a grotesque situation in Britain in which we have a surplus of nuclear weapons but a shortage of dialysis machines. The SUP debate demands that we gain personal and collective power over our lives, and that includes technology, which must be appropriated for public and community usage rather than in the service of efficiency and profit. It attacks what Winner (1986) terms 'mythinformation' concerning technology, the uncritical advocacy that computers will necessarily result in a better, fairer world.

Perhaps the social critique of technology, certainly in regard to education, is best articulated by the American sociologist Michael Apple (1988). At the centre of his work is an enduring tenet, namely the necessity to fight for and maintain a truly democratic educational system. When it comes to debating the place of new technology in education Apple warns against the ever-present inclination to decontextualize education from wider social needs. Decision-making in education is never just 'educational' since, by definition, it involves the whole 'social and ethical responsiveness of our institutions to the majority of our future citizens'. Education must constantly protect and safeguard schools by ensuring that new technology is there for 'politically, economically and educationally-wise reasons, not because powerful groups may be re-defining our educational goals in their own image'. In the past they have too readily allowed themselves to be inveigled into a premature acceptance of 'innovations' before they have had the opportunity to evaluate it in the light of the 'ideological and ethical issues concerning what schools should be about and whose interests they should serve'. Apple's argument is that discussion about the introduction of new technology into classrooms has too often trivialized matters, focusing too narrowly on the technical, the secondary issue of what computers can or cannot do, so that questions of 'Why?' have been subsumed by questions of 'How to?'. Yet technology is, potentially, a huge transformer of the labour process of both teachers and pupils and could eventually lead to the complete restructuring of education. What, Apple asks, are computers doing both *in* and *to* our schools as they redirect them to meet the easily-termed (but ill-defined) 'needs' of business. Technology is glamorized and presented as necessarily heralding progress, but precisely which relationships are being transformed and which left the same in terms of economic and cultural inequalities? Teachers (and their pupils) need to ask searching questions about causes and effects such as: Whose idea of progress? For what? Who benefits? In order to do this they need to recognize what is happening inside and outside schools with reference to technology, but also treat it as a 'text'.

The 'technology text' is one that has been produced for consumption by parents, teachers and pupils as a slogan system to convince them to change what education is for. Indeed, Apple questions whether technology is a solution to societal divisions (as it is often claimed to be) or whether it is part of them in that its expansion could exacerbate lack of social opportunities in terms of work, class, race and gender. In his analysis, technology is at the cutting edge of a massive management offensive to transform labour and render work into routine, atomized tasks; cut costs; and increase administrative controls. In a future which, rather than becoming more egalitarian and democratic, threatens to be more authoritarian, it is the duty of educators to monitor technology and the skills taught in schools. It is their task

> neither to accept such a future labour market and labour process uncritically ... nor to have our students accept such practices uncritically. To do so is simply to allow the values of a limited but powerful segment of the population to work through us. It may be good business but I have my doubts about whether it is an ethically correct educational policy.

Ethical, political and economic questions must be placed first if teachers are not to allow schools to be downgraded into production plants for new workers. Indeed, should schools really go along with new technology if, far from benefiting all, it primarily advances those who already possess cultural and economic capital? Conversely, if schools are to be given over to its requirements is it possible for us to at least attempt to redefine it in educational term? That task is one of the principal objectives of this volume.

Apple's work is particularly relevant to the continued climate of Right Wing reformism of UK education. More and more decisions are being taken out of teachers' hands, especially in connection with the content and evaluation of the National Curriculum (see Barnett's and Medway's papers in this volume) and there is increasing state intervention (in spite of the denials!). Apple contextualizes new technology as part of this rationalization, pointing to a potentially massive deskilling and depowering of both teachers and pupils. For example, teachers are given little time to think about, evaluate or re-train for new technology and they thus depend upon pre-packaged materials with the result, argues Apple, that 'rather than the machine fitting the educational needs and visions of the teacher, students and community, all too often these needs and visions are made to fit the technology itself'. Teachers are thereby deskilled in that curriculum conception is separated from execution in the following ways:

- curriculum content is something purchased as part of what Apple terms the 'political economy of commodified culture', with the school the target market for mass-produced commodities, often of dubious educational value;
- they become isolated executors of someone else's plans, procedures and evaluative mechanisms;
- an over-reliance on purchased curriculum hardware and software can result in a diminishing of local curriculum planning and an atrophying of skills.

Morever, this 'technologization' of schools could well result in teachers' jobs being placed at risk. Given the huge pressure from industry, government, parents and the computer lobby, Apple sees a great danger that new technology will transform classrooms in a manner whereby 'a technical logic will replace critical, political and ethical understanding'. The ways in which pupils are being taught to think about new technology embody ways of thinking which are primarily technical and, therefore, reductionist. There is a danger that the new technology curriculum (even the National Curriculum!) will come increasingly to focus on 'technique' rather than on 'substance' and exclude what Apple advocates, namely 'a serious understanding of the issues surrounding the larger social effects'.

In his 1987 publication Apple links the growing use of computers in schools more directly to changes in the economy. The new IT-based industries are, he argues, characterized by proletarianization and deskilling, and there is a parallel in schools in that teachers as being deskilled whilst, at the same time, pupils are cynically being told that it is their lack of computer literacy which is responsible for their poor employment prospect. However, importantly, real curriculum developments in computing increase rather than diminish inequalities of class and gender. In a telling critique of the position, however, Young and Capel (1988) see it floundering, like the Webster and Robins thesis

> in a kind of Neo-Luddite opposition to computers: the analysis renders all IT developments as outcomes of Capitalist domination. Issues of Social Literacy do not constitute a coherent curriculum but are, rather, tacked on as 'social implications'.

Learning to Read Technology

It is important to stress that whilst Technology has entered the National Curriculum as a 'single subject', information technology is an across-the-curriculum activity:

> Given the inherently cross-curriculum nature of IT capability, it is *not* intended that IT should be regarded as another subject. On the contrary, the development of IT is best achieved through a range of curriculum activities in Primary, Secondary and Special Schools — including, but not restricted to, the context of design and technological activities. (National Curriculum Technology, point A 2.1, 1990)

Indeed, three points are emphasized at the outset of National Curriculum Technology, namely:

- the IT capability is a cross-curriculum competence which should be developed through a range of curriculum activities.

- the use of IT can enhance the learning process at all levels and should develop as a normal and integral part of learning activities throughout and across the whole curriculum.
- whilst teachers need to fell confident about using IT, their general skills as teachers are of greater importance than high levels of technical 'know-how'.

Although I see all sorts of exciting possibilities of information technology being addressed across-the-curriculum and in technology being granted 'subject' status I, nevertheless, believe there is a danger that the aim of understanding the social aspects of technology could be badly handled. It should easily be relegated into an inadequate 'social impacts' course; or addressed fleetingly and incoherently in certain areas of the secondary school curriculum only (for example, in business studies and CDT). In any case the enterprise is going to be difficult to handle because

- it means addressing technology directly as a complex, multi-faceted subject of study as well as learning to operate individual technologies like micros.
- it means doing so in a way that allows different sectors of the National Curriculum to project subject-centered 'beams' or perspectives onto it in a co-ordinated manner. In my view understanding technology is a crucial part of computer literacy and implies far more than just 'knowing' about some of its social effects. It means being able to 'read' it and the conceptual basis for achieving this has only recently begun to emerge, spurred on by the publication in 1985 of the seminal collection of papers by Mackenzie and Wajcman on the social shaping of technology. These echo the ideas of Herbert Marcuse who, in the 1960s, argued that technologies are not neutral objects but rather 'historical-social projects' with in-built 'social constituents' to serve ruling interests. This theme has been picked up in *Radical Science* (1988) which, whilst stressing the progressive and radical potentiality of technology, demands that it be rendered both democratic and socially useful. To achieve this demands a hugely technologically literate populace. Indeed, the need to read the text of technology and, thereby, make visible the hidden agendas beneath its surface ideologies is made clear by Lyon (1988) when he writes that

> the 'information society' also appears to have some highly charged ideological aspects as well. Such 'Ideological aspects' may be teased out to show how the information Society concept connects Politics and Technology in a peculiarly modern way; it often obscures the vested interests involved in IT; it deflects attention from some embarrassing contradictions while at the same time giving to the coming of the

Information Society the appearance of an entirely natural and
logical social progression.

Being able to 'read' technology is being able to tease out these ideological
aspects and recognize their origins and implications. This throws a very
different light upon technology from Braverman's (1974) Labour Process
thesis which reduced technologies to artefacts and abstracted them from their
historical contexts.

In the second part of this paper I propose a way forward to studying
technology which, I hope, breaks free of the wild claims and dismissals,
internecine academic strife and vested interests characteristic of the 'voices'
reviewed above. I argue that to be truly (as opposed to basically or
functionally) computer (or, as I would prefer it, technologically) literate at
its most accomplished demands that one is empowered to 'read' the meanings
embedded (as 'dead labour', see below, p. 56) within technologies themselves:
that is, to achieve critical purchase on issues such as how they originated; the
social, historical and cultural forces that shaped them; why they were designed as they were; what they can and cannot do; what their shortcomings,
dangers and benefits are; and what their potentialities are. However, this is
not to imply that a merely technical, pragmatic body of knowledge and skills
is sufficient, to use the analogy of reading print, that would entail the
decoding of sounds and only a basic level of meaning-making. What I am
referring to is a reading which demands sophisticated decoding skills which
raise political issues and reach through to the ideological and semantic issues
buried beneath the 'givenness' of technology. I feel that computer literacy
has, to date, been defined in essentially functional terms and, as a consequence, has been trivialized. It is clearly something which must, in the light of
the advent of the Technology National Curriculum, now be set to rights (see
Mackay's paper in this volume). I am not alone in questioning the concept.
Witness Broughton (1988), for example, who writes

> Inherent in that term is the promise of generalisability comparable
> with the generativity of reading and writing. However, there is no
> evidence that programming skills transfer to other areas of psycholo-
> gical development, even cognitive ones.... The role and significance
> of the cognitive-mental processes, in development and in education,
> has been vastly over estimated.

Broughton argues that the inflated claims of the AI lobby have pene-
trated educational discourse, but the evidence suggests these cannot be substantiated. He focusses on Papert's work and argues that the stress on process
rather than product conveys a false air of liberation. The basically electronic
world of LOGO masquerades as both liberal and democratic whereas the
computer embodies a rationality which actually delimits learning possibilities.

As presently defined and operated computer literacy is, argues Broughton, far from being a liberatory force: it is no more than an invisible and insidious socialization:

> The invisible pedagogy of the computerised curriculum is systems oriented and like the hidden curriculum of Computer Literacy its concealment is essential to its primary function of socialisation.

Webster and Robins (1989) also attack the concept and see us heading for a rationalized and technocratic world in which computer literacy is being employed in order to reduce the space for liberal thought. They conclude that it

> reflects an infatuation with high technology scenarios for the future and a naive faith that computers will form the basis for additional employment, competitiveness and economic revival. The discourse of Computer Literacy embellishes and simultaneously clouds the real issue on the Government agenda: Work Literacy.

Meanwhile Apple (1986), in a paper included in this volume, argues that social literacy is an essential feature of any curriculum attempting to engender computer literacy. By this he means the confronting of the social, political and ethical issues surrounding new technology, namely:

- the relationship of computer development to military use, job loss and social disenfranchisement;
- whether computers are being used primarily to enhance or damage aspects of people's lives;
- who decides when, where and why they should be used.

Unless students are enabled to address such ethical and social issues, then the outcome will be catastrophic in that 'only those now with the power to control Technology's uses will have the capacity to act'.

We have made it clear that I dislike the term computer literacy and prefer the more generic term technological literacy. Why? Quite simply I would prefer that computers were not decontextualized and studied separately but as part of a wider culture of technology that includes, for example, television, cable and satellite, teletext and viewdata, and telephones. Moreover, I believe that learning to 'read' technology would benefit from the way cultural studies and media studies have tackled television, both in terms of its origins (for example, Williams, 1974) and its products (for example, Fiske and Hartley, 1978; Hartley, 1982; Masterman, 1980; and O'Sullivan, 1987). Indeed, in an earlier article (Beynon *et al.*, 1983) one of us argued that being able to 'read' media representations should be part of a contemporary definition of literacy.

Rather than technological literacy becoming 'another literacy', it should be incorporated into the ever-changing definition of what it is to be literate in our increasingly technologized and networked world. That means making links between print literacy, tele-literacy, social and even emotional literacy, cultural literacy and technological literacy. Clearly this is not the province of any one area of the curriculum, but is an across-the-curriculum enterprise. In summary, I argue that we must develop ways of 'reading technology' and that this is not just another bolt-on literacy skill, it is an essential if people are not to be disenfranchised and rendered powerless in a world in which being able to read print alone is no longer enough. In order to explore further how a technologically literate reading of technology might be achieved I want briefly to turn to work in print literacy and cultural studies.

Technological Literacy and Print Literacy

To tighten up on what technological literacy might entail there are benefits, we believe, in referring to the social, political and historical aspects of print literacy. There are a number of reasons for this:

- firstly, computers share with printing presses, pens and books the status of hugely influential, 'transforming' technologies (in both societal and personal, cognitive terms).
- secondly, the comparatively youthful history of computer literacy (see Capel's paper in this volume) with its heavy emphasis on basic, functional 'hands-on' skills, has many revealing parallels with the far older history of literacy in the UK (with, in the late Victorian era, its preoccupation with 'a little writing and a little reading', etc.). Indeed, the justifications for spreading computer literacy echo the justifications for spreading print literacy a century ago. Both belong to the economic efficiency model *vis-à-vis* the national need, industrial competitiveness and employability.
- thirdly, the history of print literacy has seen its definition expand from a functional model to an ideological, affective and critical one (Street, 1983). All the signs are that, with the acceptance of the necessity for the technology curriculum to address social and cultural aspects (see Barnett's and Medway's papers in this volume), computer literacy must move in the same direction. Indeed, as computer literacy is operationalized and redefined across-the-curriculum it might well be that the literature on print literacy will prove highly relevant and informative. Hughie Mackay's paper is particularly interesting in its tentative attempts to draw some parallels between print and computer literacy. He reflects what a host of writers (amongst them Clanchy, 1979; Graff, 1979; Levine, 1986; Mace, 1979; and Street, 1983) have shown — that literacy is ideologically a

double-edged sword: it can be used both to raise consciousness and to suppress it, a theme taken up in a Third World context by Paolo Freire (1972; 1973), who illustrates the closed and exploitative nature of many Functional Literacy programmes aimed at assisting nations 'to develop'. Education systems throughout the twentieth century have striven to meet the shifting definitions and demands regarding literacy that society has demanded of them (compare, for example, nearly half a century of UK literacy in the Norwood (1943), Bullock (1976) and Kingman (1988) Reports).

Technological Literacy and Cultural Studies

One field of study which I believe is hugely relevant to 'reading' technology is cultural studies, but for two quite separate reasons:

- Cultural Studies is about the identification and analysis of contemporary cultural forms. As such it can most profitably be applied to technology. Whilst it has an affinity with English, it looks beyond literary to other kinds of texts. It also departs from media studies in looking belong print and broadcast media.
- it is not a subject and is unlikely ever to become one. Rather it is a means of 'framing an agenda, a series of questions and approaches, a political and intellectual framework' (Green, 1987). Indeed, the same author goes on to say

> On one reading cultural studies exists only as a precariously won space in which many kinds of critical work, unvalued by other subjects or expelled from them, can take place. For the most part cultural studies has been found in the margins of other subjects, and in the spaces between them: at times a critique of absences in various disciplines, at others a meeting-point, aross faculties, which is not fully humanities (because locating the cultural in the development of the social formation) yet rather less social science (because wanting to analyse and interpret closely the making and taking of meaning). It can arise in productive tension with other activities — at the edges of work in english or history or sociology, or in degrees whose origins, unity and rationale still bear the marks of particular subject formations. Or, less visibly, cultural studies work is being constructed in practice-based teaching (music, drama, photography, art and design).

I believe that cultural studies writers' attempts to date in Higher Education to address technology have strong relevance for teachers implementing National Curriculum Technology because

- it provides a distinctive and coherent set of approaches to technology across-the-curriculum.
- it points to an expanded 'culturalist' definition of technological literacy based on the ability to treat and 'read' technology as a text.

The authors included in *Understanding Technology in Education* and those in this volume provide a variety of ways of reading technology. Moreover, I hope that this and the companion volumes will set in motion debates which will ensure that a comprehensive series of bench-marks (or 'attainment targets'?) will be established in respect of technological literacy to help users, and also ensure that young people are not only competent readers of a range of technologies, but also how they might best learn to 'read' technology. Clearly their teachers must themselves first become technologically literate for, as Michael Barnett has said (private communication), technological literacy presupposes in the first instance that technologists become literate and, I maintain, that means reading widely in cultural studies; the sociology of technology; media and communication studies; and the history of design and technology, as well — of course — as attaining a fuller, critical appreciation of the 'voices' reviewed in the first part of this paper. Only then can ideas be modified, rendered suitable for pupil attention, and introduced on an across-the-curriculum basis.

Understanding Technology

In *Understanding Technology in Education* we began to identify elements necessary to 'read technology' and summarized these as:

- the study of the design history of particular technologies (including the social constructivist approach), given that design embodies a series of values, ideologies and uses that must be rendered explicit if a technology is to be understood. This 'decoding of design' can be seen in the work of Chanan (1988) on the origins of the Reuters' telegraph; Albury and Schwartz (1982) on the Davy Lamp; and Fallows (1981) on the M16 rifle used in Vietnam. As Solomonides and Levidow (1985) point out, although microcomputers appear to offer a form of apparent freedom and control, the user is really forced into a form of submission by the constraints that the computer's design and implementation imposes. One instance is referred to by Huws (1988) when she writes about high-tech homeworking ('terminal isolation') mostly by women. Another is detailed by Haddon in a paper which appears in *Understanding Technology in Education* (1991) and which charts the design histories of the early Commodore and Sinclair micros. This approach to technology indicates that the emergence of an educational market compelled manufacturers to make inflated pseudo-educationalist claims when they pushed into schools micros basically designed for other purposes and, often, software manifestly unsuitable for the complex demands of teaching and learning.

- allied to the above, the unravelling of the socio-economic and political forces affecting the nature and course of technological developments (the Marxist labour process approach). By looking at the social, political and economic circumstances that give rise to a technology we can start to undermine its 'natural' or 'taken-for-granted' qualities.

- the highly distinctive feminist critique of technology, which spans work such as, for example, Cockburn (1985) (on the social history of technology as an essentially masculine set of inventions) through to Culley (1986) (on anti-sexist strategies *vis-à-vis* access to and usage of computers in schools).

- the emerging cultural studies (of 'cultural') approach which, whilst it can include each of the above, seeks to treat technology as a text. We would see Apple's work (in this volume) and Dowling's paper in *Understanding Technology in Education* (in which he argues that technologies are social processes defined by culture rather than culture being defined by its technologies) as particularly apposite examples. I believe that debates about technological literacy are starting, not ending, and they demand that teachers and their pupils are able (to quote again from the opening paper in *Understanding Technology in Education*) to

> decode the ways in which [technology] has been encoded, and to understand the nature and scope of social relations which it embodies, represents and supports. This would include an understanding of how and by whom a technology is invented, designed, marketed and introduced, what people have to know to use it how it affects the nature of work and leisure, its symbolic value, its cultural nature, who consumes it, and its effects.'

The way towards technological literacy is not merely the teaching of 'social impacts' alongside keyboard skills. The implementation of National Curriculum Technology across-the-curriculum opens up the opportunity for the humanities, for example, to address how technology is socially shaped, designed for certain purposes and, thereby, embodies certain 'meanings'. However, to treat and 'read' technology in this manner demands the appropriate conceptual tools (to return to the 'tool-kit' analogy we used in the introduction to *Understanding Technology in Education*).

A good start has been made on this by Linn (1985), whose seminal paper is included in *Understanding Technology in Education*. The following non-technological concepts allow us to gain critical purchase on aspects of technology:

- 'technicist inversion', or a set of practices which attribute consciousness to machines and mechanism to human labour power.
- 'dead' and 'living labour', or the way in which (design) labour of the past is structured into a technology and interacts with living labour. Indeed, the 'use-value' of dead labour is a conditioning force on living labour.
- 'technological immanence', or the strait-jacket of social, economic and policy-related arrangements for the production and consumption of technology.
- 'product' and 'use' models of technology, with the latter emphasizing processes, not outcomes (Papert's Turtle Geometry, for example, as a learning process).

Technology, Curriculum and Literacy

In this introduction I have argued for a non-technologist, essentially cultural discourse through which technology might be 'read'. Secondly, I have argued for a redefinition of technological literacy which would include not only learning *through* computers, but also learning *about* them. 'Reading' technology not only means an appreciation of its social shaping, but also an understanding of the kind of issues raised by the papers in this volume. The opening ones (those by Capel, Medway and Barnett) show how National Curriculum Technology might be 'read' as a text by placing it in its historical and cultural contexts, and by reviewing the debates that dictated its form and function within the National Curriculum. The second group of papers (comprising the contributions by Apple, Mackay, Grint and Chandler), whilst being highly sceptical, are certainly not dismissive of technology. Rather they point in different ways towards a 'cultural' critique of technology in general and technology in education in particular. Behind the whole volume there lies the major question previously outlined: 'What is it that teachers and their pupils respectively need to *know* (and thereby be able *to do*) to be regarded as technologically literate?' Whilst none of these authors provide a complete answer, taken together they provide a series of valuable direction indicators for future research and thinking as to what constitutes 'reading' technology in the context of education.

Richard Capel argues the need for a shift from a predominantly anthropocentric perspective on technology to a technocentric view. He regards the emergence of National Curriculum Technology as a continuation of a line of thinking which has dominated debates in the UK concerning IT/Education since the 1960s, namely one which has ignored a social, informatics approach. In that period little attention was paid to thinking in Europe where, especially in Sweden, attempts were made to break free of the technocentric model. Capel argues that technocentrism relegates people, reifies the technology and so 'delegitimizes those processes which are particularly a part of human beings and their environments such as tacit knowledge, subjective judgment, complexity and intuition'. Whereas in Europe in the recent past there has been a determined effort to broaden the technology curriculum to include psychology, sociology, industrial relations and human behaviour, in the UK Capel notes that 'the traditional academic curriculum of separate subjects has proved very limiting in attempts to broaden the approach to technology, computer studies and computer literacy'. Although the National Curriculum recognizes the need for an across-the-curriculum approach to technology it, itself, 'is a strengthening of the academic curriculum'. He regards it as a product of the history of computer education in the UK, a history dominated by mathematics teachers who were not sympathetic to social implications, and humanities teachers who were usually unable or reluctant to become computer literate. Computer awareness was a 'soft' provision usually deemed suitable only for the 'less able', 'Newsom' children. Capel's social history of computer education shows two conflicting pressures at work, namely the need, on one hand, to spread technological knowledge and improve productivity; and, on the other, counter-pressures to restrict that knowledge and control the form it took. This conflict between national, more egalitarian forces and elitist, conservative ones is seen as largely having shaped the historical development of education in and about IT in the UK and rendered it technocentric. Computers have thereby become neutral 'tools to think with' and not seen to be in any need of explanation. One step that Capel calls for is that David Noble's (1984) powerful thesis (that technologies are shaped by the wider human and social relations in which they are embedded) needs to be developed in an educational context. A social history of IT/Education, for example, would show how contradictions have been resolved, with some opportunities advanced and others stifled. The reasons underpinning these choices would afford a series of most interesting insights into both education and technology, and identify the wider forces operating upon each.

Peter Medway, too, examines the shaping of Technology in the National Curriculum and comments that it is 'bizarrely radical and conservative by turns'. He notes a number of contradictions: for example, 'design activities which are not technology are admitted while technological activities not involving design are excluded'. A major problem is that the technology curriculum is based on a 'discipline' which has no real existence outside the aspirations of curriculum designers. Indeed, 'the concept of technology on which the curriculum is based is in fact a normative, not an empirically-derived one, an artificial construct whose links to reality are tenuous and problematic'. Moreover, Medway argues, the technology curriculum, rather than being a rehabilitation of the practical, is really an academicization of it. Value is seen to reside above all in intellectual skills in spite of the attempt to identify a 'real world' framework of design and technological activity, and an acknowledgment of cognitive complexity in 'doing' as much as 'knowing'. But Medway, in spite of his many criticisms and reservations, concludes on a positive note in that the technology curriculum offers many exciting opportunities for innovative practices. The emphasis upon technology as a discipline for the production of rounded personal development keeps the subject from being part of what he describes as 'that new positivistic, career-oriented instrumentalism'. However, it remains ideologically selective and slanted in favour of business studies.

Michael Barnett, also, charts the emergence of National Curriculum Technology through the various documents leading up to the Statutory Orders and is disappointed by the final product, especially in relation to technological literacy. He notes the yoking together of design and technology and the splitting of 'Technology' and 'Information Technology' (a witless demarcation which the 'working group attempted to challenge but without success'). He shows how several of the most valuable intentions of the original working party have been jettisoned, including many of the key elements of social and economic significance in understanding the nature of technology, so much so that Barnett hopes teachers will be guided 'more by the spirit of the Interim Report rather than the letter of the Statutory Orders'. Indeed, a new academic subject may have been created whose reality 'extends no further than the school gate' and is, perhaps, best regarded as 'a somewhat circumscribed intervention in the field of general education'. It constitutes a 'narrowing of perspectives ... an approach more related to consolidation than innovation ... a syllabus framework of scarcely imaginable complexity and abstractness'. Moreover, the Final Report shows that whilst the Attainment Targets and many of the statements of attainment encourage a critical consideration of technology, the impression is not strongly conveyed that such an approach is 'desirable, necessary or even possible'. Debates concerning the social shaping and wider implications of technology must be a cross-curricular undertaking, but the National Curriculum makes it difficult to coordinate inter-subject planning. Any understanding of technology must embrace a range of issues beyond the immediate world of school, home and community, but technology as handled by the National Curriculum largely fails to accomplish this.

Michael Apple's work has already been reviewed at length and its characterizing of technology as a 'text' to be read is seminal to this volume.

Hughie Mackay's paper, too, is central to the collection in that he addresses a key issue touched on — either directly or by inference — by each of the others, namely the need for a definition of technological literacy which includes an acknowledgment of the essentially social nature of technology. To date computer literacy has focused rather more on computers that on literacy and the outcome has been a narrow definition premised on a misunderstanding of the role of technology in our lives and of our relationship to it. Alternatively it has referred to the maximum usage of micros to foster writing and pupils' talk (that is, print literacy and its first cousin, oracy) as in the case, for example, of Chandler and Marcus (1985); Robinson (1985); and NATE (1988). Mackay's emphasis is very much upon a literacy of, rather than *through*, technology, along with an argument (already rehearsed above) that the two are not unconnected. Mackay's point is that a minimal, functional technological expertise will hardly empower people: rather it will result in a false sense of power and control. Technological literacy is, at this point of the debate, easier to define in terms of what it should not be as opposed to what it should (or could) be. It is not a narrow, skills-based accomplishment to equip holders for the employment market: it should, rather, be a comprehensive understanding, an ability to 'read technology' and to utilize to the full its beneficial and democratizing potentiality. In any case, as Mackay makes clear, computer literacy courses with a technical bias (upon *doing* rather than *knowing* about) quickly go out of date. Mackay applies some of the debates that have informed print literacy to technological literacy and, thereby, raises the issue of the relationship of literacy to political, cultural and personal power. Freire's (1972) advocacy of a print literacy based on the rendering explicit of political and ideological underpinnings is applied to technology. He argues that such an approach is compatible with the DES (1982) statement that technology is 'first and foremost a cultural study'. For Mackay technological literacy is not only crucial in itself, but as a means of understanding contemporary society and our place in it.

One of the most significant features of Keith Grint's paper is the successive ways in which he 'interrogates' technology, in turn employing designer technology; technological then social determinism; and, finally, an actor network 'interpretist' approach. As it implies this highlights the interpretive processes and actions of participants and does not rely upon any objective account of the network ('the *deus ex machina* ... only exists when [people] ensure its production and reproduction'). Technology, as Grint displays, is most certainly not neutral but is 'politically impregnated [and] historically encumbered', with design choices being inevitably both social and political in nature. Technology and humans operate in conjunction and neither has a discrete impact: organizational and social relations are neither determined by technology (technological determinism) nor by social agency (social determinism), but by a close alliance of human and non-human actors. Indeed, only a limiting 'technicist' perspective assumes that we can separate the two or ignore the fact that technology is determined by its design; the social cultural aspects that have shaped it; and the subjective qualities of the actors accomplishing it. The actor network approach provides, argues Grint, a way of 'reading' technology so that its social features are more readily exposed. He exemplifies this by means of a case study of the Open University Course DT200 (*An Introduction to IT*), central to the delivery of which intention was that, through the employment of an electronic bridge, group discussion would become more egalitarian and an open, participative culture would emerge amongst the student cohort, the majority of whom would otherwise be non-participants. The hope was that 'the loneliness of the long-distance learner would be replaced by the intimacy of 1300 students and tutors in the privacy of your own home'. Grint shows how these laudable aims were, in practice, subverted by the dominance of the medium by a minority.

Daniel Chandler's thought-provoking paper is a critique of the taken-for-granted strengths and 'neutrality' of data handling, computer simulations and word-processing. He echoes Weizenbaum's (1976) charge that technology is hugely reductionist in that its emphasis on data handling underestimates the importance of ideas. He argues that the computer has purposes of its own and is certainly not neutral. Indeed, computers may include priorities which run contrary to our purpose and dictate how we 'choose' to use them, for they are ideologically loaded and 'no more neutral than the atomic bomb'. He is careful not to fall into the trap of oversimplistic conspiracy theory but, rather, maintains that it is beholden upon us all (especially teachers) to challenge technocratic values by using 'only tools and techniques which support our ethical, social and political priorities'. Teachers must reaffirm their educational purposes; identify the underlying ideology of the computer as a tool; and not give way to the educational technocrats. In the process they must reconsider what is worth doing *with* the computer. Moreover, future research must engage in comparative studies of particular examples of computer usage in classrooms and be clear about the nature of a transient ideology encoded within computer activities. Chandler's focus is on the interaction of design and application in that 'using a computer in any application can transform one's intentions according to an in-built but inexplicit ideology'. Amongst other things students, in order to be computer literate, must be aware of the constraints and of the computer as an artefact embodying an ideology and a host of invisible assumptions (that is, the 'dead labour' that went into its evolution and production). Chandler's fears are that databases remove the human element from information; computer simulations are a form of technological rationalism; and word-processing can result in a loss of freshness and spontaneity in that writing so produced 'obscures its own evolution'. Writers are in danger of becoming 'managed by the word-processor', described as 'a medium intolerant of ambiguity', and he concludes that 'it is all too easy when using a word-processor to become obsessed with surface features rather than with developing an argument or conveying an experience'.

Conclusion

In this introduction I have attempted to set the scene for the writers who now follow, writers who have interesting and important things to say about technology and, by implication, about what might constitute a new and more comprehensive definition of technological literacy. I believe they avoid the polarized 'debates' engaged in by what I have characterized as accolatory and dismissive voices and those of the technological and social determinists. Finally, by picking up Michael Apple's concept of technology as a 'text' I have indicated how we might begin to 'read' it as a precondition for first becoming technologically literate and then assisting others to become so within the context of the National Curriculum.

References

ABT, C. (1980) 'What the computer holds for children in the television-computer age', paper presented to National Council for Children, Princeton, 12 March.

ALBURY, D. and SCHWARTZ, J. (1982) *Partial Progress: The Politics of Science and Technology*, Pluto Press.

APPLE, M. (1987) 'Mandating computers', in WALKER, S. and BARTON, L. (Eds) *Changing Policies, Changing Teachers*, Open University Press.

APPLE, M. (1988) *Teachers and Texts: A Political Economy of Class and Gender Relations in Education*, Routledge and Kegan Paul.

ATHANASIOU, T. (1985) 'AI: clearly disguised politics', *Radical Science*, 18.

BAKER, C. (1983) 'The microcomputer and the curriculum', *Journal of Curriculum Studies*, 15, 2, pp. 207–14.

BAKER, C. (1984) 'A critical examination of the effect of microcomputers on the curriculum', in TERRY, C. (Ed.) *Using Micro Computers in Schools*, Croom Helm.

BAKER, C. (1985) 'The microcomputer and the curriculum: a further critique', *Journal of Curriculum Studies*, 17, 4, pp. 449–51.

BALL, S. (1982) 'Competition and conflict in the teaching of English', *Journal of Curriculum Studies*, 14, 1, pp. 1–28.

BARNES, B. and HILL, S. (1983) 'Should your children work with microcomputers — Logo before Lego?', *The Computing Teacher*, Vol. 10, pp. 10–14.

BASQUE, J. and MATTE, K. (1987) 'The integration of microcomputing in education', c/o Ministere de L'Education, Quebec.

BEVERIDGE, M. (1987) Review in British Educational Research Journal, 13/1, pp. 91–93.

BEYNON, J. (1990) 'Just a few machines bleeping away in a corner', in BLOMEYER, R.L. and MARTIN, D. (Eds) *Case Studies in Computer Aided Learning*, Falmer.

BEYNON, J. (1990) 'Researching technology', in *Report on the Computers And Education Project*, c/o Altmaster College, University of Western Ontario.

BEYNON, J. and MACKAY, H. (1989) 'IT/Education: towards a critical perspective', *Journal of Education Policy*, Falmer, Vol. 4, No. 3, pp. 245–57.

BEYNON, J. and MACKAY, H. (Eds) (1991) *Computers Into Classrooms*, Falmer Press.

BEYNON, J., DOYLE, B., GOULDEN, H. and HARTLEY, J. (1983) 'The politics of discrimination: Media Studies in English teaching', *English in Education*, 17:3, Autumn.

BLAGOVEST, S. and STENCHEV, I. (Eds) (1986) *Children in an Information Age: Tomorrow's Problem Today*, Pergamon.

BOLTER, J.D. (1986) *Turing's Man: Western Culture in the Computer Age*, Penguin Books.

BORK, A.M. (1979) 'Interactive Learning', in *American Journal Of Physics*, 47, pp. 5–10.

BORK, A.M. *et al.* (1989) Proceedings of Fifth International Conference on IT in Education, Edinburgh University Press.

BRAVERMAN, H. (1974) *Labor and Monopoly Capital*, Monthly Review Press.

BROD, C. (1984) *Techno-Stress*, Addison Wesley.

BROUGHTON, J.M. (1988) 'The Surrender of Control: Computer Literacy as Political Socialisation of the Child', in *The Computer in Education*, Teachers' College Press.

CAPEL, R. and YOUNG, M.F.D. (1988) 'Critical perspectives on IT across the curriculum: issues for theory and research', unpublished paper, Post-16 centre, London University Institute.

CHANAN, M. (1988) 'The Reuters' Telegraph', in *Science As Culture (2)*, Free Association Press.

CHANDLER, D. (1984) *Young Learners and Microcomputers*, Open University Press.

CHANDLER, D. and MARCUS, S. (Eds) (1985) *Computers and Literacy*, Open University Press.

CHANDRA, P., BLISS, J. and COX, M. (1988) 'Introducing computers into a school: management issues', *Computer Education* 12, 1.

CLANCHY, M. (1979) *From Memory To Written Record, 1066–1307*, Arnold.

COCKBURN, C. (1985) *Machinery of Dominance: Women, Men and Technical Know-How*, Pluto Press.

COWAN, R.S. (1985) 'How the refrigerator got its hum', in MACKENZIE, D. and WAJCMAN, J. (Eds) *The Social Shaping of Technology*, Open University Press.

CROOK, C. (1989) 'On defining a computer environment for innovation', paper for ESRC Seminar, Aston Business Centre, January.

CULLEY, L. (1986) 'Gender differences and computing in secondary schools', c/o Dept of Education, Loughborough University of Technology.

CULLEY, L. (1988) *Girls, Boys And Computers*, Educational Studies, Volume 14, Number 1, Carfax Publishing.

DEDE, C. (1985) 'Educational and social implications', in FORESTER, T. (Ed.) *The Information Technology Revolution*, Blackwell.

DES (1943) Norwood Report on the teaching of English, HMSO.

DES (1976) Bullock Report on the teaching of English, HMSO.

DES (1982) *Computers in Education, a Report*, HMSO.

DES (1988) Kingman Report on the teaching of English, HMSO.

DORDICK, H.S. (1986) *Understanding Modern Telecommunications*, McGraw-Hill.

DREYFUS, H.L. (1979) *What Computers Can't Do*, Harper Colophon.

EVANS, C. (1979) *The Mighty Micro: The Impact of the Computer Revolution*, Gollanez.

FALLOWS, J. (1981) 'The American Army and the M16 rifle', in MACKENZIE, D. and WAJCMAN, J. (Eds) *The Social Shaping of Technology*, Open University Press.

FISKE, J. and HARTLEY, J. (1978) *Reading Television*, Methuen.

FREIRE, Paolo (1970) *Pedagogy of the Oppressed*, Penguin.

FREIRE, P. (1972) *Cultural Action For Freedom*, Monograph Series No. 1, Harvard Educational Review.

FREIRE, P. (1973) *Education For Cultural Consciousness*, Penguin.

GARLAND, E.J. (Ed.) (1982) *Microcomputing and Children in the Primary School*, Falmer.

GIANNELLI, G. (1985) 'Promoting computer use in the classroom — the teacher is always the last to know', *Educational Technology*, April.

GLASER, B. and STRAUSS, A. (1967) *The Discovery of Grounded Theory*, Wiedenfeld and Nicholson.

GOLDEN, F. (1985) 'Here comes the microkids', in FORESTER, T. (Ed.) *The Information Technology Revolution*, Blackwell.

GRAFF, H. (1979) *The Literacy Myth*, Academic Press.

GREEN, M. (Ed.) (1987) *Broadening the Context: English, Teaching and Cultural Studies*, John Murray.

HABERMAS, J. (1987) *The Theory of Communicative Action: Lifeworld and System*, Beacon Press.

HADDON, L. (1988) 'The Home Computer: the making of a consumer electronic', in *Science As Culture*, Free Association Press.

HADDON, L. (1991), 'The Cultural Production and Consumption of IT', in MACKAY, H., YOUNG, M.F.D., BEYNON, J. (Eds), *Understanding Technology in Education*, Falmer Press.

HARTLEY, J. (1982) *Understanding News*, Methuen.

HARTLEY, J., GOULDEN, H. and O'SULLIVAN, T. (1985) *Making Sense of the Media*, Comedia.

HAWKRIDGE, D. (1983) *New Information Technology in Education*, Croom Helm.

HEAFORD, J.M. (1983) *The Myth Of The Learning Machine: the Theory and Practice of Computer-Based Learning*, Sigma Technical Press.

HEBENSTEET, J. (1986) 'Children and computers: myths and limits', in BLAGOVEST, S. and STENCHEV, I. (Eds) *Children in an Information Age: Tomorrow's Problems Today*, Pergamon.

HELLER, R. and MARTIN, C. (1982) *A Computing Literacy Primer*, Computer Science Press.

HODGES, A. (1984) *Alan Turing: the Enigma*, Unwin.

HOWE, J. (1983) 'Towards a pupil-centred classroom', in MEGARRY, J. (Ed.) *Computers and Education*, Kogan Page.

HUGHES, M. *et al.* (1987) 'Children's ideas about computers', in RUTKOWSKA, J.C. and CROOK, C. *Computers, Cognition and Development*, Wiley.

HUWS, U. (1988) 'Terminal Isolation', *Radical Science*, 2.

KARGER, H.J. (1988) 'Children and microcomputers: a critical analysis', *Education Today*, 38, 2.

KEMMIS, S. (1988) 'Educational computing: how do we know what we are getting?', paper to Educational Computing Conference, Melbourne, Victoria, July.

KUHN, T.S. (1970) *The Structure of Scientific Revolutions*, University of Chicago Press.

LARSEN, S. (1986) 'Computers in education: a critical view', in BLAGOVEST, S. and STENCHEV, I. (Eds) *Children in an Information Age: Tomorrow's Problems Today*, Pergamon.

LEVINE, R. (1986) *The Social Context of Literacy*, Routledge and Kegan Paul.

LINN, P. (1985) 'Microcomputers in education: living and dead labour', *Radical*

Science, 18, reprinted in MACKAY, H., YOUNG, M. and BEYNON, J. *Understanding Technology in Education*, Falmer, 1991.

LONDON MENTAL MODELS GROUP (1988) *Tools For Exploratory Learning*, Occasional Paper in/TER/5/88, ESRC, c/o Dept of Psychology, Lancaster University.

LYON, D. (1988) *The Information Society: Issues And Illusions*, Polity Press.

MACE, J. (1979) *Working With Words*, Writers and Readers.

MACKAY, H. (1988) 'Computer literacy: issues and debate', paper presented to IT in Education Colloquium at BERA Conference, UEA, Norwich.

MACKAY, H., YOUNG, M. and BEYNON, J. (Eds) (1991) *Understanding Technology in Education*, Falmer Press.

MACKENZIE, D. and WAJCMAN, J. (Eds) (1985) *The Social Shaping of Technology*, Open University Press.

MAKING WAVES (1988) 'The politics of communications' *Radical Science*, 16.

MASTERMAN, L. (1980) *Teaching About Television*, Macmillan.

MOORES, S. (1988) '"The box on the dresser": memories of early radio and everyday life', *Media, Culture and Society*, Vol. 10, pp. 23–40.

MORRISON, A. (1989) Computers in the Curriculum of Secondary Schools, Edinburgh, SCRE.

NATE (1988) *IT's English: Accessing English with Computers*, Sheffield.

NATIONAL CURRICULUM (1990) *Technology in the National Curriculum*, HMSO; concurrently, Curriculum Council for Wales.

NOBLE, D. (1984) Forces of Production, Alfred Knopf.

OBRIST, A.J. (1983) *The Microcomputer and the Primary School*, Hodder and Stoughton.

ONG, W.J. (1982) *Orality and Literacy: The Technologizing of the Word*, Methuen.

O'SHEA, T. and SELF, J. (1983) *Learning and Teaching with Computers: Artificial Intelligence in Education*, Wheatsheaf Press.

O'SULLIVAN, T. (1991) 'Television memories and the culture of viewing, 1950–1965', in CORNER, J. (Ed.), *The Homely Image: Essays in Television History*, British Film Institute.

PAPERT, S. (1980) *Mindstorms: Children, Computer and Powerful Ideas*, Harvester Press.

PEA, R.D. (1987) 'Logo programming and problem solving', in SCANLAN, E. and O'SHEA, T. *Educational Computing*, Wiley.

POSTMAN, N. (1984) 'Kid-friendly computers', *Parents*, 59, June.

RADICAL SCIENCE COLLECTIVE (1988) Free Association Press.

RAHTZ, S. (1987) *Information Technology In The Humanities*, Ellis Horwood.

REPO, S. (1987) 'Consciousness and popular media', in LIVINGSTONE, D. (Ed.) *Critical Pedagogy and Cultural Power*, Macmillan.

ROBINSON, B. (1985) *Micro Computers And The Language Arts*, Open University Press.

RUTKOWSKA, J.C. and CROOK, C. (Eds) (1987) *Computers, Cognition and Development*, Wiley.

SCHNEIDER, M.F. and SCHNEIDER, S. (1984) 'The computer age and family life', *Individual Psychology*, 40, March, pp. 61–70.

SEARLE, J. (1985) quoted in ATHANASIOU, T. 'AI: clearly disguised politics', *Radical Science*, 18.

SELTZER, M. (1974) 'Good morning class', *Pamparts*, Volume 8, March.

SHAYER, D. (1972) *The Teaching of English in Schools, 1900–1970*, Routledge.

SILVERSTONE, R. (1985) *Framing Science: The Making of a BBC Documentary*, BFI Publishing.

SOCIALLY USEFUL PRODUCTION DEBATE (1985) in *Very Nice Work If You Can Get It*, edited by Collective Design Projects, Spokesman.

SOLOMONIDES, T. and LEVIDOW, L. (Eds) (1985) *Compulsive Technology: Computers as Culture*, Free Association Press.

STONIER, T. and CONLIN, C. (1985) *The Three C's: Children, Computers and Communication*, Wiley.

STREET, B. (1983) *Literacy in Theory and Practice*, Cambridge University Press.

SULLIVAN, E.V. (1987) 'Critical pedagogy and television', in LIVINGSTONE, D. (Ed.) *Critical Pedagogy and Cultural Power*, Macmillan.

SUPPES, P. (1966) 'The uses of computers in education', *Scientific American*, 215, 2, pp. 206–20.

TOMLINSON, P. and QUINTON, M. (Eds) (1986) *Values across the Curriculum*, Falmer.

TURKLE, S. (1984) *The Second Self*, Granada.

VAN WEERT, T. (1987) 'A model syllabus for literacy in IT', in RAHTZ, S. (Ed.) *IT in the Humanities*, Ellis Harwood Press.

VITALE, B. (1987) 'Computers and education: main themes and a guide to the literature', paper to the International Conference on Education, Second World Basque Conference, Bilbao, October.

WAITES, B. *et al.* (Eds) (1982) *Popular Culture: Past and Present*, Croom Helm.

WALKER, D.F. (1982) *Reflections on the Educational Potential and Limitations of the Microcomputer*, Phi Delta Kappa.

WEBSTER, F. and ROBINS, K. (1986) *Information Technology: A Luddite Analysis*, Ablex Publishing Corporation.

WEBSTER, F. and ROBINS, K. (1989) *The Technical Fix: Education, Computers and Industry*, Macmillan.

WEIZENBAUM, J. (1976) *Computer Power and Human Reason*, Penguin.

WELLINGTON, J.J. (1985) *Children, Computers and the Classroom*, Harper Row.

WHITE, M.A. (Ed.) (1983) *The Future of Electronic Learning*, Lawrence Erlbaum Associates.

WILLIAMS, R. (1974) *Television: Technology and Cultural Form*, Fontana.

WILLIAMS, R. (1976) *Keywords: A Vocabulary of Culture and Society*, Fontana.

WINNER, L. (1986) *The Whale and the Reactor: A Search for Limits in an Age of High Technology*, University of Chicago Press.

WINOGRAD, T. (1985) quoted in ATHANASIOU, T. 'AI: clearly disguised politics', *Radical Science*, 18.

WINSTON, B. (1986) *Misunderstanding Media*, Routledge and Kegan Paul.

YOUNG, M.F.D. (1984) 'IT and the sociology of education: some preliminary thoughts', *British Journal of the Sociology of Education*, 5, 2, pp. 205–10.

YOUNG, M.F.D. (1991) 'Epilogue' in MACKAY, H., YOUNG, M. and BEYNON, J. (Eds) *Understanding Technology in Education*, Falmer Press.

YOUNG, M.F.D. and CAPEL, R. (1988) Critical Perspectives in IT Across the Curriculum: Issues for Theory and Research, Unpublished Paper, University of London, Institute of Education.

Chapter 2

Social Histories of Computer Education: Missed Opportunities?

Richard Capel

Introduction

This paper attempts to highlight through the use of examples the importance of a critical historical understanding of the emergence of computer studies and computer literacy. Work towards a critical social history of these areas of the modern curriculum can perhaps begin to raise significant questions about present and future developments. Most importantly, such a critical social history should be able to show how computer studies and computer literacy (and the software and hardware associated with them), as parts of educational curricula, were shaped by the wider human relations in which they were embedded.

The classic studies by David Noble regarding the social shaping of science and technology and, more specifically, of the design of machines, have helped to point the way (Noble, 1977; 1979; 1986). However, as Capel and Young have suggested, it remains a task for educational researchers to develop Noble's analysis in relation to the development and use of technology (including Information Technology) within a modernizing educational system (Capel and Young, 1988). What work has been done has tended to polarize into particular types of either technological or social determinism (Lyon, 1988; Williams, 1974). The first of these presents the reader with an analysis which implicitly or uncritically views the development of technology and the spread of its use as inevitable and inherently beneficial to society. The second tends to present an analysis which views all forms of technology as oppressive and as instruments of control, with both as an inevitable consequence of the future development of technology. What Capel and Young have begun to argue is for a view of modernization which recognizes that the twin processes of increased specialization and the growth of technology contain contradictory tendencies and present different possibilities. Most importantly, the way in which these develop are not determined in advance but depend on changes in both material conditions and the balance of political forces (Capel and Young, 1988). It should be the purpose of a critical social history of computers in education to show how these contradictions were resolved and why certain opportunities were taken up whilst others were not.

My first example looks at changes in curriculum content from the late 1960s and through the mid-1970s. It concentrates on the differentiation of that curriculum around a notion of 'ability' type and the assumed implications for computer studies and computer literacy of changes in production due to the increasing introduction of computer technology. It also describes the approaches of two early critics of computer appreciation courses at the time who argued for a much broader perspective and move away from the technocentric courses which tended to dominate the period.

The second example outlines briefly some significant changes in the use of computer technology and the growth of data-processing and management systems. It provides early examples of the development of a different approach and perspective in some European countries towards what was in this country termed computer education. Finally, it attempts to indicate some reasons for the failure, in this country at least, to begin to take up the possibilities presented by a broader 'informatics' approach.

Computer Education, Differentiation and the Division of Labour

The development of computer education in schools and the growing concern during the late 1960s and early 1970s for all students to have different amounts and forms of knowledge about computers took place against the background of what was happening in universities, colleges, the computer industry and more general educational and political developments.

In universities the development of computer science had much to do with a combination of specialists (especially electrical engineers) including a close collaboration with industry and military sectors. Early developments in schools centred around the efforts of individual mathematics teachers, the rise of 'new mathematics', collaboration with industry, and the use at times of university and college facilities (Barker, 1971, p. 9). The stimulation for the introduction of computer education was not only in connection with the practice and development of 'new' or 'modern maths', in many ways it was also an instrumental one. As a report of a working party of the British Computer Society Schools Committee stated:

> By the early 1960's any introduction of computing techniques into schools was partly stimulated by the growing career potential in the computer industry. It was soon realised that there would be a considerable staff requirement in the industry and 'computers' as a 'career subject' was introduced into some schools. (BCS, 1974, p. 3)

What came to be known as 'new mathematics', its creation in a particular form through the development of computers, and its introduction into schools, gave the school mathematics teacher a new model of the subject through which it was possible to develop practical computer education. Whilst pure and applied 'old mathematics' were characterized by 'coherent methods for showing that solutions to problems existed, and more or less *ad hoc* methods for finding the solutions', the 'new mathematics' of computation provided a coherent procedure for solving problems, which was linked through computers to the possibility of solving 'real' practical problems in the 'real' world of production (Hodgkin, 1976, p. 50). Hodgkin suggests that the 'new mathematics' arose in a specific relation to production:

> Though computer science and numerical analysis are taught in universities, offer Ph.D's and so on, this continuing relation to production, to the demands of institutions — which precisely require this 'practical' mathematics and can buy the machines (or the time) and have the people to do it - is an essential component of the new. Hence we have a demarcation determined by the relation of productive process which is self-perpetuating (as is usual where the demands of specialisation and the division of labour are strong). A firm wants a computer scientist or a traditional pure/applied mathematician, very rarely a combination of the two. (Hodgkin, 1976, pp. 53–4)

The 'new mathematics' used concepts such as 'subroutine' and was built around the idea of the coherent solution to problems based on the reduction of a mathematical deduction to a finite sequence of independent steps. Thus, unlike the 'old mathematics', it could be processed by computer (Hodgkin, 1976, pp. 50, 55). In schools the introduction of 'new mathematics' (also called modern mathematics) began with experimental exams around 1963. The justification for 'new mathematics' was based on the criteria of 'usefulness' as opposed to what was seen as the abstract characteristics of the 'old mathematics' (Broderick, 1968, p. 60). Realism, practicality and problem-solving were the terms used in conjunction with the 'new mathematics' in schools (ibid.). It was argued that 'new mathematics' unlike the 'old mathematics' needed, like other sciences, laboratory time and equipment in order to carry through the practical problem-solving approach it followed (Broderick, 1968, p. 98). The claimed usefulness and practical approach of the 'new mathematics' were used to justify the purchase of equipment or the use of computers and calculating machines.

Access to computers was becoming easier in some cases and companies were beginning to experiment with computers designed especially for education. For example, IBM (UK) began in 1966 to design and experiment with a computer which would meet educational specifications rather than commercial ones (Tinsley, 1970, p. II/85). However, the eventual design seemed to merely reflect the mathematical bias in computer education at the time. Tinsley, who was asked to conduct the trials with IBM, pointed out a few years later that although he felt the basic concept of the machine as a teaching tool was sound, the computer was, in practice, used as a calculator within a mathematical context. This, for Tinsley, was mainly a result of the machine design, in which the character set was restricted to the digits 0–9, which implied for most users a numerical (mathematical) rather than a general character-handling approach (i.e., a commercial data-processing approach which was by far the most common use of computers at the time) (Tinsley, 1972a, p. 74). The origins lay in the form of specialization which centred around, and had control over the early development of computers in education and its establishment in universities and schools.

> In the previous decade, the main influence on teaching about computers had come from University computer science departments where stress was placed on an understanding of hardware and where practical work involved mainly numerical methods within mathematics. This influence can still be felt strongly in recent syllabus submissions, particularly at CSE level, which show that the more generalised, conceptual approach has not yet been fully accepted. (Tinsley, 1972a, p. 72)

A more conceptual approach for Tinsley was contained in the 'Computer Education for All' document and represented a radical change from the previous stress on technique with its susceptability to obsolescence in the face of rapidly changing technologies (BCS, 1969; 1970). Computer appreciation courses were to be redefined in the context of an increasing commercial interest in computer education and an educational world in which the curriculum concerns of the raising of the school leaving age and the production of teaching materials to meet the 'needs' of an increasingly differentiated pupil population were highlighted. In addition the beginnings of a move away (at least in theory) from a technical focus towards what Tinsley described as a more conceptual approach, also began to open up possibilities for broader non-technical debates about what should constitute computer appreciation and awareness courses.

One of the early indications of a move towards a broader concept of computer education came from the review of computers in secondary education by the Centre for Educational Research and Development for the OECD.

> The introduction of computer education into secondary schools has, however, been on a haphazard and random basis. In the main the impetus has come from individuals, many of whom were interested in only one facet, for example, the use of computers in the teaching of mathematics. One result of this is that in too many schools computer education is restricted to mathematics lessons or even to

mathematically-gifted pupils. When this happens, many of the most
valuable rewards are lost. (CERI/OECD, 1969, p. 73)

In addition to this criticism of the narrowness of much of computer education
it also pointed to what it saw as the objectives of introducing computer
education in some form into secondary education. It supported the view that
computers gave rise to both technological and sociological developments and
that this should be a part of any broad computer education course. It listed
the main reasons for computer education in schools as being, firstly, a preparation for university work, semi-professional or vocational training, or for
employment. Secondly, computer education should be a vital element in any
social studies programme. Thirdly, according to the review, computer education 'provides a way to stimulate the interests of pupils who cannot be
reached otherwise'. Fourthly, it enables a better understanding of traditional
topics and creates opportunities to extend the school curriculum to include
areas which would not other wise be treated satisfactorily (CERI/OECD,
1969, p. 73). Much of the above would go on to characterize the developments in debates about computer education in schools over the next two
decades.

One of the most important aspects of both this review and a DES report
published two years earlier (DES, 1967) in terms of the developments in
computer education in schools, is the way the documents differentiate individuals in terms of interest, ability and aptitude and what are considered other
important personal qualities. Firstly, in relation to knowledge structured
within a division of labour; and secondly, in relation to the assumed attributes
of computer education. The report on computer education stresses that suitability for different jobs in the division of labour within the computing
industry and computer applications industry depends very much on personality and different personal qualities (see for example DES, 1967, p. 2). Support
for the review's assumption regarding computer education's ability to provide
a way to reach a certain type of pupil was also given support in a National
Council for Educational Technology report of the same period (NCET,
1969). This report divided computer education into two broad areas: firstly,
'computing for education' (more commonly referred to as computer assisted
learning (CAL)) and secondly, 'education about computing' with the report's
focus centring on 'computing for education' (NCET, 1969, p. 1). The report
puts forward that computer-based learning systems can accommodate almost
any 'type of student' and that with regard to computer-based tuition, three
areas are worth attention. The second and third are the teaching of mathematics and the 'sixth form of the future' in the context of the increasing
predominance of non-selection. However the first it states is:

The education of the 'Newsom' child, particularly in conjunction
with the projected raising of the school leaving age, raises many
problems to which it may be profitable to seek for radical solutions.

Computer based systems — which give the student the impression that he is receiving individual attention, which may keep motivation high through keeping him informed of progress, which allow him to learn by discovery, which permit him to manipulate the parameters in models of real-life situations and demonstrate the consequences of his actions, and which remain impersonal in the face of error and patient in contact with slower thinkers — appear to have many attributes worth exploring in connection with the education of this population. (NCET, 1969, p. 22)

The identifying of different pupil 'types' and the call for computer education to be included in many more pupils' general education, were part of a more general educational landscape which, especially since the Newsom Report (Newsom, 1963), the setting up of the Schools Council in 1964 and the prospect of the raising of the school leaving age, began to look to providing a different type of curriculum for what was seen as a different type of pupil.

The move away from a mathematical and technical focus on hardware in computer studies and computer appreciation towards one which began to focus more on information processing was by no means uniform. Much actual practice both in examination and non-examination courses throughout the 1970s was still machine-oriented (Makkar, 1973a; 1973b; Atkin, 1976). The concern to reflect the main use of computers in society through an increasing emphasis on information processing, especially within computer appreciation, also saw the contexts in which this processing was performed become a focus of courses. Many began to look at specific applications of computers in such areas as supermarkets, airline booking and large database applications such as health records and electricity billing (see for example Tinsley, 1972b). However, the beginnings of a move to increase the amount of coverage concerning the different applications of computers was not just a consequence of the increasing interest in teaching about information processing. In many ways it was also part of what was considered appropriate knowledge for particular groups of pupils defined as being 'below average' or 'average', who were becoming increasingly targeted with regards to the production of what were seen as appropriate teaching materials.

From the late 1960s, with the publication of the Bellis Interim Report (SET, 1969) and the British Computer Society's 'Computer Education for All' (BCS, 1969; 1970), there were calls to spread a form of computer 'appreciation' to all pupils from a position in which most computer education was concerned with academic sixth forms, with a large amount of 'pioneering work' done in private or grammar schools (for example Broderick's early work: see Broderick, 1968). The justifications for the spread of computer education to all pupils were usually put in terms which stressed the rapid spread of computers into all aspects of everyday life (see for example SET, 1969, p. 6), the assumed cross-curricular benefits of a logical approach to problem-solving encapsulated in the learning of programming and the need to dispel 'irrational fears' about computers which it was claimed many children held (see for example *Education*, 1967, p. 556).

Much of the early computer 'appreciation' courses, in line with examination courses such as CSE Mode 3 Computer Studies and Computer Science, was just that — an appreciation of the machine with an emphasis on those aspects usually associated with computer science (see Makkar (1973a) for criticism of early computer appreciation course material). Although the spread of computer knowledge to those below sixth-form level was usually in the form of a diluted Computer Science, normally designed for those considered to be potential specialists in the field, other changes in education during the 1960s and early 1970s had an impact on the form and content of this move to spread knowledge of computers to a wider section of the school population.

Differentiation of people across the division of labour in the computing industry was seen not only in terms of the work people did but also in terms of the specific attributes they were thought to possess and which it was assumed thus fitted them for a particular place in the computer industry's division of labour (see for example DES, 1967). This was nowhere stronger than in the selection of people for training as programmers. As Danziger concluded at the time when questioning the proclaimed vocational relevance of much of the existing computer courses (exam and non-exam),

> No matter how diligently a student crams the history of data processing or the elements of critical path analysis, with no matter what success in the A level or degree examinations, he will not be employed in commercial computing unless he can pass a test which measures his aptitude for computing. (Danziger, 1973)

The presumed destination of pupils into the wider division of labour across society as a whole was also used as a means of determining different levels of knowledge about computers needed by different groups of pupils. This usually consisted of a split between those who would go on to work closely with computers or who were to become computer specialists and those who would be considered future citizens who would not normally be closely involved with computers (see for example Conway, 1970, p. II/47). For some, the outcome of computer appreciation for such a citizen was seen primarily as a means of ensuring cooperation rather than obstruction *(Computer Education*, 1973, p. 25).

The Newsom Report in 1963, the setting up of the Schools Council in 1964 and the preparations for the raising of the school leaving age in 1972 meant that attention had begun to be paid to the 'needs' of the majority of the school population who were commonly referred to at the time as 'average' and 'below average'. Educated mainly in secondary modern schools they were the section of the school population who were going to make up the majority of the 'future citizens' who would need to be provided with some type of non-specialized computer appreciation course. It was in this context that the first real attempts at expanding computer education to a larger amount of the school population in the form of computer appreciation took place. Within this wider context of an attempt to meet the 'needs' of a large section of the school population, most of whom tended to be seen as 'non-academic', two important aspects stand out in relation to the attempted expansion of computer education.

Firstly, the many projects which were set up by the Schools Council and the Nuffield Foundation concerned with the production of curriculum materials for the 'average' and 'below average' young school leaver (for example Mathematics for the Majority) made the assumption that these groups of pupils were incapable of succeeding in academic courses and their associated exams. The assumption was made that they needed a different education from those who were considered 'academic' (see Young, 1975, p. 51; Cooper, 1985, p. 100).

Secondly, not only did the content of courses developed for these groups differ, but also the way in which the courses were taught took off from a different standpoint to the courses found in academic streams. Emphasis was placed on approaches to learning which reflected the progressive methods used in infant and junior schools and were associated with the work of Dewey, Piaget, Isaacs and Whitehead (see for example Anthony, 1979). Learning by 'discovery', problem-solving, an emphasis on pupil participation, the provision of concrete experiences, relevance to adult and everyday life and the attempt to dissolve subject barriers through project work and integrated studies characterized the approaches called for in courses for this section of the school population (especially for those young people staying on for an extra year because of RoSLA). Although both the form and content of the courses produced for this section of the school population were seen as meeting what was defined as their different 'needs' in relation to those considered academic (for a description of the assumed characteristics of 'non-academic' pupils see Tibble, 1970), the effect, as Young noted at the time, was to cut them off from the possibility of access to the kinds of (academic) knowledge that are associated with rewards, prestige and power in our society (Young, 1971, p. 40).

The need to apply different approaches to the teaching of what were considered 'non-academic' pupils stemmed not only from assumptions about their characteristics, values and attitudes to school (Tibble, 1970). The approaches noted above were also part of a broader educational response to perceived changes in the requirements of adult life and work being brought about by the application of computer technology to production and administration at all levels. The types of approaches noted above and embodied within the Schools Council and the Nuffield Foundation's curriculum research and development projects found support amongst many through a growing realization of modernization based upon the assumptions that for young people still at school, the key requirements of adult life will more and more be the ability not to remember facts or skills, but rather to be inventive and adaptable. They are being educated for an age in which the distinctive human contribution may no longer be the capacity to recall or reproduce existing knowledge and processes. These activities are likely to have been relegated to data-storage systems and computerised automated processes. The individual's task is likely to lie largely in the capacity to adapt, develop, diagnose and respond to new situations, whether he be manager or mechanic, housewife or office worker. In consequence, an important element of most new teaching methods in secondary schools is believed to lie in individualised problem-solving approaches. (Eggleston, 1970, pp. 31–2)

In common with other curriculum development and support, most work in computer appreciation by the end of the 1960s was directed at sixth-form level (Hutchinson, 1970, p. II/61). Very little expansion in terms of curriculum materials for computer appreciation was available for the 'average' and 'below average' child in the third, fourth or fifth forms or for the pupil who was going to have to stay on because of the raising of the school leaving age. However, by the early 1970s Dutton could report that there was a Nuffield Guide called 'Computers and Children' aimed at Junior and Middle Schools, an ICL-CES package callled '16-Scheme *Computer Studies*' aimed at general appreciation, CSE (including Mode 3) and 'O' level examinations in Computer Studies and RoSLA computer groups and finally a Scottish computer appreciation course called 'The Computer — Yours Obediently' which was a basis for general appreciation (Dutton, 1972, p. 25).

Also being developed by the National Computing Centre (NCC) in preparation for the raising of the school leaving age was a package called 'Computer Appreciation for the Majority' (Tinsley, 1972b). Prior to the NCC package, which was eventually published in 1972, concern was being raised in the computer education literature about those pupils labelled 'less able' or 'non-academic' within the wider context of calls for the expansion of computer appreciation. For some, this took the form of not only the need to expand provision for this group but also a concern at the underestimated ability of such pupils to understand what was dealt with in subjects such as computer science at an academic level and for some, their equal prowess, compared to 'academic' pupils, at problem-solving using computers. These views were held by researchers and practioners. Thomas (1970) concluded:

The initial investigation of the educational value of the terminals in both Harlington and Hayes schools suggests that some of those labelled at 11+ as 'less academically able' are as competent at problem-solving as those who were guided to a more academic curriculum. (Thomas, 1970, p. 14)

However, it must be noted that these conclusions centred around the assertion (also supported by an influential NCET report in 1969 (NCET, 1969, p. 22; Murphy, 1970, p. III/21)) that online interactive experience with the computer could enhance the performance of pupils. The claim seemed to be that it was the technology which was able to close the gap between the 'less able' and the 'academic' rather than any misrepresentation of the former's abilities. Some practitioners were also of the opinion that the abilities of the 'less able' were being underestimated.

> I understand that 'Computers' is often considered too difficult to be understood by those of average ability and below. Evidence and personal experience do not bear this out. Much of what I teach is contained in the Computer Science courses at an advanced level of study and, if presented in the right way, is easily understood and discussed by secondary school pupils of most levels of ability (Hutchinson, 1970, p. II/61).

Although much of what passed as computer appreciation was usually a diluted form of computer science with the added elements of a few applications and the consideration of the social implications of computers, the NCC package 'Computer Appreciation for the Majority' was the first real attempt to provide materials for computer appreciation to the 'average' and 'below average' RoSLA pupil. It was very much in line with Schools Council materials developed for this group. Pupils were to be involved thoughout by the use of projects, exercises and worksheets and it was concerned from a humanities perspective with basic concepts as opposed to the acquisition of technical skills. Its aim was explicitly concerned with the social and commercial applications of computers (it used the term 'information processing machines') and the syllabus reflected this with sections concerned with computer applications and case studies in addition to a section on the social implications of computers. It also in an implicit way pointed to what might be the reasons for the growth in the popularity amongst teachers within mathematics, of programming as an activity for 'below average' pupils when it stated:

> They find that simple mathematical programming has a high motivational content and has the advantage of being a structured activity of a trivial nature. It is difficult to provide such a structure for the mainly descriptive content of an appreciation course. We therefore recommend that in an appreciation course the computer be presented through the practical effects of its application rather than as a final consequence of a progressive technical study. (Tinsley, 1972b)

Finding a subject with a high motivational content for RoSLA groups was for many teachers an expressed major concern in the context of their views of the extra year being more about social control than intellectual development (see Young, 1971, p. 40).

There were a number of critical responses to both the expansion of computer appreciation to below sixth-form level and the development of syllabuses that began to move away from technical specifics to include information processing, computer applications and social and political implications (for example NCC's 'Computers and their Impact on Business and Society' (*Computer Education*, 1970); Tinsley, 1972b). The critical responses were important because they attempted to construct different types of syllabuses which argued against the then present trend of a technocentric mixture of learning hardware specifics and programming with 'bolt-on' sections concerned with applications and social and political implications.

Makkar was one of the important early critics who introduced the term 'Computer Awareness' in opposition to the more generally used term 'Computer Appreciation' (Makkar, 1973a, p. 25). This, for him, was a means of distinguishing between, firstly, appreciation courses which were already developed around the principles laid down, in for example 'Computer Education for All' (BCS, 1970), but which he considered to be watered-down computer science, and secondly, the new approach of computer awareness that he wanted to develop. He defined computer awareness as the possession 'of sufficient knowledge to enable inferences, general and social, to be made on the basis of what is seen or heard about computers' (Makkar, 1973a, p. 26). Although debate had centred on what people should know about computers and why they should know about computers, much of it was focused on a technological conception of knowledge about computers and its applications. By comparing what it was generally thought needed to be known about other technological developments such as aeroplanes, with what it was expected that non-specialists should know about computers, Makkar was able to construct an alternative view which, for him, concentrated more on a broad social and political awareness. Makkar saw the need for computer education for all as being built around two cases, the social and the political. The social case focused on the need for people to know how to 'react' when they encounter computers in computer-based services and when they encounter computers directly or indirectly. The political case, for Makkar, pointed to the need in a democracy, where decisions (for the majority of people at least) can only usually be made on the basis of general awareness, for people to be sufficiently informed to be able to influence political decisions about computers (Makkar, 1973a, pp. 25–6). A final case, the academic, recognized that as society depended on experts in various fields, specialist computer education would be needed for a minority only (p. 26). In using what it is assumed people should know about other common technological developments as a means of attempting to show that detailed technical knowledge of computers for the non-specialist is too narrow and irrelevant, Makkar states his case thus:

What does a generally aware person know about aviation for example? He knows it is faster to go by aeroplane from London to Tokyo, that by surface transport. He also knows that, generally, it costs more to fly than to go by train. He is aware that living in the vicinity of an airport means excessive noise interference. Equipped with this kind of knowledge he is able to make more or less effective use of the aviation service (the social need for awareness). He can react with confidence when he hears that a new airport is going to be built in his area (the political need for awareness). Does it help him to meet these needs better if he knows what grade of fuel is used by various types of aircraft? Will he be better educated if he knows the radio frequency used by the aircraft?

In more concrete terms, he is aware of the potential of an aeroplane.... Appreciation of this potential, then, helps him to act intelligently in a novel situation. Knowledge of applications by itself does not amount to awareness. (Makkar, 1973a, p. 26)

In attempting to move away from diluted computer science Makkar concentrated on the awareness of information systems within applications and the introduction of basic systems analysis. Makkar criticized the way in which some teachers, because they felt that children did not have the experience and maturity to deal with commercial applications, used the schools' own environment, such as the mathematics stock cupboard, to demonstrate the applications of computers in, for example, stock control (Makkar, 1975, p. 7). An overriding assumption in the teaching of pupils who were seen as 'low ability' was the need to deal with the concrete and the practical wherever possible. This applied to the general provision that was being developed by the Schools Council and to computer appreciation courses which, for example, concentrated on the concrete specifics of hardware. Makkar, in contrast, claimed that children did not necessarily need to deal with concrete objects when dealing with computer applications, only with recognizable systems (Makkar, 1975, p. 7). These commercial computer systems could be understood by pupils even though they may have had no experience of them by extracting what Makkar calls the 'irrelevant information' and then gradually introducing the computer to the simplified system (Makkar called this an 'applications system' (Makkar, 1975, p. 5)).

Another important critic of computer appreciation and computer studies as a separate subject during the mid-1970s and into the early 1980s was Longworth (Longworth, 1975; 1981a; 1981b). Longworth noted the way in which the exam-orientated British system of education affected the means by which innovations such as computer education were accepted and the slow pace of curriculum change that accompanies it. In addition he pointed to what he felt was the lack of sympathy of mathematics teachers (who dominated the teaching of computer studies and appreciation) towards what they considered to be the 'woolliness' of the social and political implications of computers and the reluctance of humanities teachers to be involved in what they saw as a science subject (Longworth, 1975, p. 750). Longworth developed a course based on the study of information rather than the computer, a change of emphasis which was supported by others in the field (for example Atchinson, 1975). For Longworth this approach became necessary because of what he saw as the 'information explosion' and the need for people to be able to organize this information in terms of logical systems of facts and ideas (Longworth, 1975, p. 750). The abilities which Longworth saw as being of new importance over and above the retention of bodies of knowledge or technical specifics was the ability to index information and find the information a person might want. The pupil should be less concerned with how the computer works and more interested in establishing it as a tool for manipulating information (a view which has been developed throughout the 1980s and now established within the National Curriculum).

Although Longworth's course was probably one of the most notable departures from what could be described as mainstream computer appreciation, it never gained wide currency. The course was wide-ranging, cutting across subject boundaries, and although Longworth stated that it could be taught by any teacher or teachers, Esterson noted seven years later that it failed to become popular because teachers were unable to teach it (Esterson, 1983, p. 187). This seemed to testify to the strength of a traditionally subject-based curriculum in this country, which was able to resist pressures to break down barriers between subjects, especially throughout the late 1960s and 1970s, for example in the work of the Schools Council (see Schools Council, 1975, pp. 40–6) and the call by the influential British Computer Society that computer-based information processing should form the central organizing element in the curriculum.

> In these days of curriculum development and the breaking down of artificial barriers between subjects, the search for such a cohesive unit has ranged over many things. Computing, as a relative newcomer to the educational scene, does not suffer from the orthodox complaints that one discipline is encroaching into the preserve of another, and yet, if it can be seen to offer something to all, it could hasten the day when watertight subjects no longer exist.... Thus, information processing could act as a central subject in the school curriculum from which other subjects find their starting point and by which the curriculum itself could be made more relevant. (BCS, 1974, p. 5)

In secondary education, the strength of subject disciplines and the narrowness of subject-based teacher training was reflected in the British Computer Society's Schools Committee document *The Computer in Secondary Education*, published in 1974. In contrast to the inclusion of the major responsibility for Information Technology within Technology within the National Curriculum, the BCS report excluded the framework of 'Technology' as a base for the study of computers on the grounds that not enough teachers possess the breadth of knowledge necessary to develop such an approach. They put forward that three methods of approach presented themselves as possible introductions to the subject of computer education. Firstly, the study of the computer as an information-processing machine and its applications and implications (BCS, 1974, p. 5). This approach had similarities to Longworth's approach. Secondly, the study of the computer as a subject in its own right which would be encompassed by a form of computer science or the broader Computer Studies. Thirdly, the study of the computer and its use within a much larger framework of 'Technology' education. Here they suggested the computer would be seen as but one of many influences by which technology affects people's lives and therefore would present a much broader picture to the student than computer science or computer appreciation. However, in excluding this approach from their consideration they note a problem which still faces education today.

> One problem of this approach is the lack of teachers with the necessary breadth of knowledge to develop it, and in spite of the research which is being carried out in a few places, it seems likely that this shortage will persist for some considerable time. For this reason, the 'Technology' approach will not be considered further. (BCS, 1974, p. 5)

From Computer Studies and Appreciation to a Broad-Based Informatics: A Missed Opportunity?

The calls for a change in emphasis away from a focus on the technical specifics of computers towards the study of information processing and the applications and implications of the use of computers were, in many ways, a reflection of the relatively rapid change from the narrow scientific and mathematical use of computers to their large-scale use in business and the development of integrated administration and management information systems.

In Europe, by the beginning of the 1970s and in contrast to the common use of the term 'computer education' in the UK, there had been the growth of a body of knowledge called 'informatics', which by 1972 was seen in many countries as a separate discipline to computer science (Buckingham, 1979, p. 56). Although, like computer education, informatics had its version of a pure subject (fundamental informatics) based around mathematics and the physical nature of processing, the development of informatics was integral to the development of the use of computers in business and administration information processing systems. In a similar way to the debate in the UK over whether computer studies and computer appreciation should reflect computer science or be more broadly based, debate in informatics also centred around whether it should be concerned with the physical data-processing systems (for example computers) or broader information systems which may include computers and which included consideration of the human and social factors involved in the design and use of information processing technology (Buckingham, 1979, p. 56). A split emerged between what was defined as 'technical informatics' with a bias towards engineering, and 'business informatics' with a bias towards management studies and business administration (Euwe, 1974).

The initial use of computers in business and administration during the 1960s was very much based on a management view of making use of the computer in distinct functional departments. This was in line with the traditional division of company activities into relatively automonous and functionally differentiated areas (for example, marketing, production, distribution and accounting) and a strongly vertical structural hierarchy with little or no formal or informal lateral information flow. As Staines noted at the time,

> The vertical orientation of company structures prevailing during the early sixties and the tendency to view company activities within the context of compartmentalised functionally defined sub units was largely responsible for the inability of management to conceive of the computer role other than as a tool of functional departments, replacing traditional processes and operations within the existing departmental (functional) boundaries. The result of this functional orientation on the part of management was a demand for computerised 'order processing systems', 'inventory recording systems', 'sales accounting systems' etc., which systems analysts designed, programmers programmed and which were duly implemented ... whilst the implementation of new systems within these functional constraints were often able to show an improvement in the behaviour of the one sub-system there are all too few instances of an evidenced contribution to the performance of the total system. (Staines, 1970, p. II/452)

By the 1970s management had realized that the development of the use of the computer in business and administration need not be limited to merely replacing or automating, for example, clerical procedures. The computer could also be used to provide information for better decision-making and control purposes (Tallis, 1978). However, this development of what came to be called 'Management Information Systems' (MIS) was dependent on the realization, by management, of the problems of lateral and vertical integration of the various separate departments within an organization (Staines, 1970, p. II/452). The subsequent move towards the integration of operations data led also to the possibility of integrated management control systems, a possibility realized a decade earlier in 1960 (Mann, 1960, p. 247).

With the development of integrated systems, the jobs associated with computers became more complex and began to involve consideration of not just the technical aspects of implementing a computer system but also the need for a greater appreciation of the organization as a whole, especially those involved in systems analysis (Staines, 1970, p. II/452). However, as Land states,

> We have been training computer professionals whose outlook is biased towards the machine.... What they have not been able to do ..., is to design applications which meet the real needs of the organisation or match the skills (and lack of skills) of all those involved in working in the organisation with the new jobs they have to carry out within the computer based system. There is increasing evidence that the most critical aspect of a computer application is its acceptance by the staff who work the system and the managers who use it. Non-acceptance spells failure, poor use involves constant and uneconomic changes to the system. From his narrow, technical base the systems designer has no way of assessing the likelihood of his design meeting the criteria of acceptance of those who have to work with the system. Indeed the systems designer often regards rejection of a system or its misuse as a fault of the user due to their stupidity and lack of appreciation of the capability of the machine. (Land, 1979, pp. 45–6)

By the late 1970s research was already being carried out into how it might be possible for those who have to work with computerized information systems to be able to take on a vital role in the design of the system (see for example Mumford, 1977).

With the development of larger integrated computerized information systems throughout Europe in the 1970s employers were increasingly critical of computer science graduates who assumed that their qualification was a sound basis for a career in the occupation of systems analysis, which was having to take account of the need for a broader field of study including psychology, sociology, industrial relations and personnel. In many cases the computer science graduate was actively discouraged from this career path and directed by employers into a narrower computer-related field (Tallis, 1978, p. 32). The broadening of the scope of informatics education and training in Europe to include consideration of social and human behaviour aspects involved in computerized information systems also had an impact in the UK at graduate level in the mid 1970s. As Land notes, when the British Computer Society's working group, set up in 1973 to develop an entirely new curriculum for a degree in data processing, reported in 1975, it published a curriculum which had a substantial part devoted to the 'human aspects' of data processing (Land, 1979, p. 47).

There were calls in 1975 at the influential IFIP Computer Education conference, for a broader view to be taken of computer education through a move towards informatics type courses which took account of the developments mentioned above (see for example Atchison, 1975). However, a crucial earlier year in this respect was 1970 when the first IFIP computer education conference took place and, at the time, was considered an important milestone in computer education in this country and in Europe (the leading figures in UK computer education attended (Scheepmaker and Zinn, 1970)). It was important for a number of reasons. Firstly, it recognized and recommended the replacement in Europe of the term 'computer science' with 'informatics' in the light of changing circumstances of the use of computers in business and administration. Secondly, informatics was seen as multidisciplinary with information processing as its focus and not the computer. Thirdly, because it generated argument in this country over whether computer studies or computer science should be replaced by a broader informatics.

A notable influence on informatics in Europe was the development of the subject in Scandinavia and in particular the work of Borje Langefors in Sweden which reflected the need for a broad concept of informatics (Buckingham, 1979, p. 56). Langefors gave one of the introductory keynote papers at the 1970 IFIP Computer Education conference, entitled 'Computer Applications in the 1970s: Consequences for Education. From Computer Science to Informatics'. In this paper he pointed to a number of important aspects of the development of informatics and education. In addition to speaking about the integration of operations into systems and the need for education to produce people capable of thinking about whole systems, Langefors stressed the need for the democratization of information within a company in order better to adapt corporate goals to the needs and desires of people, and the improvement, in terms of motivation, group communication and possibilities for innovation, of an open information system within companies (Langefors, 1970, p. I/30). He also, in contrast to much of the literature and aims for the development of computer potential in this country at the time, stressed that 'The future lies not in using computers to replace judgement. The future is for computers to support judgement' (Langefors, 1970, p. I/31). Finally Langefors, in rejecting computer science as too narrow a subject to take on board the developments noted above, stressed the need for a multidisciplinary approach to the development of informatics and the importance of information analysis and systems acceptance in organizations as part of informatics, where he considered sociology a much closer scientific field to informatics than mathematics (Langefors, 1970, p. I/32).

These calls in the conference to replace computer science with broader informatics-type courses were taken up in the UK at the time. The British Computer Society in responding to this European influence registered the name 'British Informatics Society' for possible future use (although subsequently it never used this name) (Barker, 1971, p. 17). However, the two influential bodies in computer education at the time, the Computer Education Group and the British Computer Society Schools Committee were reluctant to take any initiative in using the term informatics in any of their work (ibid.).

Barker, in summing up what he considered to be the UK reaction to pressure from Europe to use the term and broaden traditional computer courses, stated:

> The average UK attitude will be to 'laugh like drains' at the thought of using such an unfamiliar word. But I believe that 'informatics', now accepted in Europe, is the solution to many of the semantic problems which bedevil us. We have the opportunity to start with a clean slate in convincing governments and educationalists about the urgent implications of informatics without the use of that buzz word 'computer'. We would clearly delineate a field of study which is multidisciplinary and not confined to mathematics. A subject which does not necessarily need access to a computer for it to be taught. (Barker, 1971, p. 17)

However, in this country at least, the reasons for the rejection of informatics (and informatics-type courses such as those produced by Makkar and Longworth) and much of what it implied for the rapidly solidifying subject of computer studies and its non-examination counterpart, computer appreciation, was not just a matter of semantics or unfamiliarity. The particular way in which computer studies and computer appreciation developed, as this paper has begun to show, had much more to do with its initial development within mathematics, its hardware focus, a strong subject-based curriculum and a subject-based teaching profession, and an increasingly differentiated school population and associated curriculum developments.

Conclusions

This paper has attempted to outline a few major themes within the development of computer education over the last thirty years. Many of the debates mentioned in this paper still remain centre stage today, for example those concerned with information technology as a separate subject, its use across the curriculum and its assumed vocational relevance below degree level in the face of the rapidly changing uses and development of Information Technology in the manufacturing and service sectors. The traditional academic curriculum of separate subjects has proved very limiting in attempts to broaden the approach to technology, computer studies and computer literacy. Today, complaints of secondary schools producing computer labs which are used as 'computing competency factories' in isolation from the rest of the curriculum still abound (Telford, 1990). The inclusion of Information Technology (IT) in the National Curriculum is a continuation of previous attempts (for example the Microelectronics Education Programme) to spread knowledge of IT to a broader population and recognizes the need for a cross-curricular approach if IT is to be related to industrial and commercial changes. However, the

National Curriculum itself is a strengthening of the traditional academic curriculum. This combined with a limited view of the role of non-specialists, new parental pressures on schools, a lack of resources for equipment and staff and the subject traditions that are still in practice embedded in Department of Education thinking, means that changes will be slow (Capel and Young, 1988). However, IT developments across the curriculum (which at present are only at a low level of skill and knowledge) should be seen in part as a possible progressive development which could help lead to the breaking down of barriers between subjects and between academic disciplines and vocationally-related courses. Such developments could also provide the possibilities for a broader understanding of the significance of technological change for the specialist and the majority of non-specialists.

As was outlined at the beginning of this paper a helpful view of modernization is one which recognizes the contradictory tendencies and differing possibilities stemming from a need for increased specialization and the growth and development of technology. In addition, as Young has noted,

> Modernisation is not some kind of inevitable process but will take on the character of its cultural and social context. Modernisation is not necessarily progressive and democratic (reducing social divisions) or reactionary (sustaining or extending social divisions and inequalities). Its social outcomes do not depend on anything intrinsic to either technology or to the growth of specialisation in industrial and technology-based societies. (Young, 1987, p. 4)

IT and computing in educaton have to be viewed not in isolation but as related to this growth of specialization and expertise and the way in which technologies are designed to supplement or replace human work. All countries need to spread technological knowledge in order to maintain and improve their productivity. This then requires changes in education and work which can help to create new relations between specialists and non-specialists. However, in a society characterized by systematic inequalities there are also counter-pressures to restrict that knowledge and control the form it takes (Capel and Young, 1988). It is this contradictory context that has in part shaped the historical developments outlined in this paper and the form computer education took in this country.

The predominant focus of IT and computer education has been technocentric. It has had as its central focus the computer and its associated technologies with little regard for the wider human relations which produce it and on which it has an effect. Terms such as 'computer appreciation' and 'computer studies' reflect this sometime obsession with the technical aspects of the computer. As was detailed earlier in this paper, in response to changes in production, computer education attempted to move from a mathematical and computing focus to one which took account of the data-processing and information-handling use of computers in commerce and industry. However, the approach was similar in that courses tended to merely place the computer within an application stressing the role that it played within different types of organizations and the benefits (usually labour-saving) of its introduction. Over the last ten years a view of the computer as a 'tool' with which children can 'think' and work has become the dominant view of the role of IT in education. This has not moved us much further away from a focus on the technology, it has merely attempted to render it neutral and not in need of explanation. IT within the National Curriculum Technology document is based upon what could be called a cross-curricular 'tools/skills' model of IT in education (DES, 1990; Capel and Young, 1988). Such a view, however, hides the technological framework within which anyone using a computer is obliged to work and think. As Streibel has noted, the ways in which computers are designed

> force us to act as if we were rule-governed information processors. They also force us to construe thinking as cognitive problem-solving where the 'solutions' are arrived at by formal calculation, computation and rational analysis. Even if we are active and constructive and intuitive in our approach to the world, we must still analyse and reduce problems into explicit and procedural terms. Hence, we must restrict our thinking to cognitive operations. The concept of the computer as an intellectual tool is therefore not a neutral formulation because it forces us to objectify ourselves as agents of prediction, calculation and control. Personal intellectual agency has thereby been limited to the technological framework. (Streibel, 1985, p. 41)

Peter Medway has noted elsewhere in this volume the construction of a rationalistic, means-end orientated, systematic design process within Technology in the National Curriculum. Such a technological framework delegitimizes those processes which are particularly a part of human beings and their environments such as tacit knowledge, subjective judgment, complexity and intuition.

This technocentric perspective was also a predominant characteristic of the way in which industry and commerce developed the use of technology. The systems that were produced tended to be designed with the assumption that the human input to the production process was the greatest source of 'systems liability' and therefore the aim was to displace or deskill the worker (Braverman, 1974; Edwards, 1979). Cooley, in summarizing the situation within industries which could be characterized by their use of scientific management and Fordist mass-production strategies, strikes a similar note to the authors above.

> The existing systems which are predominantly technocentric tend to render human beings passive and the system active. Such systems are only regarded as 'being scientifically designed' if they are dominated

by the three predominant characteristics of the natural sciences: pre-
dictability, repeatability and mathematical quantifiability. This by
definition precludes intuition, subjective judgement, tacit knowledge,
imagination and intentionality, those peculiarly human attributes.
There is in consequence an unfortunate tendency to regard human
beings as systems' liability either to be marginalised altogether or so
constrained that they are in reality merely a passive machine appen-
dage. It is not surprising therefore that a recent issue of *American
Machinist* suggests that the ideal workers for some forms of NC
machines are mentally retarded workers, and specifically mentions a
mental age of 12. (Cooley, 1989, p. 11)

This view was part of a global system of mass production which has been
encapsulated within the term Fordism. In simple terms Fordist production
could be characterized by large factories, standardized products feeding mass
markets, the use of Taylorism and scientific management principles, bureaucracies which are strictly departmental and hierarchical, and a large amount of
dull, repetitive, unskilled work in the factory. Since the 1970s, in response to
periods of stagnation and crisis for many countries, new production strategies
which differ significantly from Fordist production have begun to develop. A
model of post-Fordism has been developed in the literature of the Left to help
understand these changes (see for example Murray's chapter in *Understanding
Technology in Education*). It is impossible in a paper of this length to give a
comprehensive account. However, many of the debates which are emerging
can provide a context for the historical accounts detailed in this paper,
especially those concerning the changing nature of work.

Probably the most well known of the post-Fordist production strategies
has been that of the Japanese. Within many Japanese industries flexible production systems are based on intensive use of advanced technology in all
stages of production coupled with a just-in-time system of stock control, less
hierarchical bureaucratic structures and new work relations. These new work
relations are based around a decline in trade unionism and an increase in
worker education, flexibility, teamwork and company loyalty mixed with
internal forms of limited worker democracy. However, the Japanese developments have also shown that at the level of the national workforce there can
develop a small population of highly skilled 'core' workers with relatively
secure employment conditions and a large population of 'peripheral' workers
with very insecure employment conditions and who are low-paid and poorly
organized.

From the literature surrounding the changes in production strategies it
is clear that the nature of work is changing at varying paces within different
industries (see for example Jones, 1988; Lane, 1988; Piore and Sabel, 1984;
Hirschhorn, 1984; Zuboff, 1988). Employers are beginning to train and re-
cruit with the objective of obtaining employees with a wide range of technical
and social skills that cut across traditional subjects and qualifications. New

production methods could require greater involvement of shop-floor workers in maintenance, monitoring, control and problem-solving, and present the need for creativity. The latter is part of moves to involve the whole workforce in quality control and innovation, rather than separating this off in research and development sections under the control of specialists. The emphasis on the creative possibilities of workers is in opposition to the Fordist tendency to concentrate on a worker's ability to exhibit standardized skills within individualized tasks. The view of organizations as hierarchical and departmentalized is declining in favour of organizations with reductions in vertical authority structures and an increase in horizontal cooperation between specialists and non-specialists from various parts of the production process. The organization is seen as a learning environment as opposed to an administrative 'machine'. A more anthropocentric view is being developed where the worker is central to the production process (as opposed to being marginalized as a 'liability'). The worker is seen as a whole person who needs to continue to learn and develop and where 'human-centred technologies' allow those peculiar human qualities and skills to develop and be drawn upon to aid more flexible and efficient production (Cooley, 1987; 1989; Brodner, 1987). Such changes, tentative and sparse as they are, offer both progressive (democratic) and regressive possibilities (increasing social divisions, for example, as with the concept of 'core' and 'periphery').

The above changes have many implications for the education and training systems of countries. If we are to work towards democratic possibilities within such changes then the education and training systems must begin to dissolve the traditional separation of the technical from the economic and the social (Capel and Young, 1988). In doing so the educational system might begin to provide holistic forms of education, which when dealing with technology provide an anthropocentric perspective as opposed to a technocentric approach. What is needed is for education to provide new combinations of knowledges which reflect the changes outlined above and bring together different specialists and non-specialists in a democratic framework premised upon a common basis for understanding each other.

The importance of the examples in this paper is that firstly they demonstrate to some extent the differentiation of knowledge based upon assumptions about the division of labour (specialists and non-specialists) and secondly they point to potentially progressive opportunities missed along the way. In many ways Makkar's call to broaden the previously technocentric approach to computer appreciation was a first attempt to combine the political and the social with knowledge about the technical. Longworth's proposals for the spread of knowledge about the study of information as opposed to the concentration on the technicalities of computers was also an attempt in its own way to bring together different subjects in a new combination. If it had been developed at the time, it would have perhaps formed a basis for a more integrated account of technological changes in our society than that which was provided by much of the computer studies/literacy of the late 1970s and

Richard Capel

1980s. The recognition by the British Computer Society of the benefits of a larger framework which they called 'technology' education also held possibilities for a broader and more integrated approach to understanding the rapid changes in society. The reasons why these opportunities were not taken up and why a more technocratic and subject-bounded approach was developed, have been clearly stated earlier in this paper.

The second historical example begins to show that there was important work taking place in Europe towards a broad approach to informatics which was not based on a technocentric approach. The work suggested that informatics should be based around the assumptions that it was important to bring together the technical and the social in the training of workers (for example, systems analysts) and to develop a democratization of information within organizations. In addition it was important for education to produce young people capable of thinking about whole systems as opposed to having knowledge related to a fragmented division of labour. Finally, that informatics was multidisciplinary and that the social sciences formed a central part in the understanding of rapid technological change. As was shown earlier in this paper, in Britain at least, the prevailing and dominant educational conditions meant that the chances of a dialogue with developments in Europe were slight.

References

ANTHONY, W. (1979) 'Progressive learning theories: the evidence', in BERNBAUM, G. (Ed.) Schooling in Decline, London, Macmillan, pp. 149–81.

ATCHINSON, W.F. (1975) Elements of Information and Information Processing for Teachers in Secondary Schools, IFIP Working Group 3.1.

ATKIN, K. (1976) 'Computer Education Group Conference: Computing and the Schoolteacher', Computer Education, June, pp. 24–7.

BARKER, J.G. (Ed.) (1971) 'Introducing informatics: a special report', Computer Education, April (special insert).

BRAVERMAN, H. (1974) Labor and Monopoly Capital, New York, Monthly Review Press.

BCS (BRITISH COMPUTER SOCIETY) SCHOOLS COMMITTEE (1969) 'Computer education for all', Computer Education, June, pp. 29–31.

BCS (BRITISH COMPUTER SOCIETY) SCHOOLS COMMITTEE (1970) 'Computer education for all', Computer Education, June (insert).

BCS (BRITISH COMPUTER SOCIETY) SCHOOLS COMMITTEE (1974) The Computer in Secondary Education, London, BCS.

BRODERICK, W.R. (1968) The Computer in School, London, The Bodley Head.

BRODNER, P. (1987) 'Towards an anthropological approach in European manufacturing', Vocational Training Bulletin, CEDEFOP, Berlin, pp. 30–9.

BUCKINGHAM, R.A. (1979) 'Educational trends in information processing in Europe', in SIMPSON, A. (Ed.) Selected Essays in Contemporary Computing, Purley, Surrey, Input Two Nine Ltd, pp. 55–60.

CAPEL, R. and YOUNG, M.F.D. (1988) Critical Perspectives in IT Across the

Curriculum: Issues for Theory and Research, unpublished paper, University of London Institute of Education.

CERI (CENTRE FOR EDUCATIONAL RESEARCH AND DEVELOPMENT) OECD (1969) 'Computers in secondary education', *Computer Education*, October, pp. 73–6.

CERI (CENTRE FOR EDUCATIONAL RESEARCH AND DEVELOPMENT) OECD (1970) 'Recommendations OECD-CERI Seminar on Computer Sciences in Secondary Schools', in SCHEEPMAKER, B. and ZINN, K.L. (Eds) *World Conference on Computer Education 1970*, papers of the first International Federation for Information Processing (IFIP) Conference, 24–28 August, Amsterdam, Groningen, The Netherlands, Wolters Noordhoff, pp. I/133–I/135.

COMPUTER EDUCATION (1970) 'NCC Computer Appreciation course', *Computer Education*, April, pp. 3–5.

COMPUTER EDUCATION (1970) 'NCC Computer Appreciation course', *Computer Education*, April, pp. 3–5.

CONWAY, D. (1970) 'The use of package programs in computer education in schools', in SCHEEPMAKER, B. and ZINN, K.L. (Eds) *World Conference on Computer Education 1970*, papers of the first International Federation for Information Processing (IFIP) Conference, 24–28 August, Amsterdam, Groningen, The Netherlands, Wolters Noordhoff, pp. II/47–II/49.

COOLEY, M. (1987) 'Human centred systems: an urgent problem for systems designers', *AI and Society*, Vol. 1, pp. 37–46.

COOLEY, M. (1989) *European Competitiveness in the 21st Century: Integration of Work, Culture and Technology*, FAST: Forecasting and Assessment in Science and Technology, Brussels, Commission of the European Communities.

COOPER, B. (1985) 'Secondary school mathematics since 1950: reconstructing differentiation', in GOODSON, I. (Ed.) *Social Histories of the Secondary Curriculum*, London, Falmer Press.

DANZIGER, C. (1973) 'Are computer courses relevant?', *Education*, 15 June, p. 677.

DES (DEPARTMENT OF EDUCATION AND SCIENCE), SCOTTISH EDUCATION DEPARTMENT AND MINISTRY OF EDUCATION FOR NORTHERN IRELAND (1967) *Computer Education: Report of an Interdepartmental Working Group*, London, HMSO.

DES (DEPARTMENT OF EDUCATION AND SCIENCE) (1990) *Technology in the National Curriculum*, London, HMSO.

DUTTON, P.E. (1972) 'Computer page', *Mathematics in Schools*, Vol. 1, No. 5, July, pp. 22–3.

EDUCATION (1967) 'Why have computer education?', *Education*, Vol. 130, 13 October, pp. 555–7.

EDWARDS, R. (1979) *Contested Terrain*, London, Heinemann.

EGGLESTON, S.J. (1970) 'Some sociological considerations', in TIBBLE, J.W. (Ed.) *The Extra Year*, London, Routledge and Kegan Paul, pp. 20–36.

ESTERSON, D. (1983) 'Computer studies and computer education', in MEGARRY, J. et al. (Eds) *World Year Book of Education 82/83*, London, Kogan Page, pp. 186–93.

EUWE, M. (1974) 'Survey of courses in informatics in the European Economic Community 1972', in DANIELS, A. (Ed.) *British Computer Society: Educational Yearbook 1973–74*, London, BCS.

HIRSCHHORN, L. (1984) *Beyond Mechanisation*, London, MIT Press.

HODGKIN, L. (1976) 'Politics and physical sciences', *Radical Science Journal*, 4, pp. 29–60.

HUTCHINSON, M.G.P. (1970) 'Computers in schools: computers and secondary education', in SCHEEPMAKER, B. and ZINN, K.L. (Eds) *World Conference on Computer Education 1970*, papers of the first International Federation for Information Processing (IFIP) Conference, 24–28 August, Amsterdam, Groningen, The Netherlands, Wolters Noordhoff, pp. II/59–II/66.

JONES, B. (1988) 'Work and flexible automation in Britain: a review of developments and possibilities', *Work, Employment and Society*, Vol. 2, No. 4, December, pp. 451–86.

LAND, F.F. (1979) 'The changing face of computer education', in SIMPSON, A. (Ed.) *Selected Essays in Contemporary Computing*, Purley, Surrey, Input Two Nine Ltd., pp. 43–50.

LANE, C. (1988) 'Industrial Change in Europe: the pursuit of flexible specialisation in Britain and West Germany', *Work, Employment and Society*, Vol. 2, No. 2, June.

LANGEFORS, B. (1970) 'Computer applications in the 1970's: consequences for education. From computer science to informatics', in SCHEEPMAKER, B. and ZINN, K.L. (Eds) *World Conference on Computer Education 1970*, papers of the first International Federation for Information Processing (IFIP) Conference, 24–28 August, Amsterdam, Groningen, The Netherlands, Wolters Noordhoff, pp. I/29–I/33.

LONGWORTH, N. (1975) 'A course on Information for the Secondary School', in LECARNE, O. and LEWIS, R. (Eds), Computer In Education, North Holland Publishing Company, pp. 749–54.

LONGWORTH, N. (1981a) 'Change and information-missing ingredients in the teaching of informatics', in LEWIS, R. and TAGG, D. (Eds) *Computers and Education*, Amsterdam, IFIP North-Holland, pp. 677–84.

LONGWORTH, N. (1981b) 'We're moving into the information society. What shall we teach the children?', *Computer Education*, June, pp. 17–19.

LYON, D. (1988) *The Information Society: Issues and Illusions*, Cambridge, Polity Press.

MAKKAR, L. (1973a) 'What is computer awareness? or (If they are ALL RIGHT, what's WRONG)', *Computer Education*, June, pp. 25–7.

MAKKAR, L. (1973b) 'Computer awareness for all, or if they are All Right, What's Wrong?', *Computer Education*, November, pp. 21–4.

MAKKAR, L. (1975) 'Computer awareness: the main aim for computer education for all', *International World of Computer Education*, Vol. 1, No. 8, April, pp. 6–8.

MANN, A.O. (1960) 'A publicly regulated system of management control services', in MALCOM, D.G., ROWE, A.J. and McCONNELL, L.F. (Eds) *Management Control Systems*, New York, Wiley.

MUMFORD, E. (1977) 'Procedures for the institution of change in work organisation (participative work design: a contribution to democracy in the office and on the shop floor)', paper given at a conference held in Moscow, International Institute of Labour and USSR Institute of Labour, March, unpublished (cited in LAND, F.F. (1979) 'The changing face of computer education', in SIMPSON, A. (Ed.) *Selected Essays in Contemporary Computing*, Purley, Surrey, Input Two Nine Ltd, pp. 43–50).

MURPHY, B.M. (1970) 'A new educational structure for the computer age', in SCHEEPMAKER, B. and ZINN, K.L. (Eds) *World Conference on Computer Education 1970*, papers of the first International Federation for Information Processing (IFIP) Conference, 24–28 August, Amsterdam, Groningen, The Netherlands, Wolters Noordhoff, pp. III/19–III/22.

MURRAY, R. (1988) 'Life after Henry (Ford)', *Marxism Today*, October, pp. 8–13 (also in MACKAY, H., YOUNG, M. and BEYNON, J. (Eds) (1991) *Understanding Technology in Education*, London, Falmer Press).

NEWSOM, J. (1963) *Half our Future*, Report of the Minister of Education's Central Advisory Council, London, HMSO.

NCET (NATIONAL COUNCIL FOR EDUCATIONAL TECHNOLOGY) (1969) *Computers for Education*, Report of a Working Party under the chairmanship of Professor J. Black, London, NCET.

NOBLE, D. (1977) *America by Design: Science, Technology and the Rise of Corporate Capitalism*, London, Oxford University Press.

NOBLE, D. (1979) 'Social choice in machine design: the case of automatically controlled machine tools', in ZIMBALIST, A. (Ed.) *Case Studies in the Labor Process*, New York, Monthly Review Press. (also in MACKAY. H., YOUNG, M. and BEYNON, J. (Eds) (1991) *Understanding Technology in Education*, London, Falmer Press).

NOBLE, D. (1986) *Forces of Production: A Social History of Industrial Automation*, London, Oxford University Press.

PIORE, M.J. and SABEL, C. (1984) *The Second Industrial Divide*, New York, Basic Books.

SCHEEPMAKER, B. and ZINN, K.L. (Eds) *World Conference on Computer Education 1970*, papers of the first International Federation for Information Processing (IFIP) Conference, 24–28 August, Amsterdam, Groningen, The Netherland, Wolters Noordhoff.

SCHOOLS COUNCIL WORKING PARTY ON THE WHOLE CURRICULUM 1971–1974 (1975) *The Whole Curriculum 13–16*, Schools Council Working Paper 53, London, Evans/Methuen Educational.

SET (SCOTTISH EDUCATION DEPARTMENT) (1969) *Computers in the Schools: An Interim Report*, Curriculum Papers 6, Consultative Committee on the Curriculum, London, HMSO.

STAINES, B.R.J. (1970) 'Fourth generation system analysts (systems analysis in the 1970s)', in SCHEEPMAKER, B. and ZINN, K.L. (Eds) *World Conference on Computer Education 1970*, papers of the first International Federation for Information Processing (IFIP) Conference, 24–28 August, Amsterdam, Groningen, The Netherlands, Wolters Noordhoff, pp. II/451–II/457.

STREIBEL, M.J. (1985) 'A critical analysis of computer based approaches to education: drill and practice, tutorials and programming/simulations, The University of Wisconsin, paper presented to the Annual Meeting of the American Research Association, Chicago, Illinois.

TALLIS, R. (1978) 'The systems analyst — past; present: future?', *Computer Education*, No. 30, November, pp. 31–2.

TELFORD, J. (1990) 'Putting IT about', *Educational Computing and Technology*, June, pp. 46–9.

THOMAS, J.B. (1970) 'Computing in schools', *Computer Education*, April, pp. 13–14.

Richard Capel

TIBBLE, J.W. (1970) 'The pupils and their teachers', in TIBBLE, J.W. (Ed.) *The Extra Year*, London, Routledge and Kegan Paul, pp. 37–53.

TINSLEY, J.D. (1970) 'A computer for schools', in SCHEEPMAKER, B. and ZINN, K.L. (Eds) *World Conference on Computer Education 1970*, papers of the first International Federation for Information Processing (IFIP) Conference, 24–28 August, Amsterdam, Groningen, The Netherlands, Wolters Noordhoff, pp. II/85–II/89.

TINSLEY, J.D. (1972a) 'Syllabuses and methods for computer education in schools', in AUSTWICK, K. and HARRIS, N.D.C. (Eds) *Aspects of Educational Technology*, Vol. 6, London, Pitman Publishers, pp. 71–8.

TINSLEY, J.D. (Ed.) (1972b) *Computer Appreciation for the Majority*, 2nd ed., Manchester, National Computing Centre Publications.

WILLIAMS, R. (1974) *Television: Technology and Cultural Form*, Fontana.

YOUNG, M.F.D. (1971) 'An approach to the study of curricula as socially organised knowledge', in YOUNG, M.F.D. *Knowledge and Control: New Directions for the Sociology of Education*, London, Collier-Macmillan, pp. 19–46.

YOUNG, M.F.D. (1975) 'On the politics of educational knowledge: some preliminary considerations with particular reference to the Schools Council', in BELL, R. and PRESCOTT, W. (Eds) *The Schools Council: A Second Look*, London, Ward Lock Educational, pp. 31–55.

YOUNG, M.F.D. (1987) 'IT and the curriculum: issues for theory and research', unpublished paper, University of London, Institute of Education.

ZUBOFF, S. (1988) *In the Age of the Smart Machine: The Future of Work and Power*, London, Heinemann Professional Publishing.

Chapter 3

Constructions of Technology: Reflections on a New Subject

Peter Medway

Introduction

Of the ten subjects prescribed as compulsory in the new National Curriculum for England and Wales (three 'core' and seven 'foundation'), nine, together with their supporting rhetorics of justification, are familiar — depressingly familiar, many feel. One subject, however, technology, represents a radical departure. Far from being slipped in unobtrusively, moreover, this incongruously innovative element has been given great prominence: the working group to write the technology curriculum was amongst the first to be appointed, and the subject, while not part of the 'core', is apparently to be assessed more rigorously than history, geography, art and the other 'foundation' subjects.[1]

It is interesting and important, therefore, to ask how this new subject got itself invented and included and what the implications are of the shape which has been given to it. By way of answer, this analysis will point to a *process* which involved, on the one hand, educational idealism and well-founded theory and, on the other, conceptual confusion, unrealistic aspirations and ideological loading, and to an *outcome* which is bizarrely radical and conservative by turns.

Readings of the New Curriculum

Hard evidence of the government's reasons for making technology compulsory for all children between the ages of 5 and 16 is unlikely to be available until the relevant papers are released in many years' time. In the meantime we can attempt to determine the field of *possible* motivations by consulting the strands of debate and advocacy over the last few years. For the case for technology education has been urged on diverse grounds, and there are a number of things which its introduction now might mean.[2]

National Curriculum technology might, for instance, be interpreted as an eleventh-hour response, long awaited by many in industry (and perhaps especially in engineering), to the long neglect of technical education in this country, a belated recognition of the need to raise its status to the prominence it enjoys in other countries such as West Germany.[3] Such reasoning might be underpinned by a more general economic and cultural concern about British lack of competitiveness and enterprise, based on a Wiener-like analysis of the depressing effect of a prevailing gentlemanly culture which despises industry and disdains practical activity.[4] If this were the motivation, the introduction of technology would have to be read as a significant *vocationalizing* of a secondary curriculum in which the major subjects had hitherto been academic, with vocational studies reserved for older students classed as less academically able. Working against this reading, however, is the consideration that nowhere else in the selection of subjects for the National Curriculum are there signs of such a vocational intent. What we see, on the contrary, at least in the subject titles (the way they are worked out in detail may be another matter), is an unreconstructed liberal curriculum of major academic and minor aesthetic subjects with physical and religious education, a curriculum in which national *economic* concerns have clearly weighed no more than they ever did in the traditional grammar school.

Alternatively, we could be seeing the creation of a new and more instrumental *academic* specialism, to begin to replace the classical subjects of mathematics, the humanities and the pure sciences from which legitimacy seems to be draining away. In the UK ever fewer teachers display much conviction in defending the traditional liberal curriculum and ever more of them readily embrace more vocational and 'applied' approaches such as those developed in the Technical and Vocational Education Initiative (TVEI),[5] while in post-compulsory and higher education students increasingly opt in favour of subjects of direct professional relevance such as accountancy and law.[6] There are signs in the UK too that, as noted in Australia by Cherry Collins, the emerging version of the academic curriculum 'is now hardly recognisable as academic by any of that tradition's major criteria. It consists of the positivistic science variant of the theory/abstraction tradition, plus a basic skill (English, seen largely as language skill), plus some preparation for rising white-collar employment areas' ('new "professional" subjects like computing, accounting, economics and legal studies').[7] The new subject of technology may have been seen as meeting a need for a discipline which would be both intellectually taxing (thus serving selection purposes) and legitimate in the eyes of a generation of career-minded students and their parents.

The craft area of the curriculum had in any case for some years been aspiring to move in this direction; the craft processes of wood and metal working had been supplemented and partly replaced first by design and then by elements of physics and engineering. Two results were clearly apparent: the area had been rising in status and recruiting more able students; and students who had previously found enjoyment, success and self-respect in the crafts (and often nowhere else) ceased to find them in the written and scientific demands of the reconstructed and renamed subject of Technology.[8] No parallel place of privilege as a foundation subject in its own right has, however, been found in the statutory curriculum for business studies, the other subject which has undergone similar academicization and status enhancement.

A final possibility is that the move was about 'the rehabilitation of the practical',[9] an attempt to redress the imbalance in the esteem accorded to skilful practice in relation to academic achievement and to acknowledge that intelligence and cognitive complexity might be manifested in doing as much as in knowing. Justificatory underpinnings might be found in studies which reveal the sophistication of thinking-in-action[10] argue for the existence of multiple forms of intelligence.[11] The impulse behind such a rehabilitation might be a democratic concern to alter the basis on which ability and worth were assessed so as to give greater access to self-respect, certification and life chances for those who operate more readily in the mode of action rather than of study and reflection.

Although it is impossible at this point to decide between such speculative explanations, they provide a useful purchase for scrutinizing the process of production and the emerging character of the new subject.

The Construction of 'Technology'

Unlike the other subjects in the National Curriculum, technology has had to be specially invented.[12] While courses called technology have previously existed, these have generally been options offered to a minority of students aged 14 and older and do not provide a basis for a general subject for all students between ages 5 and 16. Nor is there a university subject from which the main principles and content could be derived, though disciplines such as engineering and industrial design are relevant.

How then did the working group (an officially designated collection of individuals[13] charged with the task of writing 'attainment targets' and 'programmes of study' for the subject) go about their task?[14] Explaining how the technology curriculum came to be put together in the way it was is a speculative business. Its statutory formulation consists of a set of specifications (an 'Order') presented without explanation. The immediately preceding document on which the Order is largely based is the Consultation Report of the National Curriculum Council, which similarly offers little by way of rationale. Behind that in turn stand the two reports of the working group (the final one published as the main body of the *Proposals* of the Secretary of State for Education), and it is only here that we gain any significant access to the thinking of the curriculum designers. In so far as the working group's proposals have been adopted by the government in the Order (as most of them have been), we might assume that the thinking behind them has correspondingly been endorsed. (Equally, of course, we may regard the rightness or wrongness of the educational thinking as irrelevant to government, whose criteria for accepting or rejecting the proposals may well have reflected very different considerations.)

The group could have opted to begin by defining the subject philosophically and conceptually, with specifications of criteria to determine what is and is not technology. Something of this conceptualizing had evidently been done in advance, since in the Terms of Reference given to the group the title of the subject had been changed by civil servants from 'technology', the term which had featured in earlier pronouncements, to 'design and technology', though the change is thought to reflect pressure from the 'design lobby' rather than a process of searching philosophical analysis. (In the final Statutory Order the title is back to 'technology' again). In the absence of a generally agreed definition of technology, the group could not avoid some conceptual ground-clearing, and indeed they offer various criteria for and characterizations of the activity they are concerned with. Nowhere, however, do they give an explicit definition.

The group's approach was rather from a different and more pragmatic direction: the identification of a field of activity claimed to be discernible in the 'real world', and the incorporation of its essential processes and knowledge in a school curriculum. They called the field 'design and technological activity' (with 'design and technology as a unitary concept, to be spoken in one breath as it were' and to be used 'as a compound noun taking the singular form of verbs' — Interim Report, 1.6), indicating what it was less by explicit characterization than by the accumulation throughout their reports of specified features and suggestive examples.[15] It is only, in fact, by extrapolating from the curriculum — the 'attainment targets' and 'programmes of study' with their illustrative examples — that we can deduce the 'real-world' practices from which its claims to legitimacy are drawn.

This was a quite new way of doing things. The reference universes of the other major subjects may also, of course, be domains of adult activity (there has been a recent shift in emphasis in, e.g., history and science from factual knowledge and conceptual understanding to experience of the processes of practitioners), but there the activities in question are mainly those of academics. (An exception is English, which reflects the practice of novelists and other literary writers.) In technology the 'relevant practitioners' implicitly identified by the working group were, judging by the examples, operators outside the academy and mainly in the economic domain, professionals and skilled workers such as architects, landscapers, chefs and production engineers.

In deriving principles and practice from these 'realms of practical action' (Interim Report, 2.13) there would seem to have been two possibilities. Either you could list the distinctive procedures and stocks-in-trades of the different 'realms' and selectively incorporate them, or you could see all the 'realms' as displaying variant versions of a common mode of operating, which students would learn through exemplary activities which might be invented for the purpose.[16] The two strategies have rather different implications. Locating, defining and designating as educationally significant a distinct mode of being in the world brings to the subject which teaches it the legitimacy of a 'discipline' and, perhaps, pretensions to some sort of validity transcending the situations of application; the subject might, for instance, claim a fundamental role in the formation of the educated individual, as science did when it moved away from the 'science of common things' in the nineteenth century.[17] The alternative process of assembling into a curriculum diverse aspects of observed adult practice might bring to the subject both the appeal (for employers, for instance) and the stigma (for universities, for instance) of the vocational.

The working group do not state which of the two strategies they were following but it appears to have been a bit of both.[18] The grander claim is certainly there, with its status confirmed in Latin: a different *homo* is to be the presiding model, *homo faber* (the maker) instead of the *sapiens* of the academics. The essence of design and technology is identified as doing rather than knowing, the relevant educational outcome being *capability* rather than understanding. Some general characteristics are ascribed to the discipline: it typically addresses specific situations (rather than, like science, seeking general knowledge) in contexts which are marked by multiple and often conflicting constraints and inadequate information, and which thus call for the constant exercise of *judgment*. A characteristic mode of cognition is also distinguished, involving *imaging* or modelling and employing media such as drawing.

One admirable result of the group's clarification of the relationship between knowing and doing in technology is that knowledge per se has been outlawed from the assessment process in the new subject; in the practical mode, the group affirm, knowledge has its place only as a resource for acting on the world. Students are to be judged by what they can *do*. Although it will be argued below that the working-out of the curriculum does not always reflect this insight and that 'doing' turns out to include a lot of explaining, describing and commenting, and not just making things work, the assertion of the principle nevertheless represents a most important advance on earlier prescriptions for school technology.

In the thinking of the working group, if not in that of the government and the National Curriculum Council, the establishment of a general educational discipline takes precedence over vocational concerns, if we may use that term for considerations to do with personal and national *economic* advantages. The latter are certainly present, but take the 'new vocationalist' form, emphasizing general 'transferable' attitudes and personal qualities relevant to wide sectors of modern economies rather than occupationally specific competences.[19] It is the interpretation of technology as a discipline for the production of rounded personal development that keeps the subject from being a case of that new positivistic, career-orientated instrumentalism which Cherry Collins criticizes in the Australian upper secondary school. Tradition-

al humanistic values appear most obviously in the required study of manifestations of technology from other times and cultures, but also in the
emphasis on accomplishment in language.

Roles and Functions in the Design and Technology Domain

The claim to identify a distinct and coherent 'real world' domain of design
and technological activity leads to a strange conflation within one framework
of functions associated with diverse occupations, together with an apparent
blindness to the division of labour in society. Consider, for instance, the sorts
of adult activities which might correspond to the processes to be experienced
by the more advanced students aged 12–14 following the final (statutory)
version of the curriculum. (As Michael Barnett makes clear, the curriculum as
eventually presented does not fully represent the wishes of the working
group.)[20]

> Explain how they have identified needs and opportunities for design
> and technological activities and give a justification of the conclusions
> they have reached (AT1); present reasoned conclusions resulting from
> interviews and surveys on the problems faced by old people when
> shopping (ex.)

(Market researcher? Social policy or community care researcher?)

> Examine the feasibility of recycling household waste commenting on
> prices, costs and benefits, competition (AT1, ex.)

(Local authority environmental health officer?)

> Having included warmth and robustness as features of a design spe-
> cification for toddlers' clothing, choose materials that meet the spe-
> cification (AT2, ex.)

(Clothes designer for large clothing manufacturer?)

> Set up test, experiments, or trials on prototypes, mock-ups or work-
> ing models. Evaluate the results against relevant criteria leading to a
> modificaiton of their design proposal (AT2, ex.)

> Use information about materials and construction techniques in order
> to produce a design proposal for survival shelters for use after natural
> disasters (AT2, ex.)

Select and use mechanisms to bring about changes and control movement (PoS)

Designing disposable packaging (PoS, ex.)

(Product designer? Engineer?)

In making a piece of jewellery, take into account qualities such as durability and malleability of different parts of the construction and the way the material will need to be worked (AT3, ex.)

Demonstrate competence in the use of general planning and making skills as a result of understanding the materials, components, tools and equipment, and the scale of production (AT3). Use accurately measured materials by size, weight and volume. Precisely mark out materials prior to cutting. Finish the artefact e.g., fix a laminate; lay out a buffet (ex.)

When planning a meal, identifying the courses and the items/ preparation needed (PoS, ex.)

making a sauce; mixing glue; using sand to give strength to clay; using interfacing to strengthen fabric (PoS, ex.)

soldering electronic components (PoS, ex.)

(Craft worker? Chef or caterer? Home cook, DIY enthusiast, clothes maker etc.? Maintenance/repair technician?)

Conclude, after trials with the target group, that a travel guide, although adequate for leisure pursuits, should have focused on public transport and availability and cost of accommodation (AT4, ex.)

(Public information services worker? Freelance writer?)

Analyse a system to determine its effectiveness and suggest improvements (PoS); supermarket check-outs, road traffic layouts, arrangements for schools meals (ex.)

(Miscellaneous planners and managers?)

Appraise a leisure garment against criteria of visual appearance, finish, fastness of dyes, and comfort, durability, cost and efficient use of materials (AT4, ex.)

(Buyer for large store? Researcher for consumer organization? Clothing manufacture executive?)

> advertising a product, using media such as paint, ink, pens, paper, computers (PoS, ex.)

(Advertiser/graphic designer?)

> Identify markets for goods and services and recognise local variations in demand (PoS)

> Prepare a business plan, including a cash forecast and budget, and monitor performance against it (PoS)

(Business or marketing executive? Self-employed business person?)

This is a most extraordinary assemblage of functions which would almost never be exercised by one person, and in larger concerns would be spread across numerous individuals in different parts and at different levels of the organization. The range extends from shop-floor to senior executive jobs, from domestic to industrial roles, from production to R & D to negotiating with clients, and from one-off jobs in home or workshop to mass production.

What justifies the bringing together of these disparate activities is evidently the belief that they are all design and technology activities. So we are brought back to the question of what exactly these are. There are two sorts of answer. The first, as already indicated, is expressed in terms of certain general characteristics. The other is implicit in the four 'attainment targets' for the subject corresponding to the main identified components of design and technology activity: *identifying needs and opportunities* for design and technological activities (the latter, presumably, by definition, including identifying needs and opportunities for design and technological activities, which in turn ... etc.!), *generating a design* (more specifically, generating a specification, then a proposal and then a design), *planning and making*, and *evaluating*.

What is most problematic about this formulation is the lack of fit, in two main respects, with the relevant activities as we observe them in the real world. The two respects, to be discussed in what follows, are, first, that the empirical manifestations of those acitivities do not constitute a unified field or expressions of a common underlying process; and, second, that any field identified on the basis of the criteria given would include activities not recognized here.

Curricular Technology v. Real Technology

The most far-reaching requirement of this curricular specification of technology is probably that admissible activities must involve *developing an explicit design proposal.*[21] Yet, in real life and work, many of those who, like students in the National Curriculum, engage in *both* the devising *and* the production of artefacts, environments or systems do the designing entirely in their heads, either in advance or in the course of working with materials, while few ever produce and communicate a design proposal. (Those who do are not generally the ones to realize the design.) What has been made central to school technology is in real technological activity a relatively specialized function.

If one activity is overemphasized, however, others are excluded. The exclusions are weighted more heavily against technology than design. Although 'design and technology' ought to mean either all of both fields or the intersection of the two sets, the curriculum contains parts of design which do not intersect with technology, but not parts of technology that do not intersect with design. Graphic design, for instance, is admitted (as in the design of posters or magazine layouts), despite having nothing to do with technology according to any normal definition, but *making* is only allowed when linked to the identification of needs, to design and to evaluation. (The requirement that all students be involved to the age of 16 in *making* artefacts, environments and systems is a striking innovation, but its radical significance is much reduced by this proviso.)

Nor is it only normal making that is excluded: technological activity outside school includes (as the interim report acknowledges) being 'able to improve, and extend the use of, existing artefacts and systems' and 'to diagnose and rectify faults' (1.42), and also (not acknowledged) to maintain artefacts and systems. In the curriculum, however, these are admitted, if at all, only as they feature as stages within a 'holistic' design and technological sequence which runs (albeit cyclically and with recursive looping-back) from identifying a need or opportunity, through designing and making to evaluation.

The hidden criteria behind this version of 'design and technology' appear to be, then, that design activities which are not technology are admitted while technological activities not involving design are excluded. What seems to be operating here is a valorization of the conceptual; in other words, a form of academicization. Value is seen to reside above all in *intellectual* skills such as analysis, investigation and the construction of symbolic representations or models of processes and products to be realized in the future. Although the curriculum emphatically claims to be about doing, *direct* operation on the material world appears only as part of the design and technology cycle (the fabrication or realization part), the other processes of which, such as investigating, communicating and evaluating, do not in themselves produce changes in the state of affairs. Otherwise the 'doing' which this curriculum will promote refers to engaging in a set of processes, most of them not in themselves readily seen as doing or making, which will *in aggregate* result in the bringing about of change.

The label of 'academicization' must, however, be qualified in one important respect. The *modes* in which this curriculum allows conceptual activity to be displayed are very different, in welcome ways, from the traditional ones, in employing oral as much as written language along with graphical and non-linguistic form of presentation. The legitimizing of these non-traditional modes changes the criteria for what count as manifestations of academic excellence, and could have important implications for the types of students able to be successful in school. The significance of the change will depend on the way technology is realized in school curricula and on whether it manages to maintain the high status currently accorded it by government and planners.

Curricular Implications of Design-Based Technology

This particular selective bias in the technology curriculum has important effects in two areas. The first is the place of craft skills. The traditional educational justification for teaching these is perhaps rather unfairly represented:

> We recognise that it can be rewarding to work with materials through the interaction of hand and eye until the activity is effortless and the results perfect. We do not regard this perfection, however, as something to be aimed at as the sole outcome of a task. (*Proposals*, 1.18)

In fact, for many craft teachers, as opposed to, say, trainers of apprentices, it is not the attainment of perfection but the experience of struggling with materials and the care and persistence thereby developed which are the educational point. There is nothing wrong with craft skills in themselves as an element within education. The problem with traditional craft teaching — woodwork, for example — as an educational endeavour has rather been that the disciplines are learned within a context that limits their general applicability. Woodwork outside school takes place in specific situations: for instance, building a hutch for one's daughter's rabbit, using materials that are lying about and processes that she can participate in, and taking little account of aesthetic considerations; constructing a prototype of a dining chair of which one will produce ten for a commission, using sophisticated equipment and expensive materials; or erecting shuttering for a floor slab on a building site, with the help of a labourer, and working against the clock on piecework rates. School woodwork, in contrast, has purported to be context-free, as if the craft skills and values were being learned 'neutrally', in detachment from the specific demands of particular situations. In reality, however, the school woodwork task is one more particular situation, with its own peculiar set of permissions and interdictions, constraints and opportunities. To build a coffee table in school is to learn not a generalized competence capable of application anywhere but a competence for one context, school.

It was probably the customary reduction of craft teaching to a *vocational* function, in the traditional sense of one which prepares young people to fulfil lower-order industrial roles, that rightly concerned the working group. What reduces the value of craft activity, however, is not the absence of design but the absence of critical awareness of and responsibility for the purpose of the activity. Skills need to be learned in real or realistic situations of practice which students enter into for purposes which they consciously appraise and validate, so that the curriculum is not implicitly teaching them to be mere tools or 'hands' to be mindlessly deployed for someone else's purposes.

The second unfortunate implication of the way technology has been conceived is a damaging distortion. Conception in technology has been identified in practice with a rationalistic, explicit and systematic version of design (generating specifications[22] and proposals). This is despite the recognition by the working group, in their more theoretical discussion, that parctical capability typically operates in less straightforward ways dictated by the nature of its contexts of operation, which are characterized by indeterminacy and complexity, inadequate information and conflicting requirements, and call for the use of tacit knowledge and the exercise of judgment. The result is that processes of creative making and modifying which display those characteristics and denied the status of true 'design and technological' activity unless they involve a discrete, visible and communicable stage of 'designing'.

Cooking is an example of a process which comes to be devalued in this way. The activity is clearly a source of embarrassment to the curriculum planners, who allow it to appear only when wrapped up in some sort of design process. Cooking which proceeds by improvisation and adaptation in on-going *interaction* with the context, materials, equipment, time pressures etc. is no less cognitively sophisticated or effective in its outcomes than that which starts from a consciously formulated 'design' or plan. The essence of effective cooking has got very little to do with planning, investigating and the like, and the same must be said about that huge body of technological practice which keeps the made world running and constantly trims and modifies and improves it to cope with changing circumstances or as possibilities for improvement present themselves. Technology is not defined by the characteristic of planning *in advance* of action, or of operating in situations which are essentially stable and predictable; skill which is truly technological may also be displayed, for instance, in responding to runaway situations such as securing a tent which is blowing away or preventing a meltdown in a nuclear power station.

To identify the essential characteristic of technology with a rationalistic, means/end-oriented, systematic 'design' process is thus mistaken on a number of grounds. First, as a matter of fact, important sorts of technology are not like that; second, this characterization is at odds with the working group's highly enlightened account of the 'realms of practical activity' as *not* reducible to system and logic; and, third, the effect is not the rehabilitation of the practical but the academicization of some parts of it and the consigning of other parts — those which characterize the activities of many skilled workers

— to the status of subtechnology. Far from dignifying the arts of practice, the curriculum fails to recognize them and instead accords primary esteem to intellectual and communication skills.

Ideological Selectivity

Not only is the technology curriculum based on a 'discipline' which has no real existence as an integrated entity outside the aspirations of the curriculum designers; it is also a highly selective construction in which ideology plays a conspicuous part. This manifests itself most obviously in the prominence given to business.

Students' design and technological activities are required to take place in a range of contexts. Five are prescribed (though others may be utilized): 'the home, school, recreation, community, business and industry' (Order, p. 19). No justifications are offered for this particular selection. The huge area of public services is omitted from mention (although activities which might take place in, for instance, the National Health Service are not expressly excluded, almost no examples are given), while a disproportionate amount of attention is paid to business. The justification offered is that 'business and economics' is one of several 'influences on design and technological practice' (listed in Interim Report, 2.25.6) and thus needs to be understood. That argument does not, however, result in equivalent attention to the working of, say, *community* processes, structures, criteria and values, including, perhaps, the ways in which the interests of community and business and industry may be in conflict. (Social conflict appears only in a blandly distorted form: 'recognise potential conflicts *between the needs of individuals and society* — Order, p. 31, emphasis added. 'Society' is an unproblematic category and conflicts *between groups* are ignored. A parallel bias is shown in the role given to critical evaluation, which, commendably, is to help undermine students' sense of the inevitable givenness of artefacts, systems and environments, but is not to be brought to bear on *social* institutions or the procedures of business and industry.)[23]

Contained within the subject called 'technology' is, in fact, a complete, and often unrelated, business studies curriculum. For instance, by no stretch of the imagination can the following (from the programmes of study) be regarded as aspects of technology or 'design and technology': 'know that goods are bought, sold and advertised', (KS1); 'know that advertising helps promote and sell goods and services', 'recognise and represent organisational structures', 'identify markets for goods and services', 'plan a simple budget' (KS2); 'prepare a business plan, including a cash forecast and budget, and monitor performance against it', 'understand how market research can be used to measure user needs and market potential', 'recognise the relationship between price, cost, income and competition in the market for goods and services' (KS3); 'know that external influences such as level of economic development, government policy, international agencies, have effects on business activity', 'analyse business systems and organisational models', 'develop effective pricing, promotion and distribution' (KS4).

Having been carelessly excluded from the National Curriculum, business studies evidently had to be smuggled back in somewhere, and so appears extensively developed (but unannounced) in the *Proposals*. Indeed, the National Curriculum Council, in their contribution, appear more enthusiastic about the promotion of commercial enterprise qualities than specifically design and technological capability: 'Business and industry need young people who have the vision to combine enterprise, initiative and imagination with knowledge and skills to solve problems and create the nation's wealth' (Consultation Report, p. 7).

Practical v. Technological Capability

The outcome most eagerly yet unrealistically anticipated from the new subject is, in fact, not a better supply of competent practitioners in occupations involving design and technology, but a whole workforce equipped with *general practical* capability. A failure to distinguish between practical abilities in general, which could be developed by a range of subjects, and those more specific qualities which technology education in particular might be expected to produce runs through the whole series of documents. Thus the Terms of Reference describe design and technology as 'that area of the curriculum in which students design and make useful objects or systems, thus *developing their ability to solve practical problems*' — sc., in general (Interim Report, p. 86, emphasis added) — while the Secretary of State's response to the interim report welcomes the definition of the subject as 'an essentially practical activity, concerned with developing students' competence to tackle a wide variety of problems' (Interim Report, preliminary pages).

Great confusion about purposes follows from constant conceptual sliding between *practical* and *design and technological* activity, since the latter is not the equivalent but a subset of the former. *Practical* capability may be displayed in 'situations of practice'[24] which do not involve design or technology: nursing, counselling, breaking in horses, hairdressing and teaching would be examples. Part of the problem is that the working group's characterizations of design and technological capability derive from two sources which are drawn on without adequate discrimination. One source is descriptions by researchers such as Schön of skilful practice at the professional level *in a variety of occupations* not confined to those involving design and technology; the other set comes from studies of a more specific group of occupations such as engineering, industrial design and town planning, and leads the group to identify processes which are clearly and more exclusively design and technological (for example, visualization, and considering materials costs, aesthetics and the social effects of products).

Whereas a curriculum of design and technological activities can reasonably be expected to result in design and technological capability, the claim is repeatedly made that the ability will be developed to cope in practical situations more generally. Yet some situations of practice manifestly involve quite different processes, criteria, types of context, modes of cognition and ways of using knowledge, ones which are unlikely to be developed by design and technology activities. An example of this failure to discriminate is the following section of the working group's final report, in which they refer to

> the educational potential of design and technology, not least in preparing students to understand and deal with the complex problems they are likely to face in their personal and working lives in the years ahead. Many of these problems have technological origins; equally, the means of solving them, of operating effectively in fields where there is not one right answer, where judgement as much as technique is the hallmark of successful practitioners, depends upon design and technological capability. (*Proposals*, 1.47)

The claim cannot be substantiated; the technology curriculum does *not* prepare generally for those fields and will contribute to the solution only of those problems with the relevant sort of content. Moreover, the fact that a problem originated with technology in no way implies that design and technological capability will be appropriate to its solution; often, as, for instance, in addressing the problem of people put out of work by the introduction of new technology, the solution depends on deploying precisely those moral, social and political capabilities the absence of which from the original technology-driven initiative caused the problem in the first place.[25]

Despite aspirations to provide a general curriculum of the practical, the effect of the new subject is to deny validity to the most widespread forms of practical activity, which are not design-based but involve unmediated interaction with situations and phenomena. Because of the confusion, moreover, the basis on which activities are included appears quite arbitrary: if selling a service can count as 'operating in the made world', why not caring activities? If handling food is admissible, albeit within the context of 'designing' dishes and meals, why not handling plants and animals in the context of planning and realizing gardens and horticultural and agricultural enterprises?[26]

The unreasonable inflation of the claims and expectations for technology has to do with the nature of the National Curriculum as a whole. Perhaps the most intractable problems faced by the working group arose not from the philosophical and pedagogical challenge of defining a subject *de novo* but from having to do so in a political context which pre-empted certain decisions and rendered certain solutions inadmissible. Since the other practical subjects had been denied a statutory basis (including, for instance, media studies, agriculture, childcare, community service, photography and motor engineering, as well as more strictly vocational options such as welding and office practice which were formerly offered through link courses at technical colleges), the whole burden of practical education was placed on the only one which remained — as the National Curriculum Council explicitly acknowledge: the 'unique role' of technology is 'providing balance in *a curriculum based on academic subjects* — a balance in which creative and practical capabilities of students can be fully developed and inter-related' (Consultation Report, p. 7, emphasis added). In other words, the practical is to be developed here or nowhere, and that means, it seems, the whole range of 'creative and practical capabilities'.

Conclusion

The new subject of technology, then, is at odds with others which have statutory recognition. Its inclusion without apparent concern for the incongruity reflects the *ad hoc* and unprincipled processes by which the National Curriculum was constructed and represents a response to pressures and concerns which might otherwise, in a more thoughtfully designed scheme, have informed the curriculum more generally.[27] Having little in the way of precedent to work on, the curriculum designers, as I have argued, invented a new discipline and brought together as collective expressions of it a set of activities which in the 'real world' are to be found widely scattered across a diverse spread of occupations and functions. There appears little rational basis for the inclusion and exclusion of types of activity. While the new discipline embodies some traditional humanistic concerns for the understanding of culture and society, their effect is to a considerable extent neutralized by a heavy bias in favour of the domain of business.

Although most of what has been said above is critical, what is perhaps most remarkable is that, given the overall nature of the National Curriculum and the constraints within which the technology curriculum planners had to work, so much that is radical has been established in the specifications. The efforts of those on the working group and elsewhere who have a principled and well-founded understanding of the nature of design and technology and of young people's educational needs do show. For there is much to be thankful for about the technology curriculum. It offers scope for varied and enjoyable activity. Its prescriptions could have been far narrower, along the lines of traditional technical courses. It is not overloaded with technical knowledge. It gives recognition to skills rarely developed in schools hitherto. Much of what it requires to be taught is genuinely useful. There is a welcome emphasis on cooperation and work in teams. It promotes knowledge of the social impact of technology. It affords opportunity for teachers to give proper weight to ethical, environmental and aesthetic considerations, despite the simultaneous foregrounding of the market (and the fact that the aesthetic normally appears only as an aspect of 'consumer preference').

A number of things, however, are wrong with this curriculum; I wish to emphasize two that seem basic. (Michael Barnett, in this volume, identifies others, some of which are equally disabling.) The first is that the result of the attempt to construct a new educational form turns out to be, for all its encouragement of media other than language, basically another *intellectual* discipline. What is presented as experience of the practical is in fact confined within an untypical, rationalistic 'design' activity. In overemphasizing the design process, in undervaluing important aspects of real technological practice, and in combining together in 'holistic' and integrated activities functions normally exercised by different people in different contexts, the curriculum erects a spurious version of 'design and technology' which could be as artificial, as school-specific and as unrelated to real-world practice as was the traditional science lesson. The moving to centre stage of a specialized and relatively uncommon activity (the production of design proposals), and the general privileging of the conceptual, are clearly not based on an examination of the way design and technology work in the real world. The concept of technology on which the curriculum is based is in fact a normative, not an empirically-derived one, an artificial construct whose links to reality are tenuous and problematic. The appeal to real-world manifestations is a secondary, legitimating move made *post hoc* in support of the *prior* identification of what is *educationally* desirable.

The second problem lies with the attempt to address the entire principle of the practical through one subject, which therefore has to cover, and to present as closely related, an impossibly wide range of activities that are actually quite different, such as designing, fabricating, cooking and selling. The fact is that the 'realms of practical activity' represent a broad field, the curricular realization of which would require either the time equivalent of several subjects or a pervasive penetration of the curriculum as a whole. A true 'rehabilitation of the practical' would mean giving the practical a central place in the overall conception of the curriculum. It would also, however, mean rehabilitating it *as* the practical, and not as a set of new mental disciplines.

Acknowledgments

I acknowledge with gratitude the generous help I had from David Layton, Emeritus Professor of Education at the University of Leeds and a member of the Design and Technology Working Group, in his comments on an earlier version of this chapter. Despite the changes and corrections I have made since, however, what I have written does not in any way represent Professor Layton's views; I am sure he will still have numerous disagreements with the ideas expressed above.

Notes

1 'Reforms "leave arts on margins"', *Times Educational Supplement*, 4 April 1990, p. A9.

2 An account of the international movement towards the inclusion of technology in general education is given in MEDWAY PETER (1989) 'Issues in the theory and practice of technology education', *Studies in Science Education*, 16, pp. 1–24.

3 See, for instance, McCULLOCH, G.J., JENKINS, E.W. and LAYTON, D. (1985) *Technological Revolution? The Politics of School Science and Technology in England and Wales snce 1945*, Lewes, Falmer.

4 WIENER, MARTIN (1981) *English Culture and the Decline of the Industrial Spirit 1850–1980*, Cambridge, Cambridge University Press.

5 A cogent argument for the bankruptcy of the traditional liberal curriculum and the need for a reconceived *critical* vocationalism is put by SPOURS, KEN and YOUNG, MICHAEL (1988) *Beyond Vocationalism: A New Perspective on the Relationship between Work and Education*, London, Centre for Vocational Studies, University of London Institute of Education.

6 HARLAND, JANET (1988) 'Upper secondary curriculum in England and Wales: current developments and emerging structures', *Journal of Curriculum Studies*, 20, 5, pp. 407–22.

7 COLLINS, CHERRY (forthcoming) 'The changing nature of the academic curriculum', to appear in *Developing a Comprehensive Curriculum for the Senior Secondary Years*, Melbourne, Australian Council for Educational Research.

8 The version available as an optional course for students aged 14–16 was indeed felt by some to be the most difficult of all the subjects taken at that stage. BARNES, DOUGLAS *et al.* (1987) *The TVEI Curriculum 14–16: An Interim Report Based on Case Studies in Twelve Schools*, Sheffield, Manpower Services Commission, and LAYTON, DAVID, MEDWAY, PETER and YEOMANS, DAVID (1989) *Technology in TVEI: 14–18: The Range of Practice*, Sheffield, Training Agency.

9 LAYTON, DAVID (Ed.) (1984) *The Alternative Road: The Rehabilitation of the Practical*, Leeds, University of Leeds Centre for the Study of Science and Mathematics Education.

10 E.g., SCHÖN, DONALD (1983) *The Reflective Practitioner: How Professionals Think in Action*, New York, Basic Books.

11 E.g., GARDNER, HOWARD (1983) *Frames of Mind: The Theory of Multiple Intelligences*, London, Heinemann.

12 The subject is divided into two parts, called Design and Technology and Information Technology. Since the latter is rather separate and since IT is extensively discussed elsewhere in this volume, my argument will refer solely to 'Design and Technology'. See Michael Barnett's chapter in this volume for some discussion of the relationship between the two elements.

13 The group of twelve members was chaired by Lady Parkes, a home economics specialist, and included representatives of craft and design education, science and technology education, business education, computer science (higher education), local education authority administration, the Technical

and Vocational Education Initiative (TVEI), the Engineering Council, and business management.

14   The relevant official documents are as follows: the Interim Report of the National Curriculum Design and Technology Working Group was published in mimeo by the Department of Education and Science and the Welsh Office in November 1988; the group's Final Report was published with a short introduction by the Secretaries of States in June 1989 as *Design and Technology for Ages 5 to 16: Proposals of the Secretary of State for Education and Science and the Secretary of State for Wales*, DES/WO (referred to in the text as *Proposals*); the National Curriculum Council published a Consultation Report, *Technology 5–16 in the National Curriculum*, in November 1989; the government's Statutory Order for the subject were published by HMSO in March 1990 (DES/WO, *Technology in the National Curriculum*); and finally the National Curriculum Council in March 1990 published *Non-statutory Guidance* on Technology. Michael Barnett (this volume) gives a historical account of the development of the technology curriculum through these successive versions.

15   The argument in the interim report in fact goes like this. Reference is made to the 'unitary concept' of design and technology, and it appears that the term is interchangeable with 'design and technological activity'. Instead of defining what this is, the group set themselves the quite different question, 'What is it that students learn from design and technological activities . . . ?', and answer 'capability to operate effectively and creatively in the made world' and (without explanation) 'increased "competence in the indeterminate zones of practice"'. Further elucidation is in terms of the distinctions 'knowing that' v. 'knowing how', 'propositional knowledge' v. 'action knowledge' and 'homo sapiens' v. 'homo faber'. (Interim Report, 1.6, 1.9–1.10.)

16   Examples of this approach are those science courses in which a common 'scientific method' is held to be inculcated through a selection of physical, chemical and biological activities. The reality of this 'scientific method' is now widely doubted.

17   LAYTON, DAVID (1973) *Science for the People: The Origins of the School Science Curriculum in England*, London, Allen and Unwin.

18   The lack of methodological explanation is regrettable, but is not a fault for which the group can be blamed. The members had to complete their work in a very short time in moments snatched from their full-time jobs.

19   On the 'new vocationalism' see, for instance, various contributions in CHITTY, CLYDE (Ed.) (n.d.) *Aspects of Vocationalism*, University of London Institute of Education Post-16 Education Centre (formerly Centre for Vocational Studies), and particularly TERRELL, GRAHAM 'The new vocationalism', ibid., pp. 4–10. Also BATES, INGE *et al.* (Eds) (1984) *Schooling for the Dole? The New Vocationalism*, London, Macmillan.

20   The items are taken from the Order, from levels 6 and 7 in the attainment targets and from the programme of study for Key Stage 3, and relate to activity, and not just understanding. In the text, 'AT' refers to Attainment Target, 'PoS' to Programme of Study, and 'ex.' to illustrative examples. 'Key Stages' are age groupings: in terms of the age of the majority of pupils at the end of the academic year, KS1 is ages 6–7, KS2 8–11, KS3 12–14 and KS4 15–16. It is fair to acknowledge that the examples do not carry any statutory

weight, and that members of the working group are known to regret the inclusion of many that were added by the National Curriculum Council at the Consultation stage.

21 The working group specify explicitly that activities should 'each involve all the attainment targets' (stated at the head of each Programme of Study in the *Proposals*), including developing a design proposal. Although this stipulation is not repeated in the final Order, there is no doubt of the continuing centrality of an explicit design process.

22 The stipulation that a design *specification*, rather than simply a design proposal, be produced en route to the final design, was added after the Consultation and is not in the final report of the working group.

23 Michael Barnett, in his chapter in this volume, offers more extended comment on the role of critical reflection in the curriculum.

24 Schön's phrase.

25 Admittedly, at the very final stage (KS10), students must under AT10 'make reasoned judgements about what is a subject for design and technological activities and what is better dealt with in other ways'.

26 Perhaps these are in fact admissible within the terms of the Order itself and it is the emphasis of the examples and interpretive comment that creates the contrary impression. The subjects of agriculture and horticulture, however, which proved important and successful in many TVEI schemes, are never referred to in the way that home economics and textiles are as possible contributors to technology.

27 The attempt to infuse the practical across the curriculum would not be unprecedented, having been pioneered, albeit in piecemeal and untheorized form, by the Technical and Vocational Education Initiative. See the reports of the National Evaluation of TVEI Curriculum prepared by members of the University of Leeds School of Education. (A list of these is available from TVEI 9 Enquiry Point, N 805, The Training Agency, Moorfoot, Sheffield S1 4PQ.)

Chapter 4

Technology, Within the National Curriculum and Elsewhere

Michael Barnett

Introductory Remarks

Most discussions of 'technology' are beset by difficulties arising from the different meanings and associations which have attached themselves to the word itself, e.g. technology as gadgets, technology as problem solving, technology as political slogan, technology as motor of industrial change. The pervasiveness of technologies in everyday life gives rise to contrasted and potentially antithetical perspectives such as producer/consumer, 'expert'/'inexpert', winner/loser. The same pervasiveness dictates that any adequate understanding of technology must embrace issues of policy and choice both public and private: needs, priorities, accountability, material and financial resources, all these elements bearing a direct relationship to politics and power. The school curriculum has remained singularly innocent of these matters for long enough. Until Mr Baker's publicity breakthrough[1] of the early 1980s, Technology had been one of the labels describing a small low-status ghetto of craft and workshop activities. Subsequently, the focus shifted to a scarcely less narrow identification of 'technology' with computers in the classroom. For teachers and pupils alike, technological awareness was bound up with the ability to operate software (including CAL) packages.

Just as any serious consideration of curriculum policy must centre on the relationship between the school/college and the wider world, so the crucial question for technology in the curriculum is its relationship with 'real' technology out there in the world. One aim of this paper is to examine, through a critical account of the evolution of the Statutory Orders, the perspectives on this key relationship, both explicit and implicit, adopted by the designers of National Curriculum Technology.

The recent GCSE reforms and the introduction of the National Curriculum allow limited scope and even less energy for curriculum innovation at the pre-16 stage. The system appears already overburdened with multiple and possibly contradictory constraints. Any coherent national policy for the later stages of schooling will have to reexamine this area in due course; meanwhile it is the 16–19 curriculum that is up for definition (Finegold *et al.*, 1990) and in the post-compulsory context, the pre-16 details becoming significant mainly in relationship to progression. In the longer term, the break at 16+ should and probably will disappear and in this respect it is interesting to note that TVEI is targeted on 14- to 18-year-olds.

The chapter is organized in two main parts:

(i) a commentary on the various documents leading up to the Statutory Orders for National Curriculum Technology
(ii) an evaluation of National Curriculum Technology in relation to its own terms of reference and also to other possible aims including the objective of achieving a broadly based technological literacy.

The Documents

The process of defining attainment targets and associated programmes of study for National Curriculum Technology was completed by the publication in March 1990 of the Statutory Orders. The significant stages in the development of this sector of the National Curriculum have been as follows:

(a) April 1988: Terms of reference and supplementary guidance to the working group
(b) November 1988: Working group Interim Report
(c) June 1989: Final Report embodying the Secretary of State's *Proposals*
(d) November 1989: Consultation Report.

The Statutory Orders follow closely the recommendations of the Consultation Report.

The Working Party Brief

In the design of the National Curriculum, precedence has been given to the three 'core' subjects of English, Maths and Science. Technology, the first of the 'foundation' subjects to be considered, was declared by Kenneth Baker, in announcing the formation of the working group, to be 'of great significance for the economic well-being of this country. I believe that it is essential that we press ahead quickly....'.
The group were asked to consider:

• Technology for secondary pupils
• A framework for Design across foundation subjects for all pupils
• Information Technology for all pupils.

At that stage, Primary Technology had already been assigned to the Science working group, but the remit of the Technology group was soon extended to primary pupils. No reason for this switch was given but it might be surmised that an early decision by the group to yoke together Design and Technology in a seemingly indissoluble manner would have made it inevitable that they would have to take full responsibility for Technology as well as Design, in Key Stages 1 and 2. The splitting of 'Technology' and 'Information Technology' is proposed right at the outset, a witless demarcation which the working group attempted to challenge but without success.[2] The terms of reference for the working group specify technology as '... an activity which goes across the curriculum, drawing on and linking in with a wide range of subjects ... an area of study in its own right with its own objectives and content.... [but].... not necessarily ... a separately timetabled subject...'.

More specific guidance states that technology is that area of the curriculum where pupils

- design and make useful objects and systems
- draw on knowledge and skills from a range of subjects but always involving science and mathematics
- learn about the variety of modern materials and technologies in use in the industrial and commercial world
- prepare for the world of work by
    (i) learning how to work in teams
    (ii) understanding the importance of functional efficiency, quality, appearance and marketability and
    (iii) understanding the importance of working within financial and technical constraints
- are equipped with basic IT skills
- develop awareness of the use of IT ... in business office, manufacturing or commerce.

The desired outcomes are:

   (i) pupils should be able to
    - design and make artefacts and systems
    - have experience of applying design to 'real-life' tasks within typical constraints (e.g., time, money)
    - appreciate the importance of design and technology in society historically and at present, particularly as it affects the economy.
   (ii) a cross-curricular framework for IT.

In framing the proposals, the working group were to take account of

- the TGAT[3] framework of testing and assessment
- inter-subject contributions, in both directions

- best practice ... in particular developments under TVEI
- special needs
- relationship to GCSE
- progression beyond 16
- breadth, balance and relevance
- development of personal qualities (e.g., self-reliance, discipline, enterprise, social responsibility)
- equal opportunities.

In the event, the designers took far more account of certain items on this list than others. As in other subjects the first item (assessment) has been given a very high priority. Consideration of special needs and of the relationship to TVEI has been derisory while the question of progression beyond 16 has apparently been completely ignored.

The Interim Report

The long opening chapter of the Interim Report is thoughtful and well-written and conveys the sense that the working group wishes to break new ground in specifying the scope of school technology. They note that 'the national picture is one of diversity and dynamic change to an extent not found in core and other foundation subjects' (p. 1). Later on, in a related passage they draw attention to the 'present gap between best and worst practice [which] is probably greater ... than in most other subjects....' (p. 23) and refer to 'pockets of development ... which are extremely impressive. At the other extreme there are desert areas....' and look to TVEI extension to irrigate these deserts. They do not however indicate what specific features of TVEI might be helpful in this regard. Thus they recognize that TVEI can be conducive to 'good practice' but are apparently not concerned to analyze why this might be so. The working group see design and technological activities as the means by which pupils learn 'capability to operate effectively and creatively in the made world....' (p. 3). — and in a radical-sounding if cloudy phrase assert that 'The goal is increased competence in the indeterminate zones of practice'. Design and Technology is declared to be 'always purposeful (i.e., developed in response to perceived needs or opportunities..) ... [and] takes place within a context of specific constraints ... and depends on value judgements at almost every stage' (p. 4).

In the specific context of the report, the remark about value judgments serves to differentiate technology from forms of school knowledge where 'right' answers are at a premium. Numerous design solutions could be adopted which constitute satisfactory compromises between, for example, fitness for purpose, affordability and ease of manufacture. The field of value judgments around technological activity could, however, be conceived as far wider and this too is acknowledged.

> ... practical involvement is fundamental ...
>   There is, however, an additional dimension to consider and this entails *critical reflection* (my emphasis) upon and appraisal of the social and economic results of design and technological activities beyond the school....
>   Understanding of technological change and of the ways in which it is restructuring the workplace and influencing life-styles is a crucial aspect of an education in design and technology. The consequences of technological change are profound and pervasive. Furthermore, technological revolutions are irreversible; no technological change can be uninvented after it has taken place. We need to understand design and technology, therefore, not only to solve practical problems, to invent, optimise and realise solutions, but also so that we can acquire a sense of its enormous transformatory power. Used wisely, they bring new and worthwhile goals within reach. By the end of the period of compulsory education pupils should have some understanding of the value options and decisions that have empowered the technological process in the past and which are doing so today. (pp. 5–6)

This is quite strongly worded ('crucial', 'profound' and 'pervasive' etc.), though the wide social and political horizons gestured at are being viewed through a variety of filters and blinkers. A degree of technological determinism has become apparent where previously the notion of technology as a means to an end was more in evidence. 'Influencing life-styles' points towards the candyfloss ephemera of First World consumerism, the rhetoric of irreversibility and uninventability towards an uncritical triumphalism. This is, however, somewhat qualified by implication in the phrase 'used wisely', which recognizes the possibility of unwisdom, depraved value judgments, catastrophic decisions, but also, and conversely, could allow room for systems of values and practices in which the life chances of the many are not sacrificed to the life-styles of the few.

More specific thoughts about the 'additional dimension' surface later in the report.

> Features of technological change which pupils will need to know about include the emergence, often discontinuously, of new areas of technological activity associated with scientific advances (e.g., biological materials, fibre optics, superconductors); the development of new processes (e.g., frozen food processing, computer aided manufacture); as well as the evolution of new codes of practice (e.g., the Clean Air Act, the Data Protection Act, health and safety legislation). The effects of such technological changes are widespread and pupils will need to develop knowledge and understanding of these by detailed study of examples, which need not necessarily be contemporary ones. (p. 38)

This passage indicates that, at this stage, the vision of the working group was broad and ambitious when judged against current school practice. It also implies the desirability of extensive cross-curricular links and furnishes the justification for adding *secondary* history and geography (p. 9) to the more obvious contributing subjects (science, maths, CDT, business studies, HE, IT, art and design). However, in the world of the National Curriculum, breadth of vision leads to disagreeable consequences. The terms of reference require the programmes of study (PoS) to provide 'a detailed description of the content, skills and processes which all pupils need to be taught'. What then should be the knowledge base? The group concede that this is 'boundless in principle' whereas in current school design and technology practice it was 'too tightly constrained' and 'too strongly bonded to ... physics' (p. 10). Technology, as conceived in the Interim Report, poses a genuine challenge to conventional conceptions of school knowledge. If technological activity has its roots in human purposes, then the knowledge requirements will be, as in 'real life', context-dependent, and will encompass the social as well as the narrowly technical.

The working group decided to adopt a position (p. 10) 'where knowledge is prescribed in sufficient detail to give some structure in support of ... planning'. The implementation of this reasonable-sounding proposition comes to dominate, in an unfortunate manner, the final report.

The Final Report

Details of attainment targets and programmes of study are contained in the final report, which also constituted the proposals to be put out to formal consultation. As in the Interim Report, there is an extended introductory chapter but the tone and emphasis has changed markedly. There is a sense of narrowing of perspectives and hints of empty rhetoric. 'A curriculum for the twenty-first century' is a bold claim given the total lack of attention to progression beyond 16. There are also general remarks about the importance of school/industry links but no mention of TVEI in this connection. In the subsequent statements of attainment, lists of activities and programmes of study, which occupy nearly seventy tightly packed pages, it is exceedingly difficult to find any specific reference to school/industry links.

The narrowing of perspectives is signalled by an approach more related to consolidation than innovation. The attainment targets and programmes of study, 'are intended to assist ... coordination [between] art and design, business studies, CDT, home economics and information technology...'.

The framework of the proposals has been usefully summarized by the Leeds University TVEI Support Project (LUTSP); their resumé is reproduced in Appendix A. The four organically related attainment targets (ATs)[4] appear to offer a much simpler and less coercive framework than, for example, the fourteen ATs in maths or the seventeen in science. However, the decision to elaborate each AT through large numbers of statements of attainment and, more particularly, to identify no less than sixteen aspects in the knowledge and skills base leads to a syllabus framework of scarcely imaginable complexity and abstractness. This tendency is endemic in the whole National Curriculum exercise, and one sympathizes with the working group for the dilemma in which they found themselves. They may have wished to avoid being too concrete about content, in order to avoid the charge of prescriptiveness, and yet were compelled to search for some degree of specificity and detail in order to provide the basis for assessment at no less than ten levels. The various subject working groups have responded in different ways to this unappetizing challenge, with more or less depressing results, but nowhere does the TGAT tail wag the curriculum dog more vigorously than in the Design and Technology proposals. The attainment targets may be educationally defensible, practical and potentially progressive, but the rest is a morass.

The statements of attainment are fairly numerous (32 for Key Stage 1, 63 for Key Stage 2, 64 for Key Stage 3 and 85 for Key Stage 4) though modest by the standards of Science or those proposed for Geography. In these latter subjects, however, the programme of study is implicit in the attainment targets, whereas in Technology, this is set out separately in all its sixteen aspects at the ten TGAT levels. With a number of bullet points subdividing each aspect, the bullet point count mounts astonishingly (94 for Key Stage 1, 185 for Key Stage 2, 323 for Key Stage 3, 422 for Key Stage 4). The TGAT framework engenders hilarious sequences of near paraphrase in an attempt to characterize the step-by-step drive towards perfection in every aspect (and, indeed, sub-aspect) of knowledge and skill. The first element of 'Exploring and Investigating' traced through Levels 6–9 reads as follows:

> Level 6 . . . to design through exploration and analysis of contexts to identify needs and opportunities.

> Level 7 . . . to devise an effective research strategy for investigating a specific context.

> Level 8 . . . to devise an in-depth and effective research strategy for investigating a specific context.

> Level 9 . . . to research in depth with sensitivity when investigating a specific context.

The Level 10 statements of attainment present an image of the super-pupil, e.g.,

> Make sound (sic) judgements about what is properly a subject for design and technological activity and what is more properly dealt

with in other ways (for example social, economic or political measures).

Demonstrate through their choice of Working Methods and an instinctive (sic!) discernment and flair in decision taking, the wide range and quality of their design and technological capability.

The diminished sense of reality which could imagine such statements to be relevant to the appraisal of a 16-year-old is regrettably evident throughout the final report. In consequence the design and technology proposals were launched into the formal consultation procedure encapsulated in a deeply dispiriting and unsatisfactory document. It came as no surprise therefore that as a result of the consultation, the proposals were cut down to size. In this normalization process, however, it was not just the excesses that were trimmed; several of the better intentions of the original working party also became lost to view.

The Consultation Report

This document, whose proposals are replicated in the Statutory Orders, is as different from the Final Report as the Final Report was from the Interim Report. By this stage the project was out of the hands of the working group, the consultation procedure and the resulting report being the responsibility of the National Curriculum Council. Instead of an extended introductory chapter we find a crassly rhetorical Foreword whose coarse ideological shaping is only too evident.

Pupils will become aware of technological developments and the way in which technology is changing the work place and influencing life-styles. They will learn that technological change cannot be reversed and will understand its enormous power. Knowledge of technology enables citizens to be prepared to meet the needs of the 21st century and to cope with a rapidly changing society.

This crude formulation can be recognized as a totally abridged and atrophied form of para. 1.14 (pp. 5–6) of the Interim Report (cf. pp. 87–9 above). Triumphalist and uncompromisingly determinist, it presents citizens as mere vectors meeting 'needs' (whose needs and how are they recognized as needs?) and 'coping with' change. In this vision, 'citizens' do not formulate needs and are not to be agents in the conceptualization, realization and management of change. As for 'technology', an alien power, it tramps remorsely on like the legions, never to be questioned, qualified, gainsaid, refused, resisted or rejected. Nuclear power stations cannot be uninvented but this does not mean that they will prove relevant, other than as lethal scrap heaps, to the life of the twenty-first century.

> Business and industry need young people who have the vision to combine enterprise, initiative and imagination with knowledge and skills to solve problems and create the nation's wealth.

'Wealth creation' and 'enterprise' are party political slogans (Webster and Robins, 1991). It should however be self-evident that colleges, schools, hospitals and public utilities also need young people who do all those laudable things, that they contribute to the 'nation's wealth' and that they require enterprise (in its old sense before the word was hijacked by the switch-salesmen of the Department of Trade and Industry).

The consultation procedure led the National Curriculum Council (NCC) to retain the original Attainment Targets but to make many changes of detail and emphasis in the Statements of Attainment and Programmes of Study (PoS). The proposal of the working group to include the Measurement and Control and Applications and Effects aspects of Information Technology within the Design and Technology profile has been overridden and they have been returned to the software-dominated Information Technology profile component.[5] The effect of this is likely to be to retard the incorporation of hardware aspects of electronics and control into school technology teaching and to reinforce the current unsatisfactory arrangement whereby electronics is normally delivered exclusively by the science department.

More generally, the effect of exposing the proposals to practitioners is to trigger a much needed process of simplification (e.g., the sixteen aspects in the PoS are reduced to four),[6] clarification and exemplification.

Unfortunately this also leads to a degree of compromise and trivialization in an attempt to accommodate the conflicting interests of various subject specialisms.

> Several respondents felt that the language used in the proposals was too closely linked to Craft, Design and Technology making it difficult for teachers from other subject areas to recognize their contribution to technology. More detail was requested to help develop an identity for each specialist area, and simple and straightforward expression to help non-specialists understand the range of the proposals.
>
> Council has taken steps to make the proposals more accessible to the ordinary person. (Consultation Report, p. 11)

> Council has asked experienced teachers who are currently teaching technology to pupils with a range of ages and aptitudes to provide examples to supplement or replace those in the proposals of the Secretaries of State. (Consultation Report, p. 20)

The examples, which are provided as non-statutory guidance in the Statutory Orders, represent an attempt to map current practice onto what was intended to be the framework of a brand new subject. The effect is that of reframing and consolidating current practice (albeit 'best practice' as viewed by the NCC) as if the 'needs of the 21st century' could be met by maintaining business as usual in the 'five subjects'.

Anxiety lest the mechanical and physics-related aspects of technology associated with CDT should be given too much prominence leads to major readjustments of balance in the PoS. References to Energy, Structures and Mechanisms are largely expurgated and these topics are deemed to be dealt with under Attainment Targets for Science. More emphasis is placed on material which could be delivered by Home Economics, Art and Design and Business Studies staff, giving greater visibility to topics such as cookery, textiles, fashion, advertising, market research and design in the sense of visual merchandising. Clearly such activities are educationally valid, particularly if pursued in active learning modes and without gender stereotyping. However, it is debatable whether they can credibly bear much of the weight of a Technology syllabus. They can only constitute a major component of Technology at the cost of marginalizing or excluding other elements of vast social and economic significance. Examples given of 'satisfying human need' in the Level 9 and 10 PoS are 'calculating the costs of making and delivering lunches to several businesses' (why not several pensioners?) and 'setting up competing companies to *design* and sell badges'. Some might argue that these are valuable activities, but they cannot reasonably be represented as serious attacks on the commanding heights of technological understanding.

There is a great scarcity of examples referring to major technologies or industries producing capital goods. How, and by what means, are older pupils to start acquiring understanding and critical insight into, for example, mining, transport, power generation and distribution, medical and pharmaceutical technologies, the weapons industry, food processing or agribusiness? Where are the opportunities to consider technology as a major factor in the restructuring of production and in relationship to the division of labour? The attainment targets and many of the statements of attainment are framed in such a way as to permit, even encourage, a broad and critical consideration of technology and its bearing on the terms of human existence. This would, of course, require interdepartmental collaboration going outside the limits of the 'five subjects'. However, neither the Consultation Report nor the non-statutory guidance in the Statutory Orders give the impression that such an approach is desirable, necessary or even possible.

What is National Curriculum Technology for?

Let us initially consider this question in isolation from the question of what the National Curriculum as a whole might be for. The Secretary of State refers to its 'utmost economic importance' which tends to suggest that he sees it as a response to the longstanding neglect of technical and engineering subjects within the mainstream of English education (see also Peter Medway's comments in this volume). The litany of complaint inaugurated by the technical education lobby in the 1870s has remained remarkably constant over the intervening years,[7] and judged over that whole period there have been few significant successes except in the upper reaches of a highly stratified system. During this century there has been a reasonable level of investment in teaching and research in institutions of higher education. A great distance, both in resources and esteem, separates activities in this sector from what has been on offer on a day release or night school basis to groups such as craft apprentices and technicians. Beyond this, the only message that gets over to the majority of the population during formal schooling is that technology is hard, boring and really none of their business. The vast majority of women receive this message from other sources as well (Cockburn, 1991).

Against this background, there may be at least a symbolic gain in establishing something labelled as 'Technology' as a compulsory element of the curriculum. Inviting the practical subjects in from the cold and offering parity of esteem with 'academic' subjects could bolster the morale of the teachers concerned. Likewise, if pupils of all ages and stages and both genders were thereby enabled to find enjoyment and satisfaction in 'design and technological activities', this might conceivably make some of them more amenable to technological specialization at a later stage. Neither of the outcomes is likely unless the government is willing to invest in materials and equipment, INSET and course development time.

In strategic terms, what is needed to address the crisis of under-education and under-achievement in engineering-related fields? This clearly goes beyond the problems of image or perception which might be solved by repackaging current 'best practice'. Greatly increased investment could be an important factor, but unless the problems of stratification start to be tackled, this may be ineffective.

It is unrealistic to imagine that high-level (i.e., advanced and narrow) specialization can be dispensed with. The key issues for higher education are (a) *progression routes*, both in respect of access (Spours, 1988) and accreditation, and (b) in the twilight of the Taylorist/Fordist era, *flexible specialization*, in particular promoting the elimination of the 'boys in the back room', 'man in the white coat' or 'tame boffin' syndromes. A great deal of development is required with regard to intermediate levels of qualification and specialization where both access and quality of provision are important issues. More broadly, there is the question of how to promote a far wider understanding of technology. This relates to the concept of technological literacy which will be given some attention towards the end of this chapter.

Can National Curriculum Technology play any constructive part in meeting these needs? Clearly, there can be no guarantee that curriculum proposals which extend only to age 16 and ignore questions of progression beyond this point will have anything to offer to the solution of problems at intermediate and higher levels. A school subject which is compulsory for ages 5–16 is presumably designed to be a component of general education and in the case of technology this might be construed in terms of laying the basis for a form of technological literacy rooted in practical experience. It could also, particularly in the later stages, be designed as a foundation for later more specialized studies. At no point does it become clear whether the second objective is on the agenda or not. It is possible that the DES originally had both objectives in their sights, but that the second got shed along the way. Certainly there does not appear to have been any great coherence of purpose among the parties concerned. The NCC (Consultation Report, Foreword) specify the function of technology within the curriculum as 'the task of providing balance in a curriculum based on academic subjects — a balance in which the creative and practical capabilities of pupils can be fully developed and inter-related'. We might note in passing the bizarre concept of 'balance' in which a single subject among ten is to take the weight of the development of 'creative and practical capabilities', an issue discussed in more detail by Peter Medway in this volume. This looks, if anything, like a specification of technology as a component of general education and this is borne out by the examples in the Statutory Orders which have a distinctly 'low-tech' flavour — beakers, badges and fairy cakes but precious little reference to, for example, electronic hardware.

The terms of reference of the working group do however suggest that the DES might originally have had half an eye on the national crisis in advanced engineering skills. The stipulation that design activities should always involve science or maths is a pointer in this direction. Taken literally, this is a somewhat blinkered requirement, since it discounts most traditional and pre-modern technology. However, for more than a century, many economically significant technical advances have been associated with (but not necessarily derived from) developments in scientific understanding and/or the range of application of mathematical techniques. In part consequence of this, beyond the elementary stage, engineering instruction has leaned fairly heavily on science and maths. (Some would say that this emphasis, particularly on algebra, has been unnecessarily heavy, a consequence of the elitism of higher education and the professional associations.) Another possible indicator is the stipulation that pupils should learn about '*the* variety of modern materials and technologies in use in the industrial and commercial world'. The use of the definite rather than the indefinite article may be a drafting error, but if not, the delivery of the curriculum could hardly avoid at least short excursions into specialist areas of physics, chemistry and electronics. The FEU and the Engineering Council (1988) list examples of current Key Technologies as Biological Materials, Group III/V semiconductors, ceramics, ion beam implantation, optoelectric devices, mechatronics, sensors, image processing, flexible manufacturing, expert systems and condition monitoring. Now these, of course, are areas where a 5–16 syllabus could hardly do more than scratch at the surface. In the final product, only a handful of these topics feature even marginally, and then under the IT component as computer applications. As far as the Statutory Orders are concerned, the materials and hardware aspects of the new technologies might as well not exist, a consequence of a view which is content to equate 'new technology' with the software aspects of computing.

The chief assumption held in common between the Secretary of State, DES executives, the NCC and the working group is that school technology should be an 'essentially practical' activity involving designing and making, and that any necessary theorizing and reflection should be related to a 'real-world' context. The working group are however at pains to stress the 'additional dimension' of assessment, evaluation and critical reflection on the social relations of technology. It would seem that the way in which they hoped to accommodate the requirement that pupils should 'learn about' modern materials and technologies would be by a consideration of technological change (see above, p. 88). The specific examples given — biological materials, fibre optics and superconductors — are all key technologies but are conspicuous by their absence from documents subsequent to the Interim Report. They do not feature in the Science orders either.

It would seem then that whatever the original hopes or intentions, National Curriculum Technology can only be viewed and judged as a somewhat circumscribed intervention in the field of general education. It might well offer modest gains in terms of accelerating the process of transformation of the old craft subjects. This has already been under way for some years, reducing the emphasis on *making* things (never mind what — book ends, candle holders, tool clamps, ashtrays, fairy cakes — and never mind why) in favour of designing and making with a sense of context and purpose. Experience of the design process is unarguably a valuable component of an educational programme. There is a danger, however, which Peter Medway (in this volume) hints at, of schools coming to recognize a standardized set of stock 'real-life' 'opportunities for design technological activity' thus creating an orthodox academic subject whose 'reality' extends no further than the school gate.

There might also be real gains in terms of technological understanding/ literacy if full justice could be done to the working group's 'additional dimension'. This has fared badly in the curriculum design process, appearing in the Statutory Orders only in a bland and trivialized form, e.g.,

> ... understand that artefacts systems or environments reflect the circumstances and values of particular cultures and communities (Statement of Attainment, Level 8)

> understand how fashions influence the design of clothes (example to illustrate above)

The mountain roars and brings forth a (mickey) mouse! Pupils in, for example, the East End of London might well be inclined to survey their ravaged environment and reflect on the systems of values and priorities which have served to generate and perpetuate their own particular life circumstances. This, however, is probably not what the NCC had in mind. Ideological preferences apart, there are two structural problems which militate against the 'additional dimension'. The first is located within the design and technology profile component, the second in the design of the National Curriculum itself.

The working group, for defensible reasons, has stressed the holistic nature of the activity and warned against treating the four ATs as independent. Designing and Making are mandatory at all Key Stages, but these activities are not supposed to be separated from Identifying Needs and Evaluating. This serves to encourage a state of affairs in which the latter processes are only concerned with artefacts etc. which can be designed and made within the limited resources of the school. The danger is that this will fail to address the mainsprings of design and technological activity in the real economy. This may have its attractions if the idea, both literally and metaphorically, is not to frighten the children. While Noddy remains in Toyland, the concept of 'Satisfying Human Need' can sound unproblematic, even comforting. What is to be done with regard to important artefacts, environments and systems beyond the immediate confines of school, home or local community? In what context can older children start to reflect critically on e.g., crop sprays, guided missiles, nuclear waste disposal or the M25 motorway? This is not actually forbidden by the Statutory Orders, but since there is no concomitant Designing and Making Activity, these matters could only be dealt with by taking AT1 and AT4 in isolation.

Assuming, nevertheless, that room could be found for the 'additional dimension' within the secondary school timetable, the second structural problem then emerges. Consideration of the social shaping and implications of technology both here and now and in other cultures and at other times is clearly a cross-curricular activity and therefore the 'additional dimension' requires coordination within the National Curriculum between Technology and the humanities, notably History.

Coordination Within the National Curriculum

The National Curriculum is an exercise in normalization rather than innovation.[8] Its declared objective is to level up standards to those of current 'best practice'. In pursuance of this it aims, through pervasive and onerous rituals of assessment, to produce detailed performance indicators by which pupils, teachers and schools may be compared. Other than normalization on a subject-by-subject basis, there is no overall curriculum strategy from which guidelines for content could be derived, and as a curriculum of *subjects*, it is unlikely to ease the task of delivering coordinated inter-subject programmes. The curriculum is being generated piecemeal by independent subject committees reporting sequentially and possibilities for coordination will therefore be largely accidental, discernible only with hindsight. In so far as there may be an overall curriculum strategy, it remains unstated and has to be guessed at. It has often been remarked that the National Curriculum marks an attempt to revert to the 'traditional' grammar-school syllabus which has some truth except (irony of ironies) that Technology takes the place of Latin. Believers in conspiracies, surveying the choice of subjects, point to the demise of pink studies, e.g., a GCSE in Sociology will be hard to fit in. Believers in cock-ups will also note that a GCSE in Electronics would be equally difficult to accommodate.[9]

The failure to coordinate inter-subject planning places a limitation on the scope of National Curriculum Technology. The Interim Report flags the necessity of coordination with secondary History and Geography (p. 9). This requires some degree of coherence between ATs and Programmes of Study, particularly at KS4. The History final report appeared at much the same time as the Technology orders. No reference, however, is made to the material produced by the Technology group and there is no evidence that the question of coordination had ever been raised even though it is stated that 'It is largely through the study of history that pupils learn about the social origins, processes and effects of technology' (p. 181). The word technology features fairly frequently in the History final report without any explicit recognition that its meaning might be subject to a range of interpretations. The History working group have identified four 'key dimensions' to the study of history, namely Political, Economic, Social and Cultural, the Economic category subsuming Technology and Science. Each study unit therefore contains a technological sub-dimension. This offers, in principle, opportunities for coordination, but successful matches will be a matter of luck, not the result of prior planning. It is not encouraging that the cluster of study units most closely concerned with specific examples of technological development (ships and seafarers, food and farming, writing and printing, land transport) all occur in KS2, i.e., in the *primary* school.

Technological Literacy and TVEI

Richard Capel, elsewhere in this volume, expresses the hope that the 'educational system might begin to provide holistic forms of education, which when dealing with technology provide an anthropocentric perspective as opposed to a technocentric approach'. This is in effect a plea to reframe technology as a humanistic study, a deeply worthwhile but daunting objective. Somewhere along this road lies the task of developing the novel pedagogic practices which will be associated with a politically adequate concept of technological literacy. We must try and specify as precisely as possible what we want technological literacy to be for. Here the perspective adopted by John Mathews and colleagues is a useful one, proceding from the premise that, within post-Fordist relations of production, organized labour should adopt a 'protagonistic' rather than an antagonistic stance towards technological change (Mathews, 1989) and play an active role in the planning and management of workplace restructuring. Technological literacy, '. . . a capacity on the part of citizens to comprehend the essentials of technological design and the motives for change' (Mathews *et al.*, 1988) is therefore a prerequisite for 'protagonism'. In this context it would be quite inadequate to reduce technological literacy to 'computer literacy', particularly the limited versions of computer literacy which Capel criticizes.

The Interim Report might have raised hopes that National Curriculum Technology would be a reasonably fertile ground for sowing the seeds of technological literacy. It would seem that such hopes will be largely frustrated, the more innovative proposals having fallen foul of a curriculum framework whose pedagogic intention is to normalize and whose political intention is to neutralize. It would appear that the once reviled TVEI might offer a more benign setting in which to move towards basic levels of technological literacy. There is considerable overlap between the focus statements of TVEI (Appendix B) and the original specifications for National Curriculum Technology whether as represented by the DES terms of reference or by the introduction to the Interim Report. According to the latter, pupils are to learn the 'capability to operate effectively and creatively in the made world'. TVEI is broadly concerned with pupils understanding and preparing for 'the world of work'. Common preoccupations appear to be with problem solving, teamwork and some version of economic awareness and 'enterprise'. Despite this affinity, no explicit connections between NC Technology and TVEI have survived, the last even implicit link being severed when, in the interest of simplification, the Activity statements (Final Report) were suppressed. At KS4, these specified work experience, a significant feature of TVEI, among the prescribed modes of learning.

TVEI, once widely regarded as a predatory intervention on the part of the Manpower Services Commission, has now largely lived down its questionable political origins. It is less prescriptive than the National Curriculum and has structural features which actually encourage innovative practices. Thus cross-subject collaboration is mandatory as is coordination between schools and colleges across the 16+ divide. The mode of delivery of the various entitlements is a matter for local discretion, subject to negotiation. The focus statements are susceptible to a wide range of interpretation. Thus work experience could be a narrowly conceived exercise in job-tasting. Alternatively, understanding the world of work could take on the wider connotations of the 'additional dimension' and technological literacy could become the focus through which work experience and careers education are integrated into the mainstream curriculum.

Had they had time and full licence to do so, the working group might have been better employed in reviewing best practice within TVEI rather than wrestling with the intricacies of the TGAT framework. They, however, along with so many other busy and well-intentioned individuals, were in effect caged on the lumbering circus-train of the National Curriculum. How far this contraption will progress once bereft of its ideologically fuelled engine is open to doubt.[10] A few years down the line and substantial reforms will be needed. The groundwork for these could be carried out in the context of TVEI extension and the reformulation and rationalization of the post-compulsory curriculum. In the meantime, it is to be hoped that teachers, while taking due note of Peter Medway's perceptive criticisms, will be guided more by the spirit of the Interim Report rather than the letter of the Statutory Orders. If the 'additional dimension' of the Interim Report is suppressed or marginalized, then a small but significant opportunity to open up the school curriculum will have been lost. The immediate problem is that the conceptual space which it delimits is unlikely to be matched by space in the timetable, by resources or by adequate means of accreditation. There are however far deeper problems which arise from the academic division of labour (and hence of consciousness) within the educational system as a whole.

Beynon and Mackay (1989), in urging the necessity for critical analysis of the role of IT in education, remark that 'education is too important to be left to technologists'. (They might well have also said that *technology*, inside or outside the classroom, is too important to be left to technologists). The implication of this is that technology must cease to be largely a 'no-go area' for the critical social disciplines. This is also one prerequisite for building up a practical pedagogy in support of technological literacy. Another essential element is the emergence, sooner rather than later, of significant numbers of literate technologists. Effective progress towards widespread technological literacy will require a gradual but ultimately radical restructuring of practice and consciousness in every sector of education. The challenge is not just to general education and the humanities but to specialized technical instruction and to the wastelands of socially decontextualized 'problem solving' which still constitute the higher reaches of 'education' in the mathematical sciences.

Notes

1 In advocating a computer in every school (the modern equivalent of 'a chicken in every pot'?), Kenneth Baker also achieved a breakthrough in self-publicity. Arguably the most eloquent right-wing 'technoromantic' since Mussolini, Mr Baker's political career achieved lift-off with his appointment as Minister for Information Technology (a post that no longer exists). We should note that the political sponsor of IT-mania has subsequently bequeathed us the poll tax and the National Curriculum. Beynon and Mackay (1989) give a critical discussion of the 'technoromanticism' of the last decade.
2 The working group correctly note that. 'IT also forms an essential part of design and technology because it lies at the heart of many artefacts and

systems' (Interim Report, p. 65) and therefore that 'part of the assessment of IT capability must be integrated with the assessment of design and technological activity in general' (Interim Report, p. 72). However 'many respondents ... considered that the division of information technology capability in this way would be unhelpful to employers, parents and pupils' (Consultation Report, p. 25). It would presumably also be 'unhelpful' to the self-esteem of IT specialists.

3   Task Group on Assessment and Testing, established in Oct. 1987 to advise on assessment and testing within the NC.

4   A fifth attainment target related to Information Technology (which, despite the prefatory noises about coordination, is completely independent of the other four), is omitted from this list.

5   See note 2 above.

6   Developing and using systems, working with materials, developing and communicating ideas, satisfying human need.

7   An important figure in this movement, in which Thomas Huxley and Lyon Playfair were also prominent, was Sir Philip Magnus, the first Secretary of the City and Guilds of London Institute. In 1887, he wrote as follows: The facilities for scientific education are far greater on the Continent than in England and where such differences exist, England is sure to fall behind as regards those industries into which the scientific element enters. In fact I have long entertained the opinion that in virtue of the better education founded by Continental nations, England must one day — and that no distant one — find herself outstripped by these nations both in the arts of peace and war.

8   The rationale for the National Curriculum is not included in the drafting of the 1988 Education Act. It is however elaborated to some degree in early publications of the NCC e.g., *'National Curriculum' — A Guide for Parents* (1988).

9   It now appears that the constraints placed by the National Curriculum on the secondary school curriculum and timetable may turn out to be less severe than originally feared. The current Secretary of State, John Macgregor, in response to a number of pressures, including that of reality, has started to deconstruct certain parts of Mr Baker's handiwork. A recent speech (*Times*, 1 August 1990) signals his wish to limit the number of compulsory subjects at KS4 to possibly no more than English, Science, Maths, Technology and one foreign language. This, in effect, establishes Technology as the fourth 'core' subject, being the only subject apart from the original three core subjects which is certain to be compulsory throughout the 5–16 age range.

10 See note 9 above.

References

BEYNON, J. and MACKAY, H. (1989) 'Information Technology into education: towards a critical perspective', *J. Education Policy*, 4, 1, pp. 245–57.

COCKBURN, C. (1991) 'The gendering of technology', in MACKAY, H., YOUNG, M. and BEYNON, J. (Eds) *Understanding Technology in Education*, Falmer.

FINEGOLD, D., KEEP, E., MILIBAND, D., RAFFE, D., SPOURS, K. and YOUNG, M.

(1990) *A British Baccalauréat: Ending the Division between Education and Training*, Education and Training Paper No. 1, London, IPPR.

FURTHER EDUCATION UNIT and ENGINEERING COUNCIL (1988) *The Key Technologies: Implications for Education and Training*, Oxford, Opus.

MATTHEWS, J. (1989) *Tools of Change: New Technology and the Democratisation of Work*, Pluto.

MATTHEWS, J., HALL, G. and SMITH, H. (1988) Towards flexible skill formation, and technological literacy: challenges facing the Education System, *Economic and Industrial Democracy*, 9, No. 4.

SPOURS, K. (1988) *The Politics of Progression*, Working Paper No. 2, London, Institute of Education Post-16 Education Centre.

WEBSTER, F. and ROBINS, K. (1991) 'The selling of the new technology', in MACKAY, H., YOUNG, M. and BEYNON, J. (Eds) *Understanding Technology in Education*, Falmer.

Appendix A

The following is a summary of the proposals for National Curriculum Technology at the Final Report phase. It is taken from 'Design and Technology for All. Some guidance for schools', a publication of the Leeds University TVEI support project, pp. 4–5.

AT1 Identifying needs and opportunities
Through exploration and investigation of a range of contexts (home; school; recreation, community; business and industry) pupils should be able to identify and state clearly needs and opportunities for design and technological activities.

AT2 Generating a design proposal
Pupils should be able to produce a realistic, appropriate and achievable design by generating, exploring and developing design and technological ideas and by refining and detailing the design proposal they have chosen.

AT3 Planning and Making
Working to a plan derived from their previously developed design, pupils should be able to identify, manage and use appropriate resources, including both knowledge and processes, in order to make an artefact, system or environment.

AT4 Appraisal
Pupils should be able to develop, communicate and act constructively upon an appraisal of the processes, outcomes and effects of design and technological activity of others, including those from other times and cultures.

Progression

Pupils' progression from one level of achievement to the next may be as a result of:

- extending the range of performance, e.g., by working in unfamiliar resources
- more sophisticated use of familiar resources
- deeper exploration of a familiar context
- increasing interplay of knowledge, skills, judgment and personal qualities
- the ability to critically reflect and so modify a design
- weaving together contributions from a wider variety of resources

Programmes of Study

'Programmes of study describe the *means* by which pupils are able to achieve the *ends* defined by the attainment targets.' How this is done in schools is not prescribed: 'it remains for teachers to plan appropriate schemes of work in the light of their particular circumstances and knowledge of their pupils.'

The elements of design and technological activities are:

- knowledge
- skills
- contexts
- value considerations.

These elements are integrated in activities which develop design and technological capability and should be undertaken in a variety of contexts.

The programmes of study are based upon sixteen aspects:

Materials	Energy
Business and economics	Tools and equipment
Aesthetics	Systems
Structures	Mechanisms
Exploring and investigating	Imaging and generating
Modelling and communicating	Organizing and planning
Making	Appraising
Health and safety	Social and environment

Appendix B

TVEI Focus Statements

TVEI aims to ensure that the education to 14 to 18 year olds provides young people with learning opportunities which will equip them for the demands of working life in a rapidly changing society.

TVEI seeks to influence the Education of 14 to 18 year olds in 5 explicit ways:

- By making sure **the curriculum** uses every opportunity to relate education to the world of work by using concrete, real examples if possible.
- By making sure that young people get the **knowledge, competencies** and **qualifications** they need in a highly technological society which is itself part of Europe and the world economy.
- By making sure that young people themselves get **direct opportunities** to learn about the nature of the economy and the world of work — through work experience, workshadowing, projects in the community and so on.
- By making sure that young people learn how to be effective people, solve problems, work in teams, be enterprising and creative through the way they are taught.
- By making sure that young people have access to initial **guidance and counselling** and then continuing education and training, and opportunities for **progression** throughout their lives.

Chapter 5

Is the New Technology Part of the Solution or Part of the Problem in Education?

Michael Apple

The Politics of Technology

In our society, technology is seen as an autonomous process. It is set apart and viewed as if it had a life of its own, independent of social intentions, power, and privilege. We examine technology as if it were something constantly changing, and something that is constantly changing our lives in schools and elsewhere. This is partly true, of course, and is fine as far as it goes. However, by focusing on what is changing and being changed, we may neglect to ask what relationships are remaining the same. Among the most important of these are the sets of cultural and economic inequalities that dominate even societies like our own.[1]

By thinking of technology in this way, by closely examining whether the changes associated with 'technological progress' are really changes in certain relationships after all, we can begin to ask political questions about their causes and especially their multitudinous effects. Whose idea of progress? Progress for what? And fundamentally, once again, who benefits?[2] These questions may seem rather weighty ones to be asking about schools and the curricular and teaching practices that now go on in them or are being proposed. Yet, we are in the midst of one of those many educational bandwagons that governments, industry, and others so like to ride. This wagon is pulled in the direction of a technological workplace, and carries a heavy load of computers as its cargo.

The growth of the new technology in schools is definitely not what one would call a slow movement. In one recent year, there was a 56 per cent reported increase in the use of computers in schools in the United States, and even this may be a conservative estimate. Of the 25,642 schools surveyed, over 15,000 schools reported some computer usage.[3] In the United States alone, it is estimated that over 350,000 microcomputers have been introduced into the public schools in the past four years.[4] This is a trend that shows no sign of abating. Nor is this phenomenon only limited to United States. France, Canada, England, Australia, and many other countries have 'recognized the future'. 'At its center seems to sit a machine with a keyboard and a screen.

I say 'at its center' since both in industry and governmental agencies and in schools themselves the computer and the new technology have been seen as something of a savior economically and pedagogically. 'High tech' will save declining economies and will save our students and teachers in schools. In the latter, it is truly remarkable how wide a path the computer is now cutting.

The expansion of its use, the tendency to see all areas of education as a unified terrain for growth in the use of new technologies, can be seen in a two-day workshop on integrating the microcomputer into the classroom held at my own university. Among the topics covered were computer applications in writing instruction, in music education, in secondary science and mathematics, in primary language arts, for the handicapped, for teacher record keeping and management, in business education, in health occupation training programs, in art, and in social studies. To this is added a series of sessions on the 'electronic office,' how technology and automation are helping industry, and how we all can 'transcend the terror' of technology.[5]

Two things are evident from this list. First, vast areas of school life are now seen to be within the legitimate purview of technological restructuring. Second, there is a partly hidden but exceptionally close linkage between computers in schools and the needs of management for automated industries, electronic offices, and 'skilled' personnel. Thus, recognizing both what is happening inside and outside of schools and the connections between these areas is critical to any understanding of what is likely to happen with the new technologies, especially the computer, in education.

As I have argued elsewhere, educational debates are increasingly limited to technical issues. Questions of 'how to' have replaced questions of 'why.'[6] In this chapter, I shall want to reverse this tendency. Rather than dealing with what the best way might be to establish closer ties between the technological requirements of the larger society and our formal institutions of education. I want to step back and raise a different set of questions. I want us to consider a number of rather difficult political, economic, and ethical issues about some of the tendencies in schools and the larger society that may make us want to be very cautious about the current technological bandwagon in education. In so doing, a range of areas will need to be examined. Behind the slogans of technological progress and high-tech industry, what are some of the real effects of the new technology on the future labor market? What may happen to teaching and curriculum if we do not think carefully about the new technology's place in the classroom? Will the growing focus on technological expertise, particularly computer literacy, equalize or further exacerbate the lack of social opportunities for our most disadvantaged students?

At root, my claim will be that the debate about the role of the new technology in society and in schools is not and must not be just about the technical correctness of what computers can and cannot do. These may be the least important kinds of questions, in fact. Instead, at the very core of the debate, are the ideological and ethical issues concerning what schools should be about and whose interests they should serve.[7] The question of interests is very important at the moment since, because of the severe problems currently besetting economies like our own, a restructuring of what schools are *for* has reached a rather advanced stage.

Thus, while there has always been a relatively close connection between the two, there is now an even closer relationship between the curriculum in our schools and corporate needs.[8] In a number of countries, educational officials and policy-markers, legislators, curriculum workers, and others have been subject to immense pressure to make the 'needs' of business and industry the primary goals of the school system. Economic and ideological pressures have become rather intense and often very overt. The language of efficiency, production, standards, cost-effectiveness, job skills, work discipline, and so on — all defined by powerful groups and always threatening to become the dominant way we think about schooling[9] — has begun to push aside concerns for a democratic curriculum, teacher autonomy, and class, gender, and race equality. Yet, we cannot fully understand the implications of the new technology in this restructuring unless we gain a more complete idea of what industry is now doing not only in the schools but in the economy as well.

Technological Myths and Economic Realities

Let us look at the larger society first. It is claimed that the technological needs of the economy are such that unless we have a technologically literate labor force we will ultimately become outmoded economically. But what will this labor force actually look like?

A helpful way of thinking about this is once more to use the concepts of increasing *proletarianization* and *deskilling* of jobs. These concepts signify a complex historical process in which the control of labor has altered — one in which the skills workers have developed over many years are broken down and reduced to their atomistic units, automated, and redefined by management to enhance profit levels, efficiency, and control. In the process, the employee's control of timing, over defining the most appropriate way to do a task, and over criteria that establish acceptable performance, are slowly taken over as the prerogatives of management personnel who are usually divorced from the place where the actual labor is carried out. Loss of control by the worker is almost always the result. Pay is often lowered. And the job itself becomes routinized, boring, and alienating as conception is separated from execution and more and more aspects of jobs are rationalized to bring them into line with management's need for a tighter economic and ideological ship.[10] Finally, and very importantly, many of these jobs may simply disappear.

There is no doubt that the rapid developments in, say, micro-electronics, genetic engineering and associated 'biological technologies', and other high-tech areas, are in fact partly transforming work in a large number of sectors in the economy. This may lead to economic prosperity in certain sections of our population, but its other effects may be devastating. Thus, as the authors of a recent study that examined the impact of new technologies on the future labor market demonstrate:

> This transformation ... may stimulate economic growth and competition in the world marketplace, but it will displace thousands of workers and could sustain high unemployment for many years. It may provide increased job opportunities for engineers, computer operators, and robot technicians, but it also promises to generate an even greater number of low level, service jobs such as those of janitors, cashiers, clericals, and food service workers. And while many more workers will be using computers, automated office equipment, and other sophisticated technical devices in their jobs, the increased use of technology may actually reduce the skills and discretion required to perform many jobs.[11]

This scenario requires further elaboration.

Rumberger and Levin make a distinction that is very useful to this discussion. They differentiate between high-tech industries and high-tech occupations — in essence between what is made and the kinds of jobs these goods require. High-tech industries that manufacture technical devices such as computers, electronic components, and the like currently employ less than 15 per cent of the paid workforce in the United States and other industrialized nations. Just as importantly, a substantial knowledge of technology is required by *less than one-fourth* of all occupations within these industries. On the contrary, the largest share of jobs created by high-tech industries are in areas such as clerical and office work or in production and assembly. These actually pay below average wages.[12] Yet this is not all. High-tech occupations that do require considerable skill — such as computer specialists and engineers — may indeed expand. However, most of these occupations actually 'employ relatively few workers compared to many traditional clerical and service fields.'[13] Rumberger and Levin summarize a number of these points by stating that 'although the percentage growth rate of occupational employment in such high technology fields as engineering and computer programming was higher than the overall growth rate of jobs, far more jobs would be created in low-skilled clerical and service occupations than in high technology ones.'[14]

Some of these claims are supported by the following data. It is estimated that even being generous in one's projections. only 17 per cent of new jobs that will be created between now and 1995 will be in high-tech industries. (Less generous and more restrictive projections argue that only 3 to 8 per cent of future jobs will be in such industries.)[15] As I noted, though, such jobs will not be all equal. Clerical workers, secretaries, assemblers, warehouse personnel, etc. — these will be the largest occupations within the industry. If we take the electronic components industry as an example here, this is made much clearer. Engineering, science, and computing occupations constituted approximately 15 per cent of all workers in this industry. The majority of the rest of the workers were engaged in low-wage assembly work. Thus, in the late 1970s, nearly two-thirds of all workers in the electronic components industry took home hourly wages 'that placed them in the bottom third of the national distribution'.[16] If we take the archetypical high-tech industry — computers and data processing — and decompose its labor market, we get similar results. In 1980, technologically oriented and skilled jobs accounted for only 26 per cent of the total.[17]

These figures have considerable weight, but they are made even more significant by the fact that many of that 26 per cent may themselves experience a deskilling process in the near future. That is, the reduction of jobs down into simpler and atomistic components, the separation of conception from execution, and so on — processes that have had such a major impact on the labor process of blue-, pink-, and white-collar workers in so many other areas — are now advancing into high-technology jobs as well. Computer programming provides an excellent example. New developments in software packages and machine language and design have meant that a considerable portion of the job of programming now requires little more than performing 'standard, routine, machine-like tasks that require little-depth knowledge.'[18]

What does this mean for the schooling process and the seemingly widespread belief that the future world of work will require increasing technical competence on the part of all students? Consider the occupations that will contribute the most number of jobs not just in high-tech industries but throughout the society by 1995. Economic forecasts indicate that these will include building custodians, cashiers, secretaries, office clerks, nurses, waiters and waitresses, elementary school teachers, truck drivers, and other health workers such as nurses' aides and orderlies.[19] None of these are directly related to high technology. Excluding teachers and nurses, none of them require any post-secondary education. (Their earnings will be approximately 30 per cent below the current average earnings of workers, as well.)[20] If we go further than this and examine an even larger segment of expected new jobs by including the forty job categories that will probably account for about half of all the jobs that will be created, it is estimated that only about 25 per cent will require people with a college degree.[21]

In many ways, this is strongly related to the effects of the new technology on the job market and the labor process in general. Skill levels will be raised in some areas, but will decline in many others, as will jobs themselves decline. For instance, 'a recent study of robotics in the United States suggests that robots will eliminate 100,000 to 200,000 jobs by 1990, while creating 32,000 to 64,000 jobs.'[22] My point about declining skill requirements is made nicely by Rumberger and Levin. As they suggest, while it is usually assumed that workers will need computer programming and other sophisticated skills because of the greater use of technology such as computers in their jobs, the ultimate effect of such technology may be somewhat different. 'A variety of evidence suggests just the opposite: as machines become more sophisticated, with expanded memories, more computational ability, and sensory capabilities, the knowledge required to use the devices declines.'[23] The effect of these trends on the division of labor will be felt for decades. But it will be in the sexual division of labor that it will be even more extreme. As I have argued, since historically *women's work* has been subject to these processes in very powerful ways, we shall see increased proletarianization and deskilling of women's labor and, undoubtedly, a further increase in the feminization of poverty.[24]

These points clearly have implications for our educational programs. We need to think much more rigorously about what they mean for our transition from school to work programs, especially since many of the 'skills' that schools are currently teaching are transitory because the jobs themselves are being transformed (or lost) by new technological developments and new management offensives.

Take office work, for example. In offices, the bulk of the new technology has not been designed to enhance the quality of the job for the largest portion of the employees (usually women clerical workers). Rather it has usually been designed and implemented in such a way that exactly the opposite will result. Instead of accommodating stimulating and satisfying work, the technology is there to make managers' jobs 'easier', to eliminate jobs and cut costs, to divide work into routine and atomized tasks, and to make administrative control more easily accomplished.[25] The vision of the future society seen in the microcosm of the office is inherently undemocratic and perhaps increasingly authoritarian. Is this what we wish to prepare our students for? Surely, our task as educators is neither to accept such a future labor market and labor process uncritically nor to have our students accept such practices uncritically either. To do so is simply to allow the values of a limited but powerful segment of the population to work through us. It may be good business but I have my doubts about whether it is ethically correct educational policy.

In summary, then, what we will witness is the creation of enhanced jobs for a relative minority and deskilled and boring work for the majority. Furthermore, even those boring and deskilled jobs will be increasingly hard to find. Take office work again, an area that is rapidly being transformed by the new technology. It is estimated that between one and five jobs will be lost for every new computer terminal that is introduced.[26] Yet this situation will not be limited to office work. Even those low-paying assembly positions noted earlier will not necessarily be found in the industrialized nations with their increasingly service-oriented economies. Given the international division of labor, and what is called 'capital flight', a large portion of these jobs will be moved to countries such as Korea, the Philippines and Indonesia.[27]

This is exacerbated considerably by the fact that many governments now find 'acceptable' those levels of unemployment that would have been considered a crisis a decade ago. 'Full employment' in the United States is now often seen as between 7 and 8 per cent *measured* unemployment. (The actual figures are much higher, of course, especially among minority groups and workers who can only get part-time jobs or who have given up looking for paid work after so many disappointments.) This is a figure that is *double* that of previous economic periods. Even higher rates are now seen as 'normal' in other countries. The trend is clear. The future will see fewer jobs. Most of those that are created will not necessarily by fulfilling, nor will they pay well. Finally, the level of technical skill will continue to be lowered for a large portion of them.[28]

Because of this, we need convincing answers to some very important questions about our future society and the economy before we turn out schools into 'production plants' for creating new workers. *Where* will these new jobs be? *How many* will be created? Will they *equal* the number of positions lost in offices and factories, and service jobs in retailing, banks, telecommunications, and elsewhere? Are the bulk of the jobs that will be created relatively unskilled, less than meaningful, and themselves subject to the 'inexorable' logics of management so that they too will be likely to be automated out of existence.[29]

These are not inconsequential questions. Before we give the schools over to the requirements of the new technology and the corporation, we must be very certain that it will benefit all of us, not primarily those who already possess economic and cultural power. This requires continued democratic discussion, not a quick decision based on the economic and political pressure now being placed on schools.

Much more could be said about the future labor market. I urge the interested reader to pursue it in greater depth, since it will have a profound impact on our school policies and programs, especially in vocational areas, in working-class schools, and among programs for young women. The difficulties with the high-tech vision that permeates the beliefs of the proponents of a technological solution will not remain outside the school door, however. Similar disproportionate benefits and dangers await us inside our educational institutions as well, and it is to this that we now turn.

Inequality and the Technological Classroom

Once we go inside the school, a set of questions concerning 'who benefits?' also arises. We shall need to ask about what may be happening to teachers and students given the emphasis now being placed on computers in schools. I shall not talk about the individual teacher or student here. Obviously, some teachers will find their jobs enriched by the new technology and some students will find hidden talents and will excel in a computer-oriented classroom. What we need to ask instead (or at least before we deal with the individual) is what may happen to classrooms, teachers, and students differentially. Once again, I shall seek to raise a set of issues that may not be easy to solve, but cannot be ignored if we are to have a truly democratic educational system not just in name only.

Though I have dealt with this in greater detail in *Ideology and Curriculum* and *Education and Power*,[30] let me briefly situate the growth of the technologized classroom into what seems to be occurring to teaching and curriculum in general. Currently, considerable pressure is building to have teaching and school curricula be totally prespecified and tightly controlled for the purposes of 'efficiency,' 'cost-effectiveness,' and 'accountability.' In many ways, the deskilling that is affecting jobs in general is now having an impact on teachers as more and more decisions are moving out of their hands and as their jobs become even more difficult to do. This process is more advanced in some countries than others, but it is clear that the movement to rationalize and control the act of teaching and the content and evaluation of the curriculum is very real.[31] Even in those countries that have made strides away from centralized examination systems, powerful inspectorates and supervisors, and tightly controlled curricula, there is an identifiable tendency to move back toward state control. Many reforms have only a very tenuous hold at the present time. This is in part due to economic difficulties and partly due as well to the importing of American styles and techniques of educational management — styles and techniques that have their roots in industrial bureaucracies and have almost never had democratic aims.[32] Even though a number of teachers may support computer-oriented curricula, an emphasis on the new technology needs to be seen in this context of the rationalization of teaching and curricula in general.

Given these pressures, what will happen to teachers if the new technology is accepted uncritically? One of the major effects of the current (over) emphasis on computers in the classroom may again be the deskilling and depowering of a considerable number of teachers. Given the already heavy workload of planning, teaching, meetings, and paperwork for most teachers, and given the expense, it is probably wise to assume that the largest portion of teachers will not be given more than a very small amount of training in computers, their social effects, programming, and so on. This will be especially the case at the primary and elementary school level, where most teachers are already teaching a wide array of subject areas. Research indicates in fact that few teachers in any district are actually given substantial information before computer curricula are implemented. Often only one or two teachers are the 'resident experts.'[33] Because of this, most teachers have to rely on pre-packaged sets of material, existing software, and specially purchased material from any of the scores of software manufacturing firms that are springing up in a largely unregulated way. This will be heightened by the contradictory sense of professionalism and technical expertise many teachers already have.

The impact of this can be striking. What is happening is the exacerbation of trends we have begun to see in a number of nations. Instead of teachers having the time and the skill to do their own curriculum planning and deliberation, they become isolated executors of someone else's plans, procedures, and evaluative mechanisms. In industrial terms, this is very close to what I noted in my previous discussion of the labor process — the separation of conception from execution.[34]

The reliance on pre-packaged software can have a number of long-term effects. First, it can cause a decided loss of important skills and dispositions on the part of teachers. When the skills of local curriculum planning, individual evaluation, and so on are not used, they atrophy. The tendency to look outside of one's own or one's colleagues' historical experience about curriculum and teaching is lessened as considerably more of the curriculum, and the teaching and evaluative practices that surround it, is viewed as something one purchases. In the process — and this is very important — the school itself is transformed into a lucrative market. The industrialization of the school I talked of previously is complemented, then, by further opening up the classroom to the mass-produced commodities of industry. The technological 'text' joins the existing textbook in the political economy of commodified culture. And once again, financial capital will dominate. In many ways, it will be a publisher's and salesperson's delight. Whether students' educational experiences will markedly improve is open to question.

The issue of the relationship of purchased software and hardware to the possible deskilling and depowering of teachers does not end here, though. The problem is made even more difficult by the rapidity with which software developers have constructed and marketed their products. There is no guarantee that the mass of such material has any major educational value. Exactly the opposite is often the case. One of the most knowledgeable government officials has put it this way: 'High quality educational software is almost non-existent in our elementary and secondary schools.'[35] While perhaps overstating his case to emphasize his points, the director of software evaluation for one of the largest school systems in the United States has concluded that of the more than 10,000 programs currently available, approximately 200 are educationally significant.[36]

To their credit, the fact that this is a serious problem is recognized by most computer enthusiasts, and reviews and journals have attempted to deal with it. However, the sheer volume of material, the massive amounts of money spent on advertising software in professional publications, at teachers' and administrators' meetings, and so on, the utter 'puffery' of the claims made about much of this material, and the constant pressure by industry, government, parents, some school personnel, and others to institute computer programs in schools *immediately* — all of this makes it nearly impossible to do more than make a small dent in the problem. As one educator put it, 'There's a lot of junk out there.'[37] The situation is not made any easier by the fact that teachers simply do not now have the time to thoroughly evaluate the educational strengths and weaknesses of a considerable portion of the *existing* curricular material and texts before they are used. Adding one more element, and a sizable one at that, to be evaluated only increases the load. Teachers' work is increasingly becoming what students of the labor process call *intensified*. More and more needs to be done; less and less time is available to do it.[38] Thus, one has little choice but to buy ready-made material, in this way continuing a trend in which all of the important curricular elements are not locally produced but purchased from commercial sources whose major aim may be profit, not necessarily educational merit.[39]

A significant consideration here, besides the loss of skill and control, is expense. This is at least a three-pronged issue. First, we must recognize that we may be dealing with something of a 'zero-sum game.' While dropping, the cost of computers it still comparatively high, though some manufacturers may keep purchase costs relatively low, knowing that a good deal of their profits may come from the purchase of software later on or through a home-school connection, something I shall discuss shortly. This money for the new technology *must come from somewhere*. This is an obvious point, but one that is very consequential. In a time of fiscal crisis, where funds are already spread too thinly and necessary programs are being starved in many areas, the addition of computer curricula most often means that money must be drained from one area and given to another. What will be sacrificed? If history is any indication, it may be programs that have benefited the least advantaged. Little serious attention has been paid to this, but it will become an increasingly serious dilemma.

A second issue of expense concerns staffing patterns, for it is not just the content of teachers' work and the growth of purchased materials that are at stake. Teachers' jobs themselves are on the line here. At a secondary school level in many nations, for example, lay-offs of teachers have not been unusual as funding for education is cut. Declining enrollment in some regions has meant a loss of positions as well. This has caused intense competition over students within the school itself. Social studies, art, music, and other subjects must fight it out with newer, more 'glamorous' subject areas. To lose the student numbers game for too long is to lose a job. The effect of the computer in this situation has been to increase competitiveness among staff, often to replace substance with both gloss and attractive packaging of courses, and to threaten many teachers with the loss of their livelihood.[40] Is it really an educationally or socially wise decision to tacitly eliminate a good deal of the choices in these other fields so that we can support the 'glamor' of a computer future? These are not only financial decisions, but are ethical decisions about teachers' lives and about what our students are to be educated in. Given the future labor market, do we really want to claim that computers will be more important than further work in humanities and social sciences or, perhaps even more significantly in working-class and ethnically diverse areas, in the students' own cultural, historical, and political heritage and struggles? Such decisions must not be made by only looking at the accountant's bottom line. These too need to be arrived at by the lengthy democratic deliberation of all parties, including the teachers who will be most affected.

Third, given the expense of microcomputers and software in schools, the pressure to introduce such technology may increase the already wide social imbalances that now exist. Private schools to which the affluent send their children and publicly funded schools in more affluent areas will have more ready access to the technology itself.[41] Schools in inner-city, rural, and poor areas will be largely priced out of the market, even if the cost of 'hardware' continues to decline. After all, in these poorer areas, and in many public school systems in general in a number of countries, it is already difficult to generate enough money to purchase new textbooks and to cover the costs of teachers' salaries. Thus, the computer and literacy over it will 'naturally' generate further inequalities. Since, by and large, it will be the top 20 per cent of the population who will have computers in their homes[42] and many of the jobs and institutions of higher education their children will be applying for will either ask for or assume 'computer skills' as keys of entry or advancement, the impact can be enormous in the long run.

The role of the relatively affluent parent in this situation does not go unrecognized by computer manufacturers.

> Computer companies . . . gear much of their advertising to the educational possibilities of computers. The drive to link particular computers to schools is a frantic competition. Apple, for example, in a highly touted scheme proposed to 'donate' an Apple to every school in America. Issues of philanthropy and intent aside, the clear market strategy is to couple particular computer usages to schools where parents — especially middle class parents with the economic wherewithal and keen motivation [to insure mobility] — purchase machines compatible with those in schools. The potentially most lucrative part of such a scheme, however, is not in the purchase of hardware (although this is also substantial) but in the sale of proprietary software.[43]

This very coupling of school and home markets, then, cannot fail to further disadvantage large groups of students. Those students who already have computer backgrounds — be it because of their schools or their homes or both — will proceed more rapidly. The social stratification of life chances will increase. These students' original advantage — one *not* due to 'natural ability', but to *wealth* — will be heightened.[44]

We should not be surprised by this, nor should we think it odd that many parents, especially middle-class parents, will pursue a computer future. The knowledge itself is part of the technical-administrative 'cultural capital' of the new middle class. Computer skills and 'literacy', however, is partly a strategy for the maintenance of middle-class mobility patterns.[45] Having such expertise, in a time of fiscal and economic crisis, is like having an insurance policy. It partly guarantees that certain doors remain open in a rapidly changing labor market. In a time of credential inflation, more credentials mean fewer closed doors.[46] (This also works within the schools. Some teachers will support computerization because it offers a real sense of competence and control that may be missing in their jobs now *and* perhaps because it offers paths to upward mobility within the school bureaucracy as well.)

The credential factor here is of considerable moment. In the past, as gains were made by ethnically different people, working-class groups, women, and others in schooling, one of the latent effects was to raise the credentials required by entire sectors of jobs. Thus, class, race, and gender barriers were partly maintained by an ever-increasing credential inflation. Though this was more of a structural than a conscious process, the effect over time has often been to again disqualify entire segments of a population from jobs, resources and power. This too may be a latest outcome of the computerization of the school curriculum. Even though, as I have shown, the bulk of new jobs will not require 'computer literacy,' the establishment of computer requirements and mandated programs in schools will condemn many people to even greater economic disenfranchisement. Since the requirements are in many ways artificial — computer knowledge will not be so very necessary and the number of jobs requiring high levels of expertise will be relatively small — we will simply be affixing one more label to these students. 'Functional illiteracy' will simply be broadened to include computers.[47]

Thus, rather than blaming an unequal economy and a situation in which meaningful and fulfilling work is not made available, rather than seeing how the new technology for all its benefits is 'creating a growing underclass of displaced and marginal workers', the lack is personalized. It becomes the students' or workers' fault for not being computer literate. One significant social and ideological outcome of computer requirements in schools, then, is that they can serve as a means 'to justify those lost lives by a process of mass disqualification, which throws the blame for disenfranchisement in education and employment back on the victims themselves.'[48]

Of course, this process may not be visible to many parents of individual children. However, the point does not revolve around the question of individual mobility, but around large-scale effects. Parents may see such programs as offering important paths to advancement and some will be correct. However, in a time of severe economic problems, parents tend to overestimate what schools can do for their children.[49] As I documented earlier, there simply will not be sufficient jobs, and competition will be intense. The uncritical introduction of and investment in hardware and software will by and large hide the reality of the transformation of the labor market and will support those who are already advantaged unless thought is given to these implications now.

Let us suppose, however, that it was important that everyone become computer literate and that these large investments in time, money, and personnel were indeed so necessary for our economic and educational future. Given all this, what is currently happening in schools? Is inequality in access and outcome now being produced? While many educators are continually struggling against these effects, we are already seeing signs of this disadvantagement being created.

There is evidence of class-, race-, and gender-based differences in computer use. In middle-class schools, for example, the number of computers is considerably more than in working-class or inner-city schools populated by children of color. The ratio of computers to children is also much higher. This in itself is an unfortunate finding. However, something else must be added here. These more economically advantaged schools not only have more contact hours and more technical and teacher support, but the very manner in which the computer is used is often different than what would be generally found in schools in less advantaged areas. Programming skills, generalizability, a sense of the multitudinous things one can do with computers both within and across academic areas — these tend to be stressed more[50] (though simply drill and practice uses are still widespread even here).[51] Compare this to the rote, mechanistic, and relatively low-level uses that tend to dominate the working-class school.[52] These differences are not unimportant, for they signify a ratification of class divisions.

Further evidence to support these claims is now becoming more readily available as researchers dig beneath the glowing claims of a computer future for all children. The differential impact is made clearer in the following figures. In the United States, while over two-thirds of the schools in affluent areas have computers, only approximately 41 per cent of the poorer public schools have them. What one does with the machine is just as important as having one, of course, and here the differences are again very real. One study of poorer elementary schools found that white children were four times more likely than black children to use computers for programming. Another found that the children of professionals employed computers for programming and for other 'creative' uses. Non-professional children were more apt to use them for drill and practice in mathematics and reading, and for 'vocational' work. In general, in fact, 'programming has been seen as the purview of the gifted and talented' and of those students who are more affluent. Less affluent students seem to find that the computer is only a tool for drill and practice sessions.[53]

Gender differences are also very visible. Two out of every three students currently learning about computers are boys. Even here these data are deceptive, since girls 'tend to be clustered in the general introductory course', not the advanced-level ones.[54] One current analyst summarizes the situation in a very clear manner:

While stories abound about students who will do just about anything to increase their access to computers, most youngsters working with school computers are [economically advantaged], white and male. The ever-growing number of private computer camps, after-school and weekend programs serve middle class white boys. Most minority [and poor] parents just can't afford to send their children to participate in these programs.[55]

This class, race, and gendered impact will also occur because of traditional school practices such as tracking or streaming. Thus, vocational and business tracks will learn operating skills for word-processing and will be primarily filled with (working-class) young women.[56] Academic tracks will stress more general programming abilities and uses and will be disproportionately male.[57] Since computer programs usually have their home bases in mathematics and science in most schools, gender differences can be heightened even more given the often differential treatment of girls in these classes and the ways in which mathematics and science curricula already fulfill 'the selective function of the school and contribute to the reproduction of gender differences'.[58] While many teachers and curriculum workers have devoted considerable time and effort to equalizing both the opportunities and outcomes of female students in mathematics and science (and such efforts are important), the problem still remains a substantive one. It can be worsened by the computerization of these subjects.

Toward Social Literacy

We have seen some of the possible negative consequences of the new technology in education, including the deskilling and depowering of teachers and the creation of inequalities through expense, credential inflation, and limitations on access. Yet it is important to realize that the issues surrounding the deskilling process are not limited to teachers. They include the very ways students themselves are taught to think about their education, their future roles in society, and the place of technology in that society. Let me explain what I mean by this.

The new technology is not just an assemblage of machines and their accompanying software. It embodies a *form of thinking* that orients a person to approach the world in a particular way. Computers involve ways of thinking that are primarily *technical*.[59] The more the new technology transforms the classroom in its own image, the more a technical logic will replace critical political and ethical understanding. The discourse of the classroom will center on technique, and less on substance. Once again 'how to' will replace 'why', but this time at the level of the student. This situation requires what I shall call social, not technical, literacy for all students.

Even if computers make sense technically in all curricular areas and even if all students, not mainly affluent white males, become technically proficient in their use, critical questions of politics and ethics remain to be dealt with in the curriculum. Thus, it is crucial that whenever the new technology is introduced into schools, students have a serious understanding of the issues surrounding their larger social effects, many of which I raised earlier.

Unfortunately, this is not often the case. When the social and ethical impacts of computers are dealt with, they are usually addressed in a manner that is less than powerful. One example is provided by a recent proposal for a statewide computer curriculum in one of the larger states in the United States. The objectives that dealt with social questions in the curriculum centered around one particular set of issues. The curriculum states that 'the student will be aware of some of the major uses of computers in modern society ... and the student will be aware of career opportunities related to computers'.[60] In most curricula the technical components of the new technology are stressed. Brief glances are given to the history of computers (occasionally mentioning the role of women in their development, which is at least one positive sign). Yet in this history, the close relationship between military use and computer development is largely absent. 'Benign' uses are pointed to, coupled with a less than realistic description of the content and possibility of computer careers and what Douglas Noble has called 'a gee-whiz glance at the marvels of the future'. What is almost never mentioned is job loss or social disenfranchisement. The very real destruction of the lives of unemployed autoworkers, assemblers or clerical workers is marginalized.[61] The political, economic, and ethical dilemmas involved when we choose between, say, 'efficiency' and the quality of the work people experience, between profit and someone's job — these too are made invisible.

How would we counterbalance this? By making it clear from the outset that knowledge about the new technology that it is necessary for students to have goes well beyond what we now too easily take for granted. A considerable portion of the curriculum would be organized around questions concerned with social literacy: 'Where are computers used? What are they used to do? What do people *actually* need to know in order to use them? Does the computer enhance anyone's life? Whose? Does it hurt anyone's life? Whose? Who decides when and where computers will be used?[62] Unless these are *fully* integrated in a school program at *all* levels, I would hesitate to advocate the use of the new technology in the curriculum. To do less makes it much more difficult for students to think critically and independently about the place the new technology does and should have in the lives of the majority of people in our society. Our job as educators involves skilling, not deskilling. Unless students are able to deal honestly and critically with these complex ethical and social issues, only those now with the power to control technology's uses will have the capacity to act. We cannot afford to let this happen.

Conclusion

I realize that a number of my points in this chapter may prove to be rather contentious. But stressing the negative side can serve to highlight many of the critical issues that are too easy to put off given the immense amount of work that school personnel are already responsible for. Decisions often get made too quickly, only to be regretted later on when forces are set in motion that could have been avoided if the implications of one's actions had been thought through more fully.

As I noted at the outset of this discussion, there is now something of a mad scramble to employ the computer in every content area. In fact, it is nearly impossible to find a subject that is not being 'computerized'. Though mathematics and science (and some parts of vocational education) remain the home base for a large portion of proposed computer curricula, other areas are not far behind. If it can be packaged to fit computerized instruction, it will be, even if this is inappropriate, less effective than the methods that teachers have developed after years of hard practical work, or less than sound educationally or economically. Rather than the machine fitting the educational needs and visions of the teacher, students, and community, all too often these needs and visions are made to fit the technology itself.

Yet, as I have shown, the new technology does not stand alone. It is linked to transformations in real groups of people's lives, jobs, hopes, and dreams. For some of these groups, their lives will be enhanced. For others, their dreams will be shattered. Wise choices about the appropriate place of the new technology in education, then, are not only educational decisions. They are fundamentally choices about the kind of society we shall have, about the social and ethical responsiveness of our institutions to the majority of our future citizens. Here educators can be guided by the critical positions on the introduction and use of the new technology that have been taken by some of the more progressive unions in a number of countries.

My discussion here has not been aimed at making us all neo-Luddites, people who go out and smash the machines that threaten our jobs or our children. The new technology is here. It will not go away. Our task as educators is to make sure that when it enters the classroom it is there for politically, economically, and educationally wise reasons, not because powerful groups may be redefining our major educational goals in their own image. We should be very clear about whether or not the future it promises our students is real, not fictitious. We need to be certain that it is a future *all* of our students can share in, not just a select few. After all, the new technology is expensive and will take up a good deal of our time and that of our teachers, administrators, and students. It is more than a little important that we question whether the wagon we have been asked to ride on is going in the right direction. It's a long walk back.

Notes

1 NOBLE, DAVID (1984) *Forces of Production: A Social History of Industrial Automation*, New York, Alfred A. Knopf, pp. xi–xii. For a more general argument about the relationship between technology and human progress, see RESCHER, NICHOLAS (1980) *Unpopular Essays on Technological Progress*, Pittsburgh, University of Pittsburgh Press.
2 NOBLE, *Forces of Production*, p. xv.
3 OLSON, PAUL (1985) Who computes? The politics of literacy,' unpublished paper, Toronto, Ontario Institute for Studies in Education, p. 6.
4 CAMPBELL, PATRICIA B. (1984) 'The computer revolution: guess who's left out'. *Interracial Books for Children Bulletin*, 15, No. 3, 3.
5 'Instructional Strategies for Integrating the Microcomputer into the Classroom,' The Vocational Studies Center, University of Wisconsin, Madison, 1985.
6 APPLE, MICHAEL W. (1979) *Ideology and Curriculum*, Boston and London, Routledge and Kegan Paul.
7 Olson, 'Who computes?', p. 5.
8 See APPLE, MICHAEL W. (1982) *Education and Power*, Boston and London, Routledge and Kegan Paul.
9 For further discussion of this, see Apple, *Ideology and Curriculum*, Apple, *Education and Power*, and SHOR, IRA (1986) *Culture Wars*, Boston and London, Routledge and Kegan Paul.
10 This is treated in greater detail in EDWARDS, RICHARD (1979) *Contested Terrain*, New York Basic Books. See also the more extensive discussion of the effect these tendencies are having in education in Apple, *Education and Power*.
11 RUMBERGER, RUSSELL W. and LEVIN, HENRY M. (1984) 'Forecasting the impact of new technologies on the future job market', Project Report No. 84-A4, Institute for Research on Educational Finance and Government, School of Education, Stanford University, February, p. 1.
12 Ibid., p. 2.
13 Ibid., p. 3.
14 Ibid., p. 4.
15 Ibid., p. 18.
16 Ibid.
17 Ibid., p. 19.
18 Ibid., pp. 19–20.
19 Ibid., p. 31.
20 Ibid., p. 21.
21 Ibid.
22 Ibid., p. 25.
23 Ibid.
24 On the history of women's struggles against proletarianization, see KESSLER-HARRIS, ALICE (1982) *Out to Work*, New York, Oxford University Press.
25 REINECKE, IAN (1984) *Electronic Illusions*, New York, Penguin Books, p. 156.
26 See the further discussion of the loss of office jobs and the deskilling of many of those that remain in Reinecke, *Electronic Illusions*, pp. 136–58. The very

same process could be a threat to middle- and low-level management positions as well. After all, if control is further automated, why does one need as many supervisory positions? The implications of this latter point need to be given much more consideration by many middle-class proponents of technology since their jobs may soon be at risk too.

27 DWYER, PETER, WILSON, BRUCE and WOOCK, ROGER (1984) *Confronting School and Work*, Boston and London, George Allen and Unwin, pp. 105–6.

28 The paradigm case is given by the fact that, as I mentioned in the previous chapter, three times as many people now work in low-paying positions for McDonald's as for US Steel. See CARNOY, MARTIN, SHEARER, DEREK and RUMBERGER, RUSSELL (1983) *A New Social Contract*, New York, Harper and Row, p. 71. As I have argued at greater length elsewhere, however, it may not be important to our economy if all students and workers are made technically knowledgeable by schools. What is just as important is the production of economically useful knowledge (technical/administrative knowledge) that can be used by corporations to enhance profits, control labor, and increase efficiency. See Apple, *Education and Power*, especially chapter 2.

29 Reinecke, *Electronic Illusions*, p. 234. For further analysis of the economic data and the effects on education, see GRUBB, W. NORTON (1984) 'The bandwagon once more: vocational preparation for high-tech occupations', *Harvard Educational Review*, 54, November, pp. 429–51.

30 Apple, *Ideology and Curriculum* (see note 6 above) and Apple, *Education and Power* (see note 8 above): See also APPLE, MICHAEL W. and WEIS, LOIS (Eds) (1983) *Ideology and Practice in Schooling*, Philadelphia, Temple University Press.

31 Apple, *Ideology and Curriculum*; Apple, *Education and Power*; Apple and Weis (Eds), *Ideology and Practice in Schooling*. See also WISE, ARTHUR (1979) *Legislated Learning: The Bureaucratization of the American Classroom*, Berkeley, University of California Press.

32 Apple, *Ideology and Curriculum*; Apple, *Education and Power*. On the general history of the growth of management techniques, see Richard Edwards, *Contested Terrain* (see note 10 above).

33 NOBLE, DOUGLAS (1984) 'The underside of computer literacy', *Raritan*, 3 (Spring), p. 45.

34 See the discussion of this in Apple, *Education and Power*, especially chapter 5.

35 NOBLE, DOUGLAS (1984) 'Jumping off the computer bandwagon', *Education Week*, 3 October, p. 24.

36 Ibid.

37 Ibid. See also Noble, 'The underside of computer literacy,' p. 45.

38 For further general discussion of the intensification and transformation of other kinds of work, see THOMAS, ROBERT (1982) 'Citizenship and gender in work organization: some considerations for theories of the labor process', in BURAWOY, MICHAEL and SKOCPOL, THEDA (Eds) *Marxist Inquiries: Studies of Labor, Class, and States*, Chicago, University of Chicago Press, pp. 86–112.

39 Apple, *Education and Power*. For further analysis of the texbook publishing industry, see APPLE, MICHAEL W. (in press) 'Curriculum conflict in the

United States', in HARTNETT, ANTHONY and NAISH, MICHAEL (Eds) *Education and Society Today*, Falmer Press.

40   I am indebted to Susan Jungck for this point. See her excellent dissertation, 'Doing computer literacy', unpublished PhD dissertation, University of Wisconsin, Madison, 1985.

41   Reinecke, *Electronic Illusions*, p. 176.

42   Ibid., p. 169.

43   Olson, 'Who computes?', p. 23.

44   Ibid., p. 31. Thus, students' familiarity and comfort with computers becomes a form of what has been called the 'cultural capital' of advantaged groups. For further analysis of the dynamics of cultural capital, see Apple, *Education and Power*, and BOURDIEU, PIERRE and PASSERON, JEAN-CLAUDE (1977) *Reproduction in Education, Society and Culture*, Beverly Hills, Sage.

45   Olson, 'Who computes?', p. 23. See also the discussion of interclass competition over academic qualifications in BOURDIEU, PIERRE (1984) *Distinction: A Social Critique of the Judgement of Taste*, Cambridge, Mass., Harvard University Press, pp. 133–68.

46   Once again, I am indebted to Susan Jungck for this argument.

47   Noble, 'The underside of computer literacy', p. 54.

48   NOBLE, DOUGLAS (1984) 'computer literacy and ideology', *Teachers College Record*, 85 (Summer), p. 611. This process of 'blaming the victim' has a long history in education. See Apple, *Ideology and Curriculum*, especially chapter 7.

49   CONNELL, R.W. (1985) *Teachers' Work*, Boston and London, George Allen and Unwin p. 142.

50   Olson, 'Who computes?', p. 22.

51   For an analysis of the emphasis on and pedagogic problems with such limited uses of computers, see STREIBEL, MICHAEL J. (1984) A critical analysis of the use of computers in education', unpublished paper, Department of Curriculum and Instruction, University of Wisconsin, Madison.

52   Olson, 'Who computes?', p. 22.

53   Campbell, 'The computer revolution: guess who's left out?', p. 3. Many computer experts, however, are highly critical of the fact that students are primarily taught to program in BASIC, a less than appropriate language for later advanced computer work (Michael Streibel, personal communication).

54   Campbell, 'The computer revolution'.

55   Ibid.

56   An interesting analysis of what happens to young women in such business programs and how they respond to both the curricula and their later work experiences can be found in VALLI, LINDA (1983) 'Becoming clerical workers: business education and the culture of femininity', in Apple and Weis (Eds), *Ideology and Practice in Schooling* (see note 30 above), pp. 213–34. See also her more extensive treatment in VALLI, LINDA (1986) *Becoming Clerical Workers* (Boston and London: Routledge and Kegan Paul.

57   GASKELL, JANE in Olson, 'Who computes?' (see note 3 above), p. 33.

58   FOMIN, FEODORA (1984) 'The best and the brightest: the selective function of mathematics in the school curriculum', in JOHNSON, LESLEY and TYLER, DEBORAH (Eds) *Cultural Politics: Papers in Contemporary Australian Educa-*

tion, Culture and Politics, Melbourne, University of Melbourne Sociology Research Group in Cultural and Educational Studies, p. 220.

59 Michael Streibel's work on the models of thinking usually incorporated within computers in education is helpful in this regard. See Streibel, 'A Critical Analysis of the Use of Computers in Education' (see note 51 above). The more general issue of the relationship between technology and the control of culture is important here. A useful overview of this can be found in WOODWARD, KATHLEEN (Ed.) (1980) *The Myths of Information: Technology and Postindustrial Culture*, Madison, Coda Press.

60 Quoted in Noble, 'The underside of computer literacy', p. 56.

61 Ibid., p. 57. An interesting but little-known fact is that the largest proportion of computer programmers actually work for the military. See WEIZENBAUM, JOSEPH (1983) 'The computer in your future', *New York Review of Books*, 30 (27 October) pp. 58–62.

62 Noble, 'The underside of computer literacy', p. 40. For students in vocational curricula especially, these questions would be given more power if they were developed within a larger program that would seek to provide these young men and women with extensive experience in and understanding of *all* aspects of operating an entire industry or enterprise, not simply those 'skills' that reproduce workplace stratification. See CENTER FOR LAW AND EDUCATION (1984) 'Key provision in new law reforms vocational education: focus is on broader knowledge and experience for students/workers', *Center for Law and Education, Inc. D.C. Report*, 28 December, pp. 1–6.

Chapter 6

From Computer Literacy to Technology Literacy

Hughie Mackay

This chapter introduces and defines the nature and content of computer literacy. It discusses the context and background of the emergence and growth of computer literacy, and discusses various ways of implementing computer literacy in schools. It argues that computer literacy constitutes a central underpinning of contemporary policy on Information Technology in schools.

The second section introduces and discusses the notion of literacy, and some of the debates which surround it. Recent theorists of literacy have criticized functional approaches to literacy, which see literacy in terms of a set of abstracted, value-free skills which can be defined, measured and learned, and which are functional to personal and economic development. These critics emphasize the relationship of literacy to power and social relations, and the social processes whereby literacy comes to be defined in particular ways and the social context in which literacy is used.

On this basis, a critique of computer literacy is developed, drawing parallels between computer literacy and literacy as conventionally discussed: technicist computer literacy is the computer equivalent of functional literacy.

Finally, an argument is put forward that the key to computer literacy, or technology literacy, lies in understanding the social nature of technology: technologies are not merely physical artifacts, but are a part of social relations, as well as physical embodiment and constraint on social relations.

Conceived thus, technology literacy is crucial to understanding contemporary society and our place in it. The broad content of such a subject area — technology literacy as opposed to the narrow technical expertise of computer literacy — is outlined. Such an approach, it is argued, is congruent with the demands of the labour market, and *could* be possible within the parameters of the National Curriculum.

What is Computer Literacy?

By computer literacy is meant attempts to spread the uses of computing beyond specialist areas. Computer literacy is not concerned with training specifically for specialist Information Technology occupations (such as technician or programmer), nor with providing specialist Information Technology competence for such occupations as engineering. Rather, it is concerned with mass provision of some minimal introduction to computers, so that those leaving school and entering the labour market do so feeling comfortable with new technology. This has sometimes been couched in such terminology as enabling people to feel a sense of belonging in the burgeoning computer society. In other words, it is generally defined in functional terms:

> computer literacy can be considered to mean the minimum know-
> ledge, know-how, familiarity, capabilities, abilities, and so forth,
> about computers essential for a person to function well in the con-
> temporary world. (Bork, 1985, p. 33)

So what are computer literacy courses? Computer literacy courses are *practical* courses. They involve 'hands on', so that, at the end, students can *do* something. Such courses are provided by LEA adult education evening classes, in schools and in higher education.

'Computer awareness' or 'computer appreciation' courses generally have the same content as computer literacy but at a more basic level: using a keyboard, loading floppy discs, producing an elementary program, using a package such as a spreadsheet and using a printer. They sometimes take place lower down the secondary school, as a preparation for computer aided instruction (CAI) across the curriculum further up the school — this is the practice today in many schools.

Finally, mention should be made of Computer Studies, also a practical subject, and one which has been seen as of value for inculcating computer literacy. Computer Studies can be seen as the examined counterpart of computer awareness. It has had a most remarkable growth, followed by an equally rapid demise. At GCE 'O' level and CSE there were 6000 entrants in 1975 and 120,000 by 1985 (Selwood, 1988). Both GCSE and 'A' level have since declined to oblivion, in response to a number of criticisms, including that it was bad preparation for higher education, but particularly as a result of the development of computers across the curriculum as government policy and school practice — which it was seen to be militating against (Wellington, 1989). That it became so popular in such a short period suggests that it was seen as valuable in some way, perhaps as computer literacy, or as a passport to work.

Ruthven (1984) identifies three paradigms for the implementation of computer literacy in schools: computer literacy as mastery of technique, as awareness in context, and as access to tools. By considering briefly each of these we can see the various possible approaches that there are for teaching computer literacy.

Computer Literacy as Mastery of Technique

The first of these involves the teaching of knowledge and skill related directly to working with computers. City and Guilds 953, for example, defines computer literacy as ability to design and implement a programme. Ruthven (1984) cites an MSC report which, in a similar vein, states that a YTS trainee with minimum standard in computer literacy would:

(i) have had experience in switching on and setting up a disc-based microcomputer with printer
(ii) have used a disc-based system to play simple adventure games requiring full use of the keyboard
(iii) have used a disc-based system in a real or simulated work situation in order to solve pre-set problems
(iv) have an understanding of the most commonly used computer jargon
(v) have been introduced to simple programming techniques using BASIC language
(vi) have an appreciation of the computer as a machine that operates to predetermined sets of instructions (programs) to a level of complexity determined by those instructions
(vii) have some understanding of the place of computer technology in both the workplace and the home of the present and future. (Rossington, 1983, cited by Ruthven, 1984)

The underlying rationale of this approach is argued by Luehrmann (1981): computer literacy is *doing*, not 'knowing about'. Any computer literacy course, argues Luehrmann, should spend four-fifths of its time on *performance* objectives (designing, developing, and modifying), as opposed to what he refers to as merely remembering — objectives which refer to recognizing, identifying and determining. The approach, then, emphasizes practice, rather then mere awareness.

Computer Literacy as Awareness in Context

This approach accepts that technology is not divorced from human activity, which needs to be understood in terms of the environment within which it operates. An example of this approach is the 16+ examination in computer studies. Its general assessment objectives include:

(D)   knowledge and understanding of the range and scope of computer applications

(E)   understanding of the social and economic effects of the use of computerised systems on individuals, organisations and society. (16+ GCE and CSE Boards, 1983)

The Minnesota Educational Computing Consortium (MECC) found this approach dominant in its empirical survey of computer literacy courses, and recommended it as the appropriate approach — albeit including the development of positive attitudes towards computers as an integral part of the development of computer literacy (Johnson *et al.*, 1980).

Unsurprisingly, it is fairly common for technique to be taught without the context, but not the reverse.

Computer Literacy as Access to Tools

In this paradigm computer literacy is the ability to make use of the computer as a tool for communication, information handling, learning and enquiry. Computer literacy aims to enable the pupil to recognize where a computer is appropriate, and to select, design or implement a computer system; the computer is seen as a tool which can assist in carrying out certain intellectual tasks.

Dillon (1985) has said that teaching children how to operate a technology without using it in any kind of contextual application is akin to teaching how to use a pen but teaching nothing about composing, or how to use a calculator but nothing about mathematics.

Papert (1980) takes this further: the computer is not merely a tool but an object to think with. It is a source of analogies; programming can provide individuals with powerful concrete models for intellectual processes.

According to this paradigm, a computer literate culture is thus one which has accommodated the intellectual skills and strategies of computing — knowing how to use computers and when it is appropriate to do so. The emphasis of the Technology National Curriculum would seem to fall clearly within the scope of this paradigm.

Ruthven cites four different ways of implementing computer literacy in schools: (1) separation (computer literacy as a subject of its own — which is common practice at the lower end of the age range in secondary schools); (2) dispersion (the various elements of computer literacy are covered in the most appropriate place in the curriculum, e.g., programming in maths, the broader context in social studies, etc.); (2) absorption (as a part of mathematics or, preferably, technology. This is perhaps the dominant approach in the earlier days of Information Technology in education in the UK); (4) permeation (computers across the curriculum, current British government policy, which seems especially applicable at the primary level).

Computer Literacy: A Central Plank of Government Policy

Ruthven refers to the 1980s as the decade of computer literacy, and cites various policy statements to substantiate the claim. The MEP strategy statement is quite explicit: 'The aim of the Programme is to help schools to prepare children for life in a society in which devices and systems based on microelectronics are commonplace and pervasive....' (DES, 1981).

In the same year the Minister for Industry and Information Technology, Kenneth Baker, described computer manipulation as 'the fourth R', and argued that familiarization with the new technology should start as early as possible in the primary school (Baker, 1981). In 1982 the Department of Trade and Industry ran its *'IT '82'* campaign, raising public awareness about Information Technology. Commentators have referred to this as a propaganda campaign rather than a broader strategy on Information Technology (Webster and Robins, 1986). Also in 1982 the BBC launched a major computer literacy project, 'as part of a long-term commitment ... to public information in the broad field of microelectronics' (BBC, 1982). Later in the decade computer literacy was one of YTS's five core skill areas.

State or government support for computer literacy is provided in a rhetoric which emphasizes national priorities. Thatcher, at the launch of *IT '82*, said 'I believe that the future prosperity of Britain depends on our being bang up to date in the latest technology, preferably one step ahead of other countries'. Noble (1984) cites similar quotations from the USA:

> A computer literate work force is necessary to maintain our national defense and to improve our national productivity.

> A computer literate populace is as necessary to an information society as raw materials and energy are to an industrial society.

> Due to the decline in national productivity, the increase in foreign trade competition, and national defense and safety needs, computers have emerged as the major force ameliorating these conditions. Consequently, the shortage of computer specialists and knowledge-workers has raised the problem of computer literacy to the level of a national crisis.

Shirley Williams is even firmer in linking economic performance with information technology education: 'The ability of the education system to match the needs of the information society for highly educated people has now become the main determinant of a country's employment prospects' (1985, pp. 74–5). Kenneth Baker, as Secretary of State for Education, has said: 'All children as they leave school should have skills in electronic keyboard techniques so that they can operate the electronic gadgetry of this revolution since it's going to have such a dominating effect on their lives' (1983, p. 5).

ITAP (1986) recently called for computer literacy; and Baker was quite explicit that Information Technology in education has as its bottom line mass computer literacy (Baker, 1987). The crisis of the shortage of suitably skilled labour is presented as sufficiently real to obviate the need for debate: because typists must now word-process and machine-tool markers operate CNC technology, everyone must be computer literate (Robins and Webster, 1989). Barnett's paper in this volume argues against such a narrow perspective on technology.

The rise of technology to the fore in the National Curriculum, and the National Curriculum's Information Technology component, can be seen as both consequence and manifestation of this perceived centrality.

Computer Literacy and 'Information Technology in Education' Policy

I am not suggesting (as Robins and Webster (1989) seem to) that computer literacy is the totality of government Information Technology in education policy. Certainly, computer literacy exists in name on vocational courses — BTEC and YTS, for example. However, as the National Curriculum makes clear, computers across the curriculum is the essence of current policy: whilst 'technology' is a foundation subject, Information Technology 'can be taught through other subjects' (National Curriculum Council, 1988) — indeed, computer studies is not even an exemplar additional subject for GCSE warranting 10 per cent of time. Despite such policy, however, that the integration of Information Technology has hardly been achieved is suggested by the National Curriculum Design and Technology report itself: it deals with Information Technology in a separate chapter, and even this does not relate Information Technology fully either to design and technology or to the other subjects of the curriculum (National Curriculum Council Design and Technology Working Group, 1988).

What is clear, however, is that Information Technology in education *began* as computer literacy. Presumably that is now seen as either a mistake, or a necessary preparation for the 'real', more sophisticated use of Information Technology in education. Either way, computer literacy has played a crucial part in setting the agenda for current Information Technology in education policy, computers across the curriculum.

Although computers across the curriculum and CAI are official policy, its achievements are perhaps more limited than suggested by some of its advocates. I have argued elsewhere that the claims for Information Technology in education generally are far greater than the practice would warrant: the educational claims for Information Technology in education remain largely unresearched (Beynon and Mackay, 1989). The frequently cited positive effects of computers on learners' motivation (e.g., O'Shea and Self, 1983) remain unresearched (Smith and Keep, 1986); and the claims made by Papert for LOGO, probably the most exciting development in Information Technology in education, enjoy the same status: there has been little substantiation of the claims for the teaching of problem solving through programming, of the transferability of the problem solving to other areas of intellectual activity (Pea, 1987), nor that working with the computer makes students understand better how the mind works (Roszak, 1988). In short, much CAI is either too sophisticated to be more than a wish, or too simple to justify much excitement; it has been introduced at an enormous cost, on the basis of little proven educational worth.

It seems at least plausible that computers across the curriculum and CAI have been developed in part to achieve computer literacy, rather than the other way around. Such a notion is supported by evidence from a number of sources: Roszak (1988) refers to the use of LOGO in dance, poetry and art where it teaches computing, not these subjects; in may fieldwork in schools in South Wales I have found computers across the curriculum in practice to mean merely word-processing in all areas of the curriculum; and in the National Curriculum the value of basic computer skills, i.e., computer literacy, is firmly recognized — in the National Curriculum Council Design and Technology Working Group's Interim Report there is considerable reference to basic computer skills which are to be found throughout the curriculum. Information Technology may only be relevant to all subjects if one connects all subjects to procedural thinking. For example, computers are good at the trivial and mechanistic aspects of literacy teaching, so their introduction to that area of the curriculum could lead to literacy teaching emphasizing a narrow, mechanistic, view of literacy (Chandler, 1985, and in this volume; Dillon, 1985).

The Nature of Literacy

A recurrent point in the literature on literacy is the absence of any satisfactory definition of the term. The notion of literacy is highly complex, and an area which involves a range of disciplines, perspectives, and factors — psychological, linguistic and social. Broadly, the term 'literacy' is often used in a vague and imprecise way, to refer to the capacity, or relative capacity, of a person to read and write; this immediately raises the issue of how *much* reading and writing constitutes 'literacy' — merely reading, merely writing one's own name, or what? The United Nations Population Commission in 1948 defined literacy as 'the ability to read and write a simple message' (Oxenham, 1980). Sometimes, then, literacy has been defined very precisely, for example as some standard of minimal competence, or in terms of specific skills. Whatever, definitions have varied over history, between different places, and on the part of different groups and institutions.

A number of key arguments for broader or mass literacy have been made by a range of proponents over mostly fairly recent history. First, it has been argued that the ability to read and write is required by everyone for full participation in democratic society. Second, literacy is presented as something which is empowering: it allows individuals and societies to exercise greater choice and control and to develop greater knowledge. Oxenham (1980) argues that literacy has enabled humanity to maintain complex forms of organization and communication; and, indeed, to develop new systems of thought, logic, science and technology:

> the technology of literacy has served not simply the practical pur-
> poses of storing and communicating information. Vastly more impor-
> tant, it seems to have enabled the growth and development of the
> human reason and its power to combine different sources of informa-
> tion to produce even more understanding and inspiration. (p. 43)

Third, this empowering consequence of literacy possession has often been presented in the context of economic development, notably by UNESCO, and in the UK by the Adult Literacy Resources Agency (ALRA). UNESCO started by seeing literacy not as an end in itself, but soon came to emphasize the value of literacy to economic and technological development. The pro-grammes for mass literacy sponsored by these organizations have generally been based on some notion of functional literacy — in other words, associated with the employability and social integration of those who possess it. Under the UN Development Programme, functional literacy was linked to the provi-sion of training in such technological skills as motor maintenance and weaving (Levinge, 1986). Functional literacy has been adopted by individuals and groups of a variety of political perspectives, in military, diplomatic and educational circles. During the 1970s literacy's role in social and economic development survived as an article of faith, despite the absence of supporting evidence (Levine, 1986):

> Whether intentionally or not, functional competence has been defined
> in such a way that it is just sufficient to bring its possessor within the
> reach of bureaucratic modes of communication and authority.... Its
> net effect might well be to domesticate and subordinate the previous-
> ly illiterate person further rather than to increase his or her autonomy
> and social standing. (Levine, 1986, p. 41)

Indeed, Levine goes on to argue:

> The social and political significance of literacy derives from its role in
> creating and reproducing (or failing to reproduce) the social distribu-
> tion of knowledge. (p. 46)

Although commonly presented and perceived as liberating, literacy has made people less powerful as well as providing them with greater control —

Henry II, for example, used literacy to render his barons powerless — he employed clerks who wrote documents which his barons could not read and were not concerned about; they continued to rely on seals and other non-written practices, and two generations later experienced the consequences (Clanchy, 1979); whilst the printing press disenfranchised some while enabling those in power to exercise control. Heath (1983) identifies the different functions which literacy has served for different social classes and ethnic groups; and Graff (1979), in his account of literacy instruction in nineteenth-century Canada, argues that in certain contexts literacy may function more as a means of social control than of social mobility, but under the guise of offering social mobility, overcoming poverty, and providing self-fulfilment. Levine (1986) explains how literacy is used to mystify — for example by lawyers or civil servants — as well as to demystify.

One crucial question is whether literacy is merely a technical matter. Opposing such a perspective, it has been argued that literacy depends on context and can serve a variety of functions. It consists of both ability and the uses to which it is put: literacy transforms the ways in which people think and how they see the world; once made literate people see things differently, and thus literacy constitutes a technology of transformation and development — of individuals and societies. Literacy is inseparable from comprehension and context (Williams, 1961); it relates to understandings of reality, and is embedded in social practices and cultural and institutional contexts. Rather than being an abstract set of value-free, neutral, technical skills which can be taught in isolation from their social context, and being associated with progress and economic development, literacy is thus ideological (Street, 1987). As a social skill, which is used between people and institutions, the use of literacy depends on social circumstances; hence there can be no absolute standard for attainment; adequate literacy depends on the context of a given individual and society (Oxenham, 1980).

> What practices are taught and how they are imparted depends on the nature of the social formation. The skills and concepts that accompany literacy acquisition, in whatever form, do not stem in some automatic way from the inherent qualities of literacy, as some authors would have us believe, but are aspects of a specific ideology.... Many representations of literacy, however — and, I suspect, of 'computer literacy' — rest on the assumption that it is a neutral technology that can be detached from specific social contexts. (Street, 1987, p. 34)

Street goes on to argue that if we take literacy as relating to a set of conceptualizations and beliefs, rather than simply a technical skill, then imparting this to others is more clearly the transfer of culture rather than merely of technology. Buckingham explains Street's argument:

The skills and competencies which accompany the acquisition of literacy do not simply follow from the 'inherent' qualities of the written word: they are socially constructed in the practice of that literacy, and hence cannot be seen as neutral or merely 'technical'. What literacy 'means' depends on the processes by which it is learnt, the purposes for which it is used, and the institutions in which it takes place. (Buckingham, 1988, p. 45)

Street contrasts the 'autonomous' model of literacy with his 'ideological' model. The autonomous model (about which he says less) is based on the assumption that literacy has a neutral or technical character, and that it can be isolated from its social context and treated as an independent variable with inherent, autonomous characteristics. It assumes an association between literacy and progress, civilization and individual liberty. In this vein, for example, Anderson (1966) argues that a society requires a 40 per cent literacy rate for economic 'take off'. Street's ideological model, in contrast, focuses on the social institutions in which the meaning of literacy is constructed, the significance of literacy for specific social groups (as opposed to the claims that are made by others for it), and the ideological and political nature of literacy practice (as opposed to its autonomous nature). Levine (1986) argues that any notion of functional literacy is inevitably ideological, in that it depends on prior assumptions about social welfare, rights and responsibilities.

Freire (1972) is a key writer to refute technical approaches to literacy instruction, as propounded by (for example) UNESCO. He takes literacy from its Western context, and translates it for the Third World context. He argues that the political and ideological functions of literacy should be made explicit at all stages — he argues that one function of literacy is the inculcation in others of the notion of illiteracy; he sees UNESCO's functional literacy as enabling exploitation and incorporation. Freire's approach, in contrast, involves working with students in devising a curriculum — in other words, it is an action curriculum approach; the teacher is the stimulus or catalyst, to enable students to understand their cultural heritage and political awareness — literacy then is not just a skill, but is something which introduces the learner to a new culture; people thus develop a radical consciousness — and the function of the literacy teacher is to make people see the world in a way which their teacher sees as correct. Clearly, such a perspective is not without its problems — by whom and how truth is to be established to be such, and how such a process relates to individuals' consciousness.

What, then, are the implications for computer literacy of these issues which arise in the social theory of literacy? This question will be addressed in two senses: first, it points us to a number of ways in which we can explain the computer literacy phenomenon — there are many parallels between the two movements. Second, it gives us some ideas about what a different computer literacy, which I call 'technology literacy', might encompass.

Applying the Debate about Literacy to Computer Literacy

The debate about literacy leads us to ask similar questions about computer literacy: how is computer literacy propagated; how is it presented to us; what are the social forces behind it; who is defining the nature of computer literacy; which institutions are involved?

It is interesting that with computer literacy we have the first occasion on which a mass education movement has followed so closely on the heels of a technological innovation (Beynon and Mackay, 1989): in the case of print, steam engines, cars, TV, radio, or the telephone there were no such movements; and none of these technologies was equated with functional literacy, as is computer literacy. There seems to be a close parallel with the situation in the post-1870 era, when schools were devoted to mass literacy. Why, then, do we see the drive towards computer literacy when earlier technologies created no such shift?

Although Information Technology is prevalent in all walks of life, computerized telephones, watches, or washing machines require no computer understanding by the user. With a cash point or library, for example, what one needs to know about a computer is minimal; most of us learn about telephones, cars, and televisions as we grow up without too much trouble.

Information Technology is undoubtedly pervasive, and parents, employers and the government support it (Linn, 1985; Robins and Webster, 1989). On one level we can say that the last of these, government policy, is the factor responsible — and I have discussed how computer literacy *is* a central plank of government policy. This policy, however, which includes the National Council for Educational Technology (NCET)'s National Development Programme in Computer-assisted-learning (NDP CAL), the Department of Trade and Industry's microcomputers into primary schools initiative, the Microelectronics Education Programme (MEP), the Microelectronics Education Support Unit (MESU) and the National Council of Educational Technology (NCET) — does not emerge from a vacuum and inevitably become implemented.

That it does so, I shall argue, is because of its particular ideological nature (Slack, 1984). It enjoys the appeal and credibility it does because it engages successfully with the elements of particular dominant and popular discourses.

First, it draws on the fear of the uninitiated that they will be left behind by the 'computer revolution': if you are not computer literate, you will be disadvantaged; 'the computer is here to stay, so get on board'. Such is the rhetoric of both government publicity (e.g., the DTI campaign *IT '82*) and private advertising (e.g., for home computers: see Adamson and Kennedy, 1986).

Second, it draws on the psychological fear or distaste for interacting with computers which some people have (Turkle, 1984). If someone does not want to become involved with computers they are labelled 'computerphobic'. Such a fear is presented as a handicap as great as not reading or writing, and one which can be broken down by computer literacy.

Third is the political argument: technologists must be accountable to the public, and this demands that the public is technologically literate. The public needs to be informed about new technology, as citizens in a democracy, to determine how computers will shape our lives. To control new technology, we need first to understand it; if computers remain a mystery to the public, the public will remain ignorant and be prey to vested interests (Webster and Robins, 1986; 1991).

A key underpinning of arguments for computer literacy is that we are living in or moving towards a post-industrial or information society. Are we, however, witnessing the emergence of a new social order? Few would disagree that the emerging information society is increasingly referred to in popular fiction, the media and social science (Bell, 1973; Masuda, 1981; Lyon, 1987; 1991). Its key features as identified by Bell (1973) are the shift towards a service economy; the emergence of a pre-eminent class of professional and scientific and technical groups (replacing entrepreneurs and skilled workers); the increasingly codified nature of knowledge (the rise of 'systems'); the supplanting of labour and capital by knowledge and information as the 'central variables' of society; the introduction of Information Technology; increasing prosperity and the demise of class struggle. Some of the claims for the coming information society seem implausible or absurd (e.g., Stonier, 1983); and among the problems behind the thesis are the questions which its proponents do *not* ask: how the new order relates to power, how technology is socially shaped, the nature of the forces behind the information technology, and its debated and contested nature (Lyon, 1987).

The arguments for computer literacy have been inextricably linked to the alleged needs of the labour market — as the arguments for literacy have been inextricably linked to the development of commerce and industry (Oxenham, 1980). Rather than fulfilling these, I shall argue, computer literacy as we know it fails miserably in that aim: to most future workers, whether their jobs will involve working with computers or not, computer literacy is largely a waste of time.

Underlying computer literacy is the notion that a high-tech job requires a high level of skill on the part of employees.

> A computer literate populace is as necessary to an information society
> as raw materials and energy are to an industrial society. (Deringer and
> Molnar, 1982, p. 33)

It is important, however, to distinguish high-tech *industries* from high-tech *occupations*: plenty of jobs in the former are routine assembly or even management (Robins and Webster (1989) detail how few top managers of the large electronics corporations have any background in Information Technology);

and even the high-tech occupations (e.g., systems analyst or computer programmer), it has been claimed, are becoming deskilled (Kraft, 1979; Greenbaum, 1976; Mackay and Lane, 1989). At the same time, computers have become more 'people literate', or 'user-friendly'.

In general, the more advanced the technology, the simpler it is to use; and the skills required to use it are not to be compared to reading and writing. In contrast with computer literacy courses which, when they look at new technology and work, look at the tiny minority of professional or high-tech occupations, new technologies often require less skill.

> as machines become more sophisticated, with expanded memories, more computational ability, and sensory capabilities, the knowledge required to use the devices declines (Rumberger and Levin, 1984, cited by Apple, 1986)

New machines may look impressive, but it is a mythology that computers enhance all jobs they touch, transforming them into 'mind jobs', filled with responsibility (Braverman, 1974). One way to measure the skill requirement of a technology is by the amount of time required to train its operator. On this basis we find that new technology often deskills (Thompson, 1983). More helpful than the empirical argument that technology sometimes deskills and sometimes extends skill is to look at the broader historical, macro context within which technology is introduced. Given the competitive nature of the world market economy, it would be surprising if new technologies did not sometimes extend managerial control over the workforce, reducing worker skill and autonomy. Again, there is a parallel with literacy: the Taunton and Exeter Commissions in the 1880s, in the light of possible insurrections, advocated the teaching of more science and literacy, and thus sought to extend the power of the Victorian manager over the workforce. Braverman (1974), in particular, has argued that innovation has been largely guided by a desire to simplify the worker's role. On the other hand, management is not solely concerned with the control of labour (Child, 1985); and it has been argued that contemporary labour markets require a more skilled and flexible workforce than in the past (Friedman, 1977; Murray, 1991). Such post-Fordist arguments about the end of mass production and the increasing skill requirements of work are not without their critics (Pollert, 1990; *Science as Culture*, 1990). However, even where work is requiring greater skills, these are hardly supplied by a narrow computer literacy: if problem-solving, communicating, analytical, autonomous workers are required by the labour market, then a narrow computer literacy is going to make little contribution.

Finally, it has been argued that the focus on skills shortages is ideological in that it individualizes unemployment: it implies that the problem is not structural unemployment, but individuals with outdated or inappropriate skills (Robins and Webster, 1989). If people were trained in the sunrise technologies, runs the argument, they would have jobs and industry would no longer be held back. Clearly, such an argument blames the victim, and blames education for failing to equip children with skills useful to industry.

That computer literacy makes no sense in terms of the labour market does not mean that it is not required by employers. Dore (1976) has pointed out that the demand for more qualified labour bears little relation to the technical requirements of jobs: rather, it is the product of the inflationary spiral of credentialism. Computer literacy is thus able to create its own necessity; mythology becomes reality (Noble, 1984). Functional illiteracy comes to be broadened to include computers (Apple, 1986; Noble, 1984).

Through these and other ways, the need for computer literacy for everyone comes to be accepted as reasonable, even reassuring — for participation or survival in the burgeoning social order.

Computer literacy is clearly congruent with the interests of particular parties. These include manufacturers (of hardware and software) who are trying to enter the educational market; and those working in education whose careers are tied in with the growing demand for INSET in the area — at a time when other sectors of schooling are facing the consequences of resource constraints and demographic decline.

By looking at the ideology of computer literacy and the social forces behind it, we can see that Information Technology, not just computer literacy, is socially constructed: Information Technology is a myth, rather than an agreed, objective reality; and the myth works as some form of social control. This parallels the absence of any one agreed definition of literacy, and how definitions have always been dependent on the ideological interests and functions of the institutions involved (Resnick and Resnick, 1979, cited by Buckingham, 1988).

Behind computer literacy is the intention to draw an analogy with better known forms of literacy; and to assert that what happens there should also be attempted in relation to computing. Computer literacy is presented as on a par with other literacies. Yet a brief consideration of the notion of literacy shows us that literacy is not merely syntax, or even an objective skill; nor can computer literacy, as any other literacy, be a neutral, abstracted skill. As it has been taught, however, computer literacy has consisted of an introduction to basic skills — very similar to basic literacy, 'a little reading and writing' — or as Kenneth Baker, as Minister for Industry and Information Technology, would have it, 'the fourth R'. To some in the nineteenth century literacy was fine if it was to enable the worker to read machine manuals and to understand written orders, but someone with political understanding was seen as a danger; literacy was defined to exclude the latter, as is computer literacy today.

Computer literacy, like literacy, is not benign. Others have argued that computer literacy will actually *increase* inequalities, within and between nations — as literacy has done (Clanchy, 1979; Graff, 1979). Evidence suggests that Information Technology in education will exacerbate the class bias of schooling: the distribution of home personal computers is far from even across social class, allowing advantage to those with such resources at home, whilst poorer schools are perhaps dependent on increasingly limited resources (Apple, 1986). Research also shows that blacks have less access to Information Technology in education (Apple, 1986). Finally, others report on the re-inforcement and exacerbation of gender inequalities through the use of Information Technology in education (Culley, 1986; 1991; Ciann *et al.*, 1988; Beynon, 1991).

New technology is not just machines, or boxes, and software. Innis (1951) has discussed how changes in communications technology alter the way we think and what we think about — again, paralleling literacy. Any technology embodies forms of thinking, which orientate a person to approach the world in a particular way — often ways of thinking which are primarily technical. The more new technology transforms the classroom in its own image, the more a technical logical understanding may replace a critical, political and ethical understanding. The focus comes to be on technique rather than substance, on 'how to' rather than 'why?' (Apple, 1986). Robins and Webster (1989) argue that Information Technology in education is about education for a technocracy, and reflects and promotes a technocratic rationality. A decline in creativity is a consequence: pupils gain computer literacy at the risk of becoming cultural cripples (Chandler, in this volume; Roszak, 1988).

Implicit in computer literacy, then, is attitude learning:

> Rather than idiosyncratic teachers, computers can implement a cen-
> trally imposed curriculum with rigidly defined rules and dependence
> on binary logic. This indoctrinates workers to accept an infallible
> rationality, beyond change, embedded in the machine.... Hence the
> computer literacy movement emerges as part of a broader effort to
> reassert authoritarian control. (Magrass and Upchurch 1988, p. 11)

Robins and Webster (1989) argue that behind calls for computer literacy are alleged limitations in the products of the education system: deficiencies in 'numeracy' amongst school leavers; lack of awareness of 'industry'; incapacity to 'communicate'; and inappropriate attitudes to 'enterprise'. Information Technology is not neutral, but expresses and reinforces prevailing relations of power; as Information Technology moves into the classroom it takes these with it. Those working in the area of literacy have discussed how all literacies entail the capacity to exchange a coded form of information; many social transactions involve such exchange; and so the encoding and decoding skills are socially priced; and acquiring them comes to reflect or to be incorporated in prevailing institutional arrangements. As well as the technical skills, then, any new literacy exposes the pupil, trainee or student to new values and claims to authority. In this sense, computer literacy, as first aid, is ideological (Levine, 1988; Street, 1987).

Whilst the rhetoric of computer literacy is to empower (i.e., confront prevailing practice), it seems more plausible that it is, rather, a tool to further public acceptance. Computer literacy trains pupils as passive users, not to enable participation in design, or in other crucial areas of technology (Barnett, in this volume). By focusing on the technical, computer literacy stifles debate and depoliticizes.

Again paralleling arguments for literacy is the democracy argument — that technologists must be accountable to the public and this demands that the public is technologically literate. Minimal technical knowledge, however, will not in any way empower the citizenry; it can at the most lead to a false sense of power and control; to be empowered there is a need for enabling mechanics and structures. Again, paralleling the history of literacy, we see computer literacy masquerading as access to participation, though providing something rather different.

Implicit in computer literacy is that control of the technology requires technical expertise. Technologists and the public, though, are interested in different questions: the former ask how a technology works; and the latter what it can do for them or what its effects will be. The latter's questions are often seen as irrelevant by the former, whose job is the development of the technology, and who have an interest in the technology *qua* technology. Control of technology would involve political understanding of the technology, rather than a highly limited technical understanding — for example of a little of the BASIC programming language.

Further, Information Technology is a set of very rapidly changing technologies; the speed of innovation is without precedent. Consequently, computer literacy courses with a technical emphasis are quickly out of date. So, whereas the rhetoric of computer literacy implies that the incumbent is technologically literate in a generic sense, computer literacy constitutes a very specific area of literacy.

One reason for the paucity of computer literacy is that its basis rests on some notion of technological determinism. By technological determinism I mean the notion that technology is somehow outside society, follows its own trajectory, and has effects on society — at its strongest, that it is a key determinant of the society (Mackenzie and Wajcman, 1985). Yet the reality is *not* that we are entering a technologically determined, inevitable, information society. The nature of the technology and its effects are contested, negotiated and flexible (Lyon, 1987). In contrast to such an approach, those bits of computer literacy which look at context look at the *effects* of Information Technology; they do not, however, investigate the socially shaped nature of technology (Mackenzie and Wajcman, 1985). Technologies are developed for particular purposes, within the context of particular power relations, and are thus inevitably political (Winner, 1980). By ignoring this, computer literacy 'mystifies in the name of demystification' (Noble, 1884, p. 62).

Towards a Technology Literacy

There is nothing necessarily wrong with some notion of computer literacy — in that others have argued that literacy is not just about reading and writing: as well as print literacy one can have visual literacy, political and economic literacy, media literacy, etc. (Buckingham, 1988). Pattison (1982), in particular, argues that the notion of literacy should not be tied to specific technologies or practices such as reading and writing; and regards literacy of electronic media as merely another addition to the diversity of available literacies.

Computer literacy, however, is as ambiguous and complex as any other literacy (Levine, 1986). I have looked at who is defining computer literacy, for whom and in what terms. My argument, however, is not that we do not need or want computer literacy; but that technology and technology literacy are *more* important than is credited. Technology is a crucial social factor, and technology literacy increasingly important.

It is interesting to think about what a functional computer or technology literacy might be: what are the implications of being computer illiterate? What knowledge of technology do people need to get by? What are the demands for technology literacy in our society? What do people see technology literacy as providing? What is useful about it?

Despite the general absence of research findings to answer these questions, it seems at least plausible that we need literacy, and not merely in relation to specific technologies or practices, for example reading or writing. The emphasis should be not on mere artefacts, but on how these relate to social processes; and this should be done in a way that empowers, rather than enslaves.

In a general sense, society will benefit from having people sufficiently technologically literate to answer such questions as:

- Who controls the technology?
- What is it used to do?
- Whose needs and interests does it serve?
- Whose life does it enhance?
- Who decides where and what technology is used?
- What can technology *not* do?
- What do people need to know to use a technology?
- How does technology affect the nature and quantity of work?
- How does technology relate to power and control — across the globe, within the state, and in the workplace?

An ability to answer these questions would constitute a real technological understanding (which Devon (1987) calls 'technological sense'), which is required for a technological society to work — as opposed to technological expertise (Devon, 1987). Now, such an approach is clearly congruent with some of the thinking of the DES on technology: a good technology course

teaches specific concepts that are central to technology but which
impinge upon the lives of all.... Without an informed appreciation
of these concepts, intelligent participation in many aspects of social,
educational or political dialogue which relates to everyday life is
necessarily curtailed.

It also

gives insights into the general nature of technology in society and its
current importance in adult affairs ... technology is therefore, first
and foremost, a cultural study. (DES, 1982, pp. 27–8)

As Medway argues in his paper in this volume, the Technology National
Curriculum provides an opportunity for enhancing the status of the practical
in education; and of extending definitions of intelligence, from knowledge, to
making and doing, and social skills. The aim which is to be tested is capability, not knowledge.

Nor is such an approach incompatible with the requirements of the
labour market. Employers want employees who possess transferable
intellectual and personal skills: the ability to analyze complex issues, to
identify the core of a problem, to use information effectively, to work
cooperatively with others, and to communicate. *These* are employers' selection criteria (Buckroyd and Cornford, 1988; Mackay and Lane, 1989), not the
possession of a narrow, basic technical skill.

The failure of computer systems has been commented on extensively
(Mowshowitz, 1976; Price Waterhouse, 1989); in general, they fail not because of technical faults, but at the point of their interfaces with people:
technology never exists as a black box, isolated from humans; its efficient
performance requires an understanding of the social (Department of Industry,
1982). Looking at this from the perspective of technologists, an education
merely in technicalities, however indispensable that technical knowledge, will
not equip the technologist for power. The Finniston report on engineers
argued firmly that engineers needed not a different training in a technical
sense, but that their personal abilities failed to match the requirements of their
employers — motivation, ability to work in a team, to communicate, etc.
(Finniston, 1980). Elsewhere in Europe we see recognition of the need for
'hybrid' Information Technology professionals: the education and training of
Information Technology professionals in many European countries draws
more on sociology and has less emphasis on mathematics and the narrowly
technical (see Capel, in this volume).

Teaching a computer language does not *mystify* Information Technology's social relations; but it does not begin to demystify them (Robins and
Webster, 1989). Using a keyboard, trivial computer literacy, does not mean
that pupils grasp the nature of 'the Information Technology revolution' —

what about the relationship of the technology to the military, corporate information networks, the emerging international division of labour, the gender division of labour, national sovereignty, and state surveillance, for example? Trivial computer literacy is perhaps the contemporary equivalent of the notion of a little reading and writing being a good thing for the working class. Reading technology, however, can be much more than that. Apple (1986) argues that technology is a text; to read it you have to learn how it has been written (Smith, 1978; Hill, 1988).

I have tried to develop an argument which is premised on the centrality of technology in society today: technology is here to stay, it will not go away, and nor would most of us want it to. It *is*, however, a part of the social order. It can, further, take a variety of forms and be employed in a variety of ways — and it is social processes which thus shape technology. New technology needs to be developed and harnessed in ways which are beneficial to society, and education has a particular responsibility in relation to such a project. Computer literacy as it has hitherto been practiced, however, ignores the social arrangements and interests which give rise to the forms of technology we have, and the possibilities of technologies to better meet human need. We need public debate about how technologies might be understood and used in ways which enrich our lives. This would be a first step towards a truly computer literate society (Noble, 1984). Our task, as educationalists, is to make sure that when Information Technology enters the classroom it is there for educationally sound reasons.

References

16+ GCE AND CSE BOARDS' JOINT COUNCIL FOR 16+ NATIONAL CRITERIA (1983) *Recommended 16+ National Criteria for Computer Studies.*

ADAMSON, I. and KENNEDY, R. (1986) *Sinclair and the 'Sunrise' Technology*, Harmondsworth, Penguin.

ANDERSON, C.A. (1966) 'Literacy and schooling on the development threshold: some historical cases', in ANDERSON, C.A. and BOWMAN, M.J. (Eds) *Education and Economic Development*, Cass.

APPLE, M.W. (1986) *Teachers and Texts: A Political Economy of Class and Gender Relations in Education*, London, Routledge and Kegan Paul.

BAKER, K. (1981) 'IT: Information technology in schools', *Industry/Education View*, 7:2.

BAKER, K. (1983) *Information Technology — the Path to Greater Freedom or to 1984*, London, Department of Industry.

BAKER, K. (1987) Address to conference on IT in education, Barbican, London, February.

BELL, D. (1973) *The Coming of Post-Industrial Society*, New York, Basic Books.

BEYNON, J. (1991) 'Computers, dominant boys and invisible girls: or, Hannah, it's not a toaster, it's a computer', in BEYNON, J. and MACKAY, H. *Computers into Classrooms: More Questions than Answers*, Falmer.

BEYNON, J. and MACKAY, H. (1989) 'Information technology in education: towards a critical perspective', *Journal of Education Policy*, 4, 3, pp. 245–57.

BLACKBURN, R.M. and MANN, M. (1979) *The Working Class in the Labour Market*, London, Macmillan.

BORK, A. (1985) *Personal Computers for Education*, New York, Harper and Row.

BRAVERMAN, H. (1974) *Labor and Monopoly Capital: The Degradation of Work in the Twentieth Century*, New York, Monthly Review Press.

BBC CONTINUING EDUCATION TELEVISION (1982) *Computer Literacy Project*, London, BBC.

BUCKINGHAM, D. (1988) 'Television literacy: a critique', paper presented to the International Television Studies Conference.

BUCKROYD, B. and CORNFORD, D. (1988) *The IT Skills Crisis: The Way Ahead*, Manchester, National Computing Centre.

CHANDLER, D. (1985) 'Computers and literacy', in CHANDLER, D. and MARCUS, S. *Computers and Literacy*, Milton Keynes, Open University Press.

CHILD, J. (1985) 'Managerial strategies, new technology and the labour process', in KNIGHTS, D., WILMOTT, H. and COLLINSON, D. *Job Redesign: Critical Perspectives on the Labour Process*, Aldershot, Gower.

CIANN, G. *et al.* (1988) 'Stereotyping in relation to the gender gap in participation in computing', *Educational Research*, 30, 2, pp. 98–103.

CLANCHY, M. (1979) *From Memory to Written Record, 1066–1307*, London, Arnold.

COX, M.J. and RHODES, V.J. (1988) 'Training primary school teachers to use computers effectively in the classroom — an investigation into inservice provision', paper presented at Fifth International Conference on Technology and Education, Edinburgh.

CULLEY, L. (1986) *Gender Differences and Computing in Secondary Schools*, Department of Education, Loughborough University of Technology.

CULLEY, L. (1991) 'Gender equity and computing in secondary schools: issues and strategies for teachers', in BEYNON, J. and MACKAY, H. *Computers into Classrooms: More Questions than Answers*, Falmer.

DES (1981) *MEP — the Strategy*, London, DES.

DES (1982) *Technology in Schools*, London, HMSO.

DES/WO (1987) *The National Curriculum 5–16: A Consultation Document*, London and Cardiff, DES and Welsh Office.

DEPARTMENT OF INDUSTRY (1982) *Programme for Advanced Information Technology: The Report of the Alvey Committee*, London, HMSO.

DERINGER, D.K. and MOLNAR, A.R. (1982) 'Key components for a national computer literacy program', in SEIDEL, R.J. *et al.* (Eds) *Computer Literacy: Issues and Direction for 1985*, New York, Academic.

DEVON, D.F. (1987) 'In praise of computer literacy', *Bulletin of Science, Technology & Society*, 7, 1 & 2, pp. 338–43.

DILLON, D. (1985) 'The dangers of computers in literacy education: who's in charge here?', in CHANDLER, D. and MARCUS, S. *Computers and Literacy*, Milton Keynes, Open University Press.

DORE, R. (1976) *The Diploma Disease*, London, Allen and Unwin.

FINNISTON, M. (1980) *Engineering our Future: Report of the Committee of Inquiry into the Engineering Profession*, London, HMSO.

FRANCIS, A. (1986) *New Technology at Work*, Oxford University Press.

FREIRE, P. (1972) *Pedagogy of the Oppressed*, Harmondsworth, Penguin.

FRIEDMAN, A. (1977) *Industry and Labour*, London, Macmillan.

GILL, K. (1985) *Work, Unemployment and the New Technology*, Cambridge, Polity.

GRAFF, H.J. (1979) *The Literacy Myth: Literacy and Social Structure in the Nineteenth Century City*, New York, Academic.

GREENBAUM, J. (1976) 'Division of labour in the computer field', *Monthly Review*, 28, 3.

HEATH, S.B. (1983) *Ways with Words*, Cambridge University Press.

HILL, S. (1988) *The Tragedy of Technology*, London, Pluto.

INNIS, H. (1951) *The Bias of Communication*, University of Toronto Press.

IT ADVISORY PANEL (1986) *Learning to Live with IT*, London, HMSO.

JOHNSON, D.C. et al. (1980) 'Computer literacy — what is it?', *The Mathematics Teacher*, 73, 2, pp. 91–6.

KRAFT, P. (1979) 'The industrialisation of computer programming', in ZIMBALIST, A. *Case Studies in the Labour Process*, London, Monthly Review Press.

LEVINE, K. (1986) *The Social Context of Literacy*, London, Routledge and Kegan Paul.

LEVINE, K. (1988) 'The tools in a language', *The Guardian*, 21 January.

LINN, P. (1985) 'Microcomputers in education: dead and living labour', *Radical Science* 18, pp. 58–101; reprinted in MACKAY, H., YOUNG, M. and BEYNON, J. *Understanding Technology in Education*, Falmer, 1991.

LUEHRMANN, A. (1981) 'Computer literacy — what should it be?', *The Mathematics Teacher* 74, 9, pp. 682–6.

LYON, D. (1987) *The Information Society: Issues and Illusions*, Cambridge, Polity.

LYON, D. (1991) 'The information society: ideology or utopia?', in MACKAY, H., YOUNG, M. and BEYNON, J. (Eds) *Understanding Technology in Education*, Falmer.

MACKAY, H. and LANE, S. (1989) 'Towards a sociology of systems analysis', paper presented at Labour Process Conference, Manchester, April; and ESRC PICT Software Workshop, Manchester, July. To be published in MURRAY, F. and WOOLGAR, S. *Social Perspectives on Software*, Boston, Mass., MIT Press.

MACKENZIE, D. (1984) 'Marx and the machine', *Technology and Culture*, 25, pp. 473–502.

MACKENZIE, D. and WAJCMAN, J. (Eds) (1985) *The Social Shaping of Technology*, Milton Keynes, Open University Press.

MAGRASS, Y. and UPCHURCH, R.L. (1988) 'Computer literacy: people adapted for technology', *Computers and society*, 18, 2.

MASUDA, Y. (1981) *The Information Society as Post Industrial Society*, Tokyo, Institute for the Information Society.

MOWSHOWITZ, A. (1976) *The Conquest of Will*, Reading, Addison-Wesley.

MURRAY, R. (1991) 'Life after Henry (Ford)', in MACKAY, H., BEYNON, J. and YOUNG, M. *Understanding Technology in Education*, Falmer. First published in *Marxism Today*, October 1988, pp. 8–13.

NATIONAL CURRICULUM COUNCIL (1988) *General Report*, London and Cardiff, DES and Welsh Office.

NATIONAL CURRICULUM COUNCIL DESIGN AND TECHNOLOGY WORKING GROUP (1988) *Interim Report*, London and Cardiff, DES and Welsh Office.

NOBLE, D. (1984) 'The underside of computer literacy', *Raritan*, 3, pp. 37–64.

ONG, W. (1982) *Orality and Literacy*, London, Methuen.

O'SHEA, T. and SELF, J. (1983) *Learning and Teaching with Computers*, Brighton, Harvester.

OXENHAM, J. (1980) *Literacy: Writing, Reading and Social Organisation*, London, Routledge and Kegan Paul.

PAPERT, S. (1980) *Mindstorms: Children, Computers and Powerful Ideas*, Brighton, Harvester.

PATTISON, R. (1982) *On literacy: The Politics of the Word from Homer to the Age of Rock*, Oxford University Press.

PEA, R.D. (1987) 'LOGO programming and problem solving', in SCANLON, E. and O'SHEA, T. *Educational Computing*, Chichester, Wiley.

POLLERT, A. (Ed.) (1990) *Farewell to Flexibility?*, Oxford, Blackwell.

PRICE WATERHOUSE (1989) 'The return of the dinosaurs', *Computing*, 25 September, pp. 26–7.

RESNICK, D.R. and RESNICK, L.B. (1977) 'The nature of literacy: an historical exploration', *Harvard Educational Review*, 47, 3, pp. 370–85.

ROBINS, K. and WEBSTER, F. (1988) *Computer Literacy: Who Needs It?*, unpublished paper, CURDS, University of Newcastle and Oxford Polytechnic.

ROBINS, K. and WEBSTER, F. (1989) *The Technical Fix: Education, Computers, Industry*, London, Macmillan.

ROSSINGTON, D. (1983) 'Computers make learning easy' *Youth Training News*, 3, p. 5.

ROSZAK, T. (1988) *The Cult of Information: The Folklore of Computers and the True Art of Thinking*, London, Paladin.

RUMBERGER, R. and LEVIN, H.M. (1984) 'Forecasting the impact of new technologies on the future job market', Project report No. 84-A4, Institute of Research on Educational Finance and Government, School of Education, Stanford University.

RUTHVEN, K. (1984) 'Computer literacy and the curriculum', *British Journal of Educational Studies*, XXXII, 2, pp. 134–47.

SCIENCE AS CULTURE (1990) 8: Special volume on post-Fordism.

SELWOOD, I. (1988) 'The rise and fall of computer studies', *Computer Education*, June, pp. 2–3.

SLACK, J. (1984) 'The information revolution as ideology', *Media, Culture and Society*, 6, 3, pp. 247–56.

SMITH, D. and KEEP, R. (1986) 'Children's opinions of educational software', *Educational Research*, 28, 2, pp. 83–8.

SMITH, F. (1978) *Reading*, Cambridge University Press.

STONIER, T. (1983) *The Wealth of Information: A Profile of the Post-Industrial Economy*, London, Thames-Methuen.

STREET, B.V. (1984) *Literacy in Theory and Practice*, Cambridge University Press.

STREET, B.V. (1987) 'Models of "computer literacy"', in FINNEGAN, R. *et al. Information Technology: Social Issues*, Sevenoaks, Hodder and Stoughton.

THOMPSON, P. (1983) *The Nature of Work: An Introduction to Debates on the Labour Process*, London, Macmillan.

TURKLE, S. (1984) *The Second Self: Computers and the Human Spirit*, New York, Simon and Schuster.

WEBSTER, F. and ROBINS, K. (1986) *Information Technology: A Luddite Analysis*, New Jersey, Ablex.

WEBSTER, F. and ROBINS, K. (1991) 'The selling of the new technology', in MACKAY, H., YOUNG, M. and BEYNON, J. (Eds) *Understanding Technology in Education*, Falmer.

WELLINGTON, J.J. (1989) *Education for Employment: The Place of Information Technology*, Slough, NFER/Nelson.

WILLIAMS, R. (1961) *The Long Revolution*, London, Chatto and Windus.

WILLIAMS, S. (1985) *A Job to Live: The Impact of Tomorrow's Technology on Work and Society*, Harmondsworth, Penguin.

WINNER, L. (1980) 'Do artefacts have politics?', *Daedalus*, 109, pp. 121–36.

WOOD, S. (1982) *The Degradation of Work: Skill, Deskilling and the Labour Process*, London, Hutchinson.

Chapter 7

Sniffers, Lurkers, Actor Networkers: Computer Mediated Communications as a Technical Fix

Keith Grint

This paper considers the social aspects of computer mediated communications (CMC) for participation in group discussion. The culture of participation in educational and decision-making forums poses a contradiction between the mass participation that ought to occur and the minority participation that usually does. Some recent research suggests that CMC can rescue non-participants from their silence and facilitate a more egalitarian participative culture through the equivalent of a technological fix or an electronic bridge. However, a small empirical case study of a CMC-based Open University (OU) course, that focuses on the social and technical aspects of Information Technology, suggests that the socially constructed issues of participation cannot be reconstructed simply by a 'technological fix' because it is itself socially constructed. Adapting the arguments of the actor network and an interpretivist approach to technology, I argue that the accounts of participation and non-participation undermine claims that CMC serves as a *deus ex machina*, indeed, for some people CMC appears to be an electric fence rather than an electronic bridge. Success and failure, then, depend not on whether there is a god in the machine but on the strength of the actor network and the interpretation of the machine.

Introduction

Since the time of Pericles it has been argued that one of the best ways to learn, to fulfil self-potential and to generate effective discussion and decision-making, based upon some measure of agreement, is by active participation. Through participation, it is claimed, individuals make the most of their own talents which are developed in and through social interaction. Concomitantly, the group benefits from the pooling of knowledge and ideas, and from the positive commitment to the decisions made through the participative process. Such arguments underlie a wide range of perspectives and substantive developments: from theories of legitimacy (Weber, 1986, pp. 212–301) to theories of political authority (Mill, 1982; Macpherson, 1966) to theories concerning the efficacy of small groups (Trist *et al.*, 1963) and democratic leadership (Lewin, 1958; Likert, 1961). In sum, the organizational culture engendered by participative decision-making and discussion groups is allegedly the resolution of both personal, organizational and pedagogic problems. We are left with a generalized cultural expectation that participation ought to be pursued, contrasted with a generalized cultural reality that participation is more like a minority sport than a mass event: however much participation might be good for you, many people appear to avoid it wherever possible.

Mansbridge (1983) argues that the critical block to participation is the fear of public ridicule, and whilst it may be the case that participation *builds* individual confidence, the leap across the ridicule threshold is one that some simply cannot cross. Certainly Sniderman (1974) has argued that participation is caused by, and does not advance, high self-esteem; hence there can be few advantages derived from a system built upon a closed circle of self-esteem and participation. However, since conventional decision and discussion groups are seldom designed or organized with the aim of facilitating supportive participation it is hardly surprising that little participation is inculcated (Crittenden, 1988; Held, 1987).

Is there a technical solution to the problem of participation lying in wait in the wings? Can information technology solve the problem by transcending human delimitations and injecting a technological fix in the shape of CMC? According to some advocates (Kiesler *et al.*, 1984; Kaye, 1989; Mason, 1989), CMC can provide a whole battery of electronic bridges and ladders to enable non-contributers to bypass some of the conventional blockages: no powers of public oratory are required; no skills of interruption or loquaciousness are prerequisites; rapid exits from unpleasant situations are viable and, perhaps above all, no physical appearance or meeting is required. In short, CMC seems to offer an electronic mask to transcend a number of factors that tend to delimit participation. Without collapsing headfirst into technical determinism the general assumption is that CMC has certain 'impacts' upon educational forms, and many of these are beneficial.

However, the assumption that technology has such 'impacts' upon society, or that technical innovations like CMC are either 'progressive' or 'neutral' are assumptions that may be questioned. Whether technology has 'effects' depends, *inter alia*, on how technology is defined. In turn, the actual definition of technology tends to vary with author: from a delimited concern with machinery through to the entire corpus of organizational features, and all points in between (Winner, 1977, pp. 8–12). Quite often the definition of technology remains implicit and therefore obscure. As a result, technology can become the reserve category which explains all aspects that cannot be explained by other factors, or the bewildering variety of definitions simply confounds any attempts to assess the 'impact' of technology (see Davis and

Taylor, 1976, pp. 390–1). Many sociologists would want to argue that technology, qua apparatus, cannot explain anything anyway since technology is itself socially constructed and the effect of technology depends upon the use made of it. Still others would want to deny the apparent neutrality afforded to technology, for rather than technology being inert it may be seen as inherently political in nature: it is not simply a means to any end but a means that already encapsulates particular preferences (Winner, 1985). All these arguments, of course, resurface within that most slippery of agendas, technological determinism.

What I want to consider in the first part of this article are attempts to avoid technical determinism that, in my opinion, are less than successful, and an alternative based generally on the actor network theory which rejects the division between human and non-human actors and conceptualizes the two apparently discrete phenomena as fused elements in a seamless web: a human-technology alloy. Additionally, I want to draw upon interpretive approaches to technology which suggest that the characteristics of technology do not inhere within an artefact but are the transient results of social definitions. This interpretive actor network approach provides a way of disassembling the technology so that its social features are more readily exposed but in a way that does not strip out such features from their technological materialization. Once the elements of the network are disassembled we will then be in a better postion to reassemble them into a whole — and this reconstruction is critical; after all, neither the human nor the non-human elements of an actor network can operate in isolation.

Having adumbrated the alternative it will then be used to examine a case study of OU students involved in the course DT200, *An Introduction to Information Technology: Social and Technological Issues.* The relative novelty of much of the technology involved in CMC ensures that little in the way of empirical or theoretical work is currently published. Indeed, the OU's course in Information Technology (DT200) is the only large-scale experiment in the UK where CMC, in the form of computer conferencing and electronic mail, is a primary format for social and pedagogic contact (for international comparisons and assessments of the OU scheme see Mason and Kaye, 1989; for CMC in a business environment see Dennis *et al.*, 1988). Students contact their tutors and fellow students through a home-based computer using a modem and communications software, transmitting messages down the telephone lines to the mainframe computers of the OU. Communication may take the form of electronic mail messages or participation in a series of course-oriented local, regional and national computer conferences where messages bear the surname and initial of the author but not their gender nor (excluding the full time OU staff) their status. Logging on to the DT200 databases and asynchronous electronic conferences is strongly recommended and a prerequisite to the completion of certain parts of the course. However, as shall be demonstrated shortly, the perceived disadvantages of actively participating in the conferences far outweigh the advantages for most of the respondents and tend to deter the majority from active participation. Hence, although over 75 per cent of all DT200 students logged on to the major conference only about 25 per cent actually contributed anything. An even smaller number acquired the disreputable status of 'Modem Sniffers' or 'CoSy Addict' (CoSy is the COmmunications SYstem software) because of their apparent dependence on the system; the rest merely 'lurked', reading the conference messages passively and from the safe anonymity of their homes. Some of the conferences were concerned purely with socializing, others with the technical or social aspects of the information technology presented in the course; in all cases students were encouraged to ask questions, offer their own views and expertise, and engage in the kind of debate that allegedly occurs within more conventional universities. Part of the motivation of the course team was to develop an integrated course on Information Technology which considered both social and technical issues, though there is no attempt to argue that the two features are inseparable. The OU had at last become the Electronic Campus: the loneliness of the long-distance learner would be replaced by the intimacy of 1300 students and tutors in the privacy of your own home.

Much of the material for this article is derived from a series of unstructured interviews with twelve OU students which lasted between one and two hours, but before I attempt to represent their experiences I shall first examine the theoretical perspectives on the relationships between the social and technical and having criticized technological determinism, social determinism and political or 'designer technology' I shall argue for an interpretive actor network approach. First let me set out the first position I wish to attack: technological determinism.

Technological Determinism

At its simplest, technological determinism considers technology to be an exogenous and autonomous development which coerces and determines social and economic organizations and relationships; it appears to advance spontaneously and inevitably in a manner resemblant of Darwinian survival, in so far as only the most appropriate innovations survive and only those who adapt to such innovations prosper. This is particularly prescient when Information Technology is considered, for the march of the microchip appears omnipotent and to deny this is to deny both reality and the future. Whether that future is to be one of Toffler's (1980) utopia or Burnham's (1983) Orwellian nightmare is secondary to the inescapable essence of the future. This perspective has a long history as well as an apparently radical future, from Saint-Simon and Comte (Kumar, 1978) to the more recent arguments of Leavitt and Whisler, Bell (1960; 1973), Kerr *et al.* (1964) and Blauner (1964). Yet, as Mackenzie and Wajcman (1985) suggest, since not all technical 'advances' are enacted, since the same technology appears to have different 'effects', and because this implies that the specification of cause is an extremely complex task, all models of technical determinism are suspect.

While some of the more general discussions concerning technological determinism have sought to highlight the way that the power of technological advance tramples all before it, there are some rather more sophisticated résumés which leave a degree of freedom for social groups to manoeuvre (Pool, 1983; Freeman, 1987) Robey (1977), for example, argues that a more contingent relationship between technology and organizational effects exists in which organizations within unstable environments used computer technology to buttress a decentralized structure while organizations with stable environments used computers to centralize control. Similarly, Dutton (1988) has asserted that new technology tends to buttress or 'reinforce' whichever group is already in control of a particular organization: bias merely becomes automated. Yet even these 'softer' forms of technical determinism are 'technicist' in that they imply we can separate the technical from the social and agree upon the technical capabilities and effects of the technology, in this case the computer system. But neither attitudes, control structures, nor the form, effects and use of technologies are determined, they are all elements in the negotiated order of work. As Woolgar (1989) has argued, the technologies themselves are not stable entities with fixed and determinate 'uses'; rather the entire design, development and implementation process of a technological artefact is socially constructed to the extent that the point at which an artefact is 'completed' is itself subject to stabilization rituals. This does not imply that we should abandon concern for the technology itself and concentrate upon issues outside the 'black box' — on the contrary. Nor does it mean that 'social determinism' is the solution to the problems of technical determinism.

Social Determinism

The opposite form of determinism is the social variety. This approach assumes that technological artefacts and changes are themselves socially constructed or that social relationships are, in any case, derived from, and ultimately determined by, cultural or social aspects, not technological aspects (Gallie, 1978; Silverman, 1970; Goldthorpe *et al.*, 1968; 1969). In this approach social reality was produced and reproduced in and through the meaningful actions of subjective individuals to the extent that there could be no direct connection between allegedly objective structures and human actions and attitudes. Rather, all social action was mediated by the subjective and interpretive understandings of individuals, and by the social relationships between individuals. In the context of technology, therefore, what was important was the mediating and subjectivist qualities of actors: what counts as technology is an accomplishment of the actors.

Nonetheless, it is important that we retain technology as one facet of the social-technical web because the claim that technology does not have any independent effects does not mean it has *no* significance, though 'significance' does not imply the same as 'impact'. Technologies and humans invariably operate in conjunction with each other, and since the result of this conjunction is not the equivalent of adding one to the other but enacts an alloyed fusion of human and non-human, we can only distinguish between the social and the technical to the extent that the 'alloy' contains elements of both. It becomes misleading, therefore, to argue that one or the other has a discrete impact.

Political Technology and Designer Technology

Somewhere between the polarities of technological determinism and social determinism lies a disparate amalgam of approaches that concede to both technology and social forces variant degrees of consequence (Trist and Bamforth, 1951; Winner, 1977; 1985; Noble, 1979; Wilkinson 1983; Rose *et al.*, 1986; Pfeffer, 1982). This variety of different approaches to technology suggests that 'the uses and consequences of technology emerge unpredictably from complex social interactions' (Markus and Robey, 1988, p. 588). However, one of the prime aims of the designer of technical artefacts is to limit such contingencies through the design process itself.

The most recent attempt to articulate a perspective bearing some resemblance to this ideal has been that of Rose *et al.* (1986), Clark *et al.* (1988) and McLoughlin and Clark (1988). Their studies of technological change in the telecommunications industry suggest that one form of exchange equipment facilitates individual working patterns while another lends itself more to team approaches, and that the relative impact of technological and social forces tends to alter, the further away individuals are from the immediate work task. Technology in this perspective, therefore, becomes conceptualized as politically impregnated, as historically encumbered and as one among many potentially independent variables. But once 'the stages leading to the choice of a particular system are accomplished, then social choices become frozen in a given technology' (Clark *et al.*, 1988, p. 32). However, I would suggest that the limitation placed upon the social aspects of technology, that is to the design and implementation process, underestimates the significance of both the alloyed nature of technology and actors' interpretations of the alloy. Inasmuch as technology embodies social aspects it is not a stable and determinate object (albeit one with political preferences inscribed into it), but an unstable and indeterminate artefact whose precise significance is negotiated and interpreted but never settled. For example, telephones themselves were used originally to broadcast concert music and it was not axiomatic that the telephone would ultimately be restricted primarily to a two-way personal communication system (Finnegan and Heap, 1988), nor that it would serve as a communication channel for students undertaking distance education. Its use originally, and indeed its use now, was and is the result of negotiations, not determinations, derived both from the embodied politics of the artefact and the actor network within which it exists.

Winner's (1977; 1985) argument, that 'technical things have political qualities', is a another example of this 'designer technology' approach. What Winner is anxious to attack is the assumption that technology is neutral and, therefore, that the impact and importance of technology depends wholly upon the use to which we put it. In the context of this debate we could represent this 'technical neutrality' argument, which Winner considers naive, as the assumption that the technology of computer mediated communications need not lead to greater or less participation since the designers of CMC build in particular preferences which are necessarily achieved: some CMC systems are designed as, and therefore operate as, hierarchical, others are participative. This does not mean users of the systems are axiomatically aware of the embodied politics of the designer, and where they remain ignorant of them they may well account for their experiences through the determining, but apparently neutral, effects of the technology. Part of the explanation for the rise of this naive view, in Winner's view, is the distaste for technological determinism: since it is not the case that social developments are driven by technological developments, it has become a commonplace to assume that technology has no impact in and of itself. Rather, technology is socially constructed. Yet this underlines its inherently political nature, for if technology is not the product of autonomous creation then it must become entrammelled in the political ribbons of its designers and users.

One of Winner's own examples (1985) relates how the New York architect, Robert Moses, designed bridges so low that buses, and therefore the black and poorer white sections of New York, could not gain access to Jones Beach. Thus, what appear to be the results of 'neutral' technological developments actually embody the political preferences of the designer. Here, then, technological determinism reappears as 'designer determinism': control over the design and construction process of the artefact ensures the required result; or does it?

Actor Networks and Contingent Technology

Contrary to the implications of 'designer determinism' whether the poor are kept away from Jones Beach, and if they are whether that is determined by Moses's low bridges or something else, is also open to interpretation (Woolgar, 1990). At its most banal one might want to question *whether* the poor were deterred, and if they were *what* deterred them? Might it be that they had no desire to go there, or that the bridges were only interpreted as a minor impediment in a whole system or network of human and non-human obstacles? I might not end up at the Queen's Garden Party this year but it will not be just because the gates will deter me. Contrary to Winner's assumption, the preferences fo designers, makers and users do not lead in any unmediated way to particular outcomes, for the position and power of current users mediates between design and outcome and is channelled in part by the unintended consequences of social life. What is crucial, then, is to retain the ambiguity of technology in the sense that organizations and social relations are neither determined by technology nor are they determined by social agency; organizations are the contingent result of a permanently unstable network of human and non-human actors. Technology and its properties, then, are not fixed or determinate but contingent.

The actor network model (Callon, 1986; Latour, 1988; Law, 1988), which has been adopted principally as a way of explaining the development and stabilization of forms of technology, is particularly useful in this context. Fundamentally, the approach suggests that power depends upon the construction and maintenance of a network of actors; crucially, and contrary to the implications of Clegg's (1989, pp. 202–7, 225) otherwise useful review, these networks involve both human and non-human 'actors'. Perhaps 'elements', rather than 'actors' might be considered as a better description here because it avoids the reification implied by non-human actors. The approach is constructed on the premise that we should not distinguish between human and non-human elements but talk instead of the 'heterogeneous entities that constitute a network' (Bijker *et al.*, 1987, p. 11). The implication, for this particular example, is that the educational organization of the DT200 course should not be perceived as, or explained through, the activities of humans alone nor through discrete technologies but through the alliances fo human and non-human actors. These non-human actors may, for example, take the form of technology or material facets of institutions — buildings etc. In effect, we should not analyze the success or failure of, say, individual students in the course, in terms of the superior human aspects or the better technology. Nor is it viable to link the two in some form of discrete but parallel resources: it was not the students *and* the CMC technology but the students *using* the CMC technology. That is, we should consider the unity of human and non-human actors in terms of a 'seamless web' as Hughes (1979) calls it or 'heterogeneous engineering' in Law's (1986) terms.

As a further illustration, it would be erroneous to explain and apportion blame to the actions of an individual shooting people at random in the street in terms of the weapon *or* the murderer. The gun lobby would have us believe that the guns are innocent tools in the hands of maniacs; their opponents will try to persuade us that it is the ease of access to weapons that facilitates such actions. But both perspectives can be undermined if we assert that only when *maniacs unite with guns* do we have such problems: gunless maniacs do not shoot people anymore that peopleless guns do; but the fusion of human and non-human can lead to devastating results. This does not mean that we can abandon the interpretive approach in favour of an 'objective' analysis of weapons systems and psychopathology. What counts as a weapon that should be prohibited, and which individuals are liable to use them against other humans, are not issues that 'experts' have been able to agree on.

What should be stressed here is the contingent nature of such networks and, implicitly therefore, the constant need for the network to be reproduced. Networks do not maintain themselves, even though a viable method of extending the time span of a network is to inscribe it into material form. For example, the radical Paris government built its subway bridges too small to allow the coaches of the private railroad companies to pass through, thereby literally ossifying its contingent political control. As Latour argues:

They shifted their alliance from legal or contractual ones, to stones, earth and concrete. What was easily reversible in 1900 became less and less reversible as the subway network grew. The engineers of the railway company now took these thousands of tunnels built by the subway company as destiny and as an irreversible technical constraint (1988, pp. 36–7)

Actor networks, then, feature human and non-human actors in a contingent and seamless web of relationships, which, through certain strategies — especially the transformation or institutionalization of human resources into non-human resources, either material (e.g., in technologies) or symbolic (e.g., in law) — may reduce the degree of inherent contingency. Let me move on now to apply this theoretical perspective to the case study.

The DT200 Case Study

In what follows I discuss the results of a series of semi-structured interviews with twelve students, eight men and four women, from the OU's DT200 course. The gender division replicates that for the course as a whole which began with over 1300 students, and while I make no claims that this small group is representative of the total course, their accounts of participation and non-participation in CMC are useful illustrations of the value of the theoretical approach. Equally important, the problems encountered by this group pose substantial practical limitations to the optimistic position and conventional analysis: Information Technology does not offer a technological 'fix' for the issue of participation — the problem is socially and culturally constructed but embedded within a network of human and non-human actors. In this case the network comprises the student, her or his domestic relations and environment, the computer, modem, communications software, telephone lines, the Open University computer network, and the other students and tutors etc., with their related human and technical associations. The problem of participation cannot, therefore, simply be transcended by electronic wizardry. If there ever was a god in the machine this one has been eaten by it and secreted in and through the entire network. Figure 1 is a representation of the DT200 actor network.

Figure 1 DT200 Actor Network

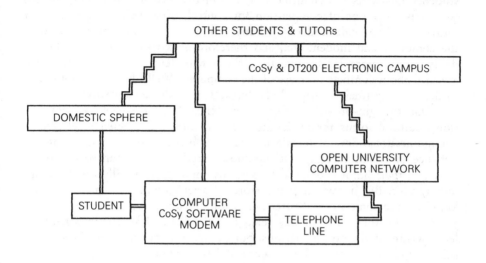

Domestic Networks

Let us begin with the domestic network, not because this has priority or superordinate status over any other element in the DT200 network but because this is the starting-point for most OU students. Perhaps the most commonly articulated explanation for the lack of participation amongst OU students, both in this particular group and more generally, is that of time. As part-time students, they are already 'doubling up' their existing consumption of time by undertaking normal work hours, either as conventional employees or as full-time homeworkers. As such, the rationing of time is usually very strictly determined by personal and academic demands, but seldom by the 'time saving' advantages of technology. As Cowan (1983) has argued elsewhere, technology seldom liberates time and is usually adapted to reproduce the status quo. Similarly, what is significant here is not the availability of the technology but how using it meshes with or overrides other aspects of students' domestic, work and academic networks. For example, the freeing of time for OU activities depends crucially, for those with partners and/or dependent children, upon partner support and/or sympathetic children. As Charlie explained about his wife's attitude, 'Sometimes she objects to me doing my computing but I say to her: "sorry dear its the OU".' Although most husbands of female students were tolerant, if not exactly supportive, of their partner's educational activities, more male spouses regarded their wives' studies as a diversion from conventional responsibilities than did wives of male students. Thus Jane said that her husband 'was not very happy with the idea ... he's supportive in the sense that he doesn't mind me doing it — as long as his dinner is not late!' This was most evident when it involved female students' control over technological apparatus, though since many of these students' husbands and children were also involved in similar technology the issue was more one of competition for control rather than competition for knowledge. Few male students had any serious competition for control over the computer and modem etc., and therefore networks involving male students appear more intransitive than those with female students. As Brian revealed about conflicts over use of the computer, 'Well I have to admit I tend to defer to my [male teenage] kids, but not generally to my wife'.

One thought-provoking feature was the inappropriateness of conventional cultural forms for mediating between men and women in electronic communications. Several female interviewees mentioned the disquieting experience of communicating with unknown students, who turned out to be males, in their homes, albeit at one remove and electronically on the visual display unit. But it was, in Jane's words, 'easier to talk to men that I don't know via the computer ... after all, you don't know what they are like do you?' Partly, they thought this related to the cultural associations between letter writing and amorous liaisons, but equally it concerned the invasions of privacy induced through the network and the unknown consequences such innocent exchanges would have on third parties who were unaware of the context within which electronic conferencing occurred. Julia's comment manifests this uneasiness:

> I don't like getting messages from men, that is I don't mind getting messages from men, but I'm very tentative about telling my husband. I'll say 'Brown' or 'Walker' was on; and I have this difficulty about accepting that a man I don't know is talking to me ... I gloss over it and tell him its another student.

Male students did not voice any such uncertainties, suggesting that what occurs between men and women through CMC does not so much represent reality as the raw material for different creations and interpretations of 'reality'.

Here is a fine example of the value of the network analogy since it is only the control executed on men by women through the network of students and computer systems that provided the structure for the interaction. In fact, most students noted that the ambiguous status of respondents, i.e., their genderless state, did not impair communications but once the gender was known there did tend to be a qualitative change in perceptions towards conventional assumptions about, amongst other things, the levels of expertise associated with men and women. In short, the unequal access to and control over the actor network, in both its human and non-human facets, i.e., the differing degrees of domestic responsibility, control over the computer and interpretations of electronic socializing, were a significant aspect of differing levels and forms of participation.

Students

One of the most frequently asserted participatory advantages of CMC is the flattening of status hierarchies and the consequential expansion in the number and quality of, as well as attention to, the contributions. According to Kiesler *et al.* (1984) and Hilz *et al.* (1982), the reduction (though not elimination) of status hierarchies encourages a greater level of participation, which in turn promotes greater focus upon the message rather than the messenger, though it also raises the problem of taking all information as legitimate. If readers are uncertain as to the status of any individual messenger they may be coerced into assuming that all messages are potentially valid until proved otherwise. Thus, rather than being swayed by the messenger, readers may be swayed by the message. The interviewees had some sympathy with this point, particularly in so far as the system only revealed the surname and initial of each contributor. As Charlie remarked, 'the way he was "talking" I thought he was a tutor ... and I mean if it comes from the tutor it must be right'. This equivocal line is reproduced by George's initial denial and subsequent confirmation of the significance of status: 'I don't actually associate anything with the person, I only relate to the text ... but because you know he is a tutor you read it with more intensity'. This general lack of distinction between tutors and students encouraged students to participate in debates with tutors, though not so much with the course team whose distinctive CoSy name underline separated them off from the rest of the participants. Yet many also felt distinctly uneasy about some contributions and, over time, allocated their own unofficial status hierarchy, such that known individuals, especially the 'CoSy addicts' or 'Modem Sniffers', were systematically ignored while others were always sought out and respected. For Julia, for example, 'I like to know who to believe ... F.G. Howard is never going to be believed in a month of Sundays; when he comes on you think — oh God!' Indeed, where a particularly useful or outrageously awful message was found several students used the personal résumé facility to reconstruct the invisible status. Once more, then, the technical construct which minimizes social status differences did nothing to determine the interpretation placed on messages by students, rather the status system was reconstructed through the actor network.

Another aspect of status that emerged in some influential ways was that of gender. The socially constructed 'technical incompetence' of women, as interpreted by men, has a long history and shows little sign of diminishing (Cockburn, 1983; Cowan, 1983; Dex, 1988; McNeil, 1987; Grint, 1990). But the technical success of women students on the course, as measured by completion of various tasks and which compared very favourably with male students, was considered as a non-event by several students of both sexes, and by some men as an explicable but atypical event. Most technical expertise was seen by a majority of the male interviewees to be deposited within men and manifest in their general assumption that technical contributions were from men, whereas cries for help were assumed to be from women. Exceptional women, on the other hand, were perceived to be just as competent as men — but only *because* they were exceptional and unrepresentative of women generally. Indeed, course success was seen as a result of a well structured teaching mechanism rather than evidence of innate abilities since, as Charlie put it, 'Women tend to read the instructions first, men tend to plough on because they think they are more familiar with the technology.'

Part of the rationale behind DT200 is the desire to make explicit these links between technological and social facets: to demonstrate that to assume that technology is neutral is itself a political assumption. As the first unit concludes:

> The point is that to consider fully issues about the implications of IT for people's lives, and of how it has been or might be shaped, you need to look not just at technical expertise or high-level social or political theory, but at the overlapping social and technological factors that are in practice combined in any application of IT. (Finnegan and Heap, 1988, p. 58)

It is, then, rather ironic that one of the reasons for the limited levels of participation in the course conferences is the extent to which the technical aspects are imbued with neutrality and the prerequisite for relevant participation is technical expertise. Irrespective of all advice to the contrary, the majority of students perceived CMC to be a mode of communication configured to transmit technical expertise. It was not just that most individual problems were regarded as technical in origin, nor was it just that the profusion of 'trivia' within the computer conferences deterred all but the addicts, rather it was that technical information was *interpreted* as objective, accurate and useful; all else, and in particular the expression of attitudes or 'politically or socially' oriented contributions, were *interpreted* as not merely biased, but almost irrelevant. Some of the ambiguities of this perspective are nicely captured within George's account of the conferences:

> Some of it's worth reading ... especially the social stuff ... they get on certain themes and crucify the whole thing ... the social spiel I find difficult to believe quite honestly ... they do tend to rabbit on about some mysterious philosopher of yesteryear and to me its just chewing gum for the eyes.

It is important here to note that the devaluation of contributions perceived as non-technical goes beyond the general concern that CMC provides for a poor socializing medium. Instead it reflects more the assumptions of Marcuse (1964) and Habermas (1971) in their various critiques of instrumental or technical reason. It is not just that technology is perceived as neutral but that technology is interpreted as impervious to political control, as unstoppable and deterministic. Thus, since only technical expertise is regarded as sufficiently valuable to form the basis for contributions, and since very few students regard themselves as possessing such expertise, the conferences were left to self-appointed technical experts and CoSy addicts. For Colin, much like the rest, 'the technology is just a tool, its neutral', whereas social arguments were, in Brian's perspective, 'coloured by one's position in life'. Paradoxically, it is this putative neutrality that ensures the need for a more sociological analysis — if the technology is neutral then something else must explain its development in political directions. Furthermore, since technology is perceived as neutral the technological contributions are considered in a Manichean framework: they are either right or wrong, whereas social scientific contributions are either more or less interesting (usually less) but almost never right or wrong. This is a manifestation of a philosophical approach to technology that denies itself: since technology is perceived to be neutral there can be no philosophy of technology; without a philosophy of technology there can be no debate. Technology, rather than actively fostering, let alone determining, greater levels of participation amongst students, appears to be an impediment to it.

Participation is limited, then, because within this particular actor network it is perceived as fundamentally inappropriate to the issue involved. At the level of culture and philosophy students do not participate because participation is regarded as an irrational activity: if technology never lies why argue with it? It might appear a viable system where the substantive issues are not ostensibly technological, but the other facets of the actor network imply that this too is unlikely.

Computers, Modems and Lines

One of these facets relates directly not to the issues involved in the academic debates and but to the links between students and the computer conferences hosted on the mainframes at Milton Keynes. These linkages rely upon telephone lines which are often regarded as not being particularly conductive to the transmission of data signals (rather than voices) because, while distortion in conventional conversation is just a problem, corruption within data signals makes it impossible to read (I shall return to this professed qualitative distinction below). Although regarded as generally primitive, modems were taken to be relatively reliable in transmitting rapid two-way communications. The review undertaken by Mason (1988), based in part upon the survey of 75 per cent of the initially registered students, suggests that 18 per cent of the calls to the OU's help desk were hardware related, while less than half of 1 per cent were related to the modem operation and 59 per cent related to software problems — almost half of which concerned the CMC aspect of the course. Exactly what this represents in terms of the proportion of students involved is difficult to say. Two-thirds never experienced problems with modem operation but only 22 per cent had never experienced problems in logging on to the mainframe (this excluded those who never actually logged on at all — around 8 per cent of the original number). It is also worth noting that the highest proportion of messages within the conferences was almost invariably within the 'Gremlin' section (a specific topic initially restricted to software and hardware bugs etc.) where errors in the documentation rather than software bugs appeared to be the main complaint.

From the interviews it would appear that a considerable degree of concurrence with the survey data exists. Many students complained of similar problems particularly with gaining access to the computer conferences and several bemoaned the 'noise' on the telephone lines which may corrupt data transfers. As I mentioned above, 'noise' on the line during a human conversation makes understanding difficult; 'noise' on the line during a data transmission can make the information difficult to read on the VDU. However, the point at which a connection counts as 'too poor to read' is not something determined by the technology but by the user's interpretation and assessment of the problem. As George remarked: 'you frequently get a touch of garbage here and there'; but the point at which 'a touch' becomes illegible lies within the observer rather than the technology.

The communications software used is the widely adopted Kermit but this is 'front-ended' by a specially written package — OUCOM — which provides for automatic logging on and a menu-based system of commands. The difficulties facing students were usually laid by them at the door of British Telecom, especially BT's somewhat archaic exchanges in certain parts of the area. Ironically, the worst complaints about line 'noise' did not emanate from the areas which actually operated non-digital exchanges but the accounts provided by students suggest such an explanation was popular. However, few of them declined to participate simply because of the problems of accessing the mainframes and Mason (1989, p. 140) suggests that overall no more than around 5 per cent gave up through what they took to be technical problems.

CoSy and the Computer Conferences

Computer conferences are deemed to embody significant advantages over conventional dialogue and one of the most popular lies in the massaging and appropriation of time. The absence of real-time exchanges, as asynchronous conversations and contributions become the norm, is commonly regarded as an advantage of CMC. This facility not only provides for contributions and attention as and when the contributor feels ready, but also ensures that contributions may be considered over time, and therefore become more rational and responsive. Thus, the supporters of CMC claim, a technical system offers up the probability of a more rational social exchange than is possible under conventional systems of face-to-face exchange. But this is to split off the technical from the social aspects of the network and implies, first, that the technical can be objectively altered so that it will have a measurable and objective impact upon the social; second, that the success of the network will be enhanced, or at least remain unaffected, by such change to one aspect of it. In fact, although many interviewees thought CMC's asynchronous components useful for electronic mail, most also considered it debilitating in terms of the spontaneous triggering of ideas associated with synchronous exchanges. In George's terms:

> I think spontaneous comment frequently gets to the root of the thing as opposed to the clinical sanitizing of what you say just in case it upsets somebody ... it's the volatility of conversation that makes it interesting.

Indeed, several students only contributed to conferences if they could do so in real time, either online or by constructing the contribution offline for immediate delivery online. Online response by private line may be extremely expensive if the comments are more than spontaneous, and the combination of time and monetary resources demanded by conference contributions seems to have deterred large-scale use by all but the CoSy addicts and modem sniffers. Furthermore, where students did reply, the constraints of online writing in terms of time, money and the simultaneous acts of typing and thinking merely made an already difficults situation into a near impossible one for many. After all, as Julia argued:

> With face to face you don't have to put your thoughts into words. With CMC you have to write the whole thing out first ... with face to face their response tells you when you can stop.

Thus, although the promoters of the system generally considered it as technically advanced and socially useful the student users tended to define it as awkward and inhibiting. We do not have to argue that one of these two groups is correct and the other incorrect; what is important is the upshot of interpretive assumptions which construct different technologies.

An influential element in the consumption, or rather the misconsumption, of time was the colossal amount of information available through the conference system. The storage and retrieval of contributions in the computer memory which delimits the extent of misinterpretation or missed communications can clearly be of great benefit to many aspects of debate, but this advantage simultaneously leads to the possibility of sensory overload as all opinions are held in the computer memory and the sheer volume of data makes accessing it financially prohibitive and psychologically unnerving. The limited time available to students is further compressed by the quantity and quality of data available within the conferences. Anyone logging on to a conference after the first couple of months is faced with an apparently impossible task of catching up on the items. This, in conjunction with the sheer number of conferences available and the message-copying facilities, provides an enormous barrage of data that the hard pressed students are seldom in a position to overcome. Clearly, computers are not unique in their storage capacities: conventional libraries hold far more information than any mainframe. But any student walking into a library would not expect to read the entire contents during their degree, nor would they walk out of the library just because there happen to be 2000 lines of text to read on any particular topic. Indeed, it is not uncommon for the opposite to occur with students complaining bitterly (and rightly) about the *absence* of material rather than a surfeit. One way to account for this contrast is to reflect upon the interpretive significance of knowledge forms and their linkage into cultural networks. Students have already been taught how to access, use and interpret material held in a conventional library in paper form, but that interpretive acumen is largely absent in regards to electronic forms of information. Now the crucial point here is not how much information actually lies in the conferences but the students' interpretations of the amount. For most there was simply too much, for a minority there was not enough. The problem is exposed by Peter's analogy: 'It's the Pearl Harbour example — lots of information coming in but it's lost in the noise'. Similarly, the conventional library sits squarely at the centre of the educational network of student, teacher, library, lecture hall etc. Such a network does not maintain itself but its maintenance has become an everyday practical accomplishment by the human actors in the network. Yet the network within which electronic information is stored is not nearly so robust nor are most new students accomplished at maintaining it through use.

The perceived trivialization of conferences, and its concomitant wasting of students' scarce resources of time and money, was particularly inappropriate, according to the interviewees, because these bespoiling characteristics are normally associated with face-to-face tutorials. Since face to face tutorials involve considerable travel, time and money to be expended by most OU students, the degeneration of such meetings into what became known as 'rhubarb sessions' was particularly resented. A common explanation for this vegetation rather than stimulation appears to be the cultural requirements for void-filling: the normative patterning of social interactions by which lapses in dialogue are considered as embarrassing silences, pregnant pauses and general collective failure. But within CMC the asynchronous aspect and the invisibility of electronic lurkers ought to ensure that gaps in communications remain unnoticed, or at least camouflaged. In Deborah's words, 'I don't feel obliged to participate because they don't know I'm there do they?'

It is ironic that a primary aim of instigating CMC in the Open University has been to transform the loneliness of the long-distance learner to the intimacy of the electronic campus, yet the common interpretation of the technology by students is one which buttresses the academic communication at the expense of the social communication. The network may have been designed to facilitate student socialization but it ends up being avoided by a majority because of this very activity by a minority. Here, then, is a valuable reminder of the limitations of designer technology, with the users rejecting the 'official' version of the technology and employing their own criteria for use and success.

Others

If a consensus existed as to the technical features of CoSy would this actually lead to greater levels of participation? Well it may do in the conventional assumption that CMC transcends the trials and tribulations of public speaking by making listeners and watchers invisible. As Kiesler *et al.* (1984), Hilz *et al.* (1982), and Mason (1988) note, the absence of conventional interrupting and attention-gaining techniques should facilitate participation by individuals whose limited confidence and skills in verbal exchanges may inhibit their participation.

But there are problems. In the first place, face-to-face contributions for those less troubled by public articulation is an exercise demanding relatively little effort: cultural norms may require continuous dialogue but the norms connote little about the quality of contributions. In contrast, most inter-viewees suggested that before CMC contributions were made a good deal of text construction and content analysis was undertaken. Partly this was due to the cultural associations between written language and linguistic accuracy — the writing of letters, essays and articles was always associated with the slow and serious development of ideas and arguments, not the throwaway remarks and conjectures associated with verbal interchanges. It may be that with greater experience, literacy and CMC contributions become disassoci-ated, such that conferences begin to resemble tape recordings of conventional dialogue, but the transition from formality to informality may be a long and twisting road.

A second aspect of importance was the very essence of this road: not only was the electronic road crooked, it was contextless. In ordinary speech most interviewees expressed the concern common to indexical positions that constant readjustment to statements and important forms of tacit knowledge were built into the communication through the context in which it appeared and through the non-verbal methods and patterns of communication. But CMC messages had neither of these facilities and remained frozen in time and space, and permanently in the public domain; messages therefore had to make explicit as much as possible and to make the content absolutely unambiguous. Since this was regarded as impossible to achieve in reality, and anything approaching the ideal involved considerably more work than any verbal communication, the advantages of invisible messengers did not compensate for the disadvantages. Messages are, for Peter at least, very private things:

> When you're putting a message up its quite personal really, its for
> people you don't know ... and they might think 'what a silly

> so-and-so putting that down'. They don't know where you are — it's slightly irrational really ... when you write letters you're used to composing them — it takes me hours.

In short, rather than technological developments sweeping away the significance of the social it merely facilitated a reconstruction of it in a different dimension.

A related issue, paradoxically perhaps, is the very nature of invisibility. Contributions in face-to-face groups tend to be delivered to known faces and become instantaneously lost. Not so CMC contributions which are posted up on networked computer boards visible to hundreds and perhaps thousands of unknown individuals. Moreover, while contributors can, and frequently do, deny their own verbal contributions on the grounds of mishearing or misunderstanding, the temporal permanence of conference messages means that the apparent invisibility of the messenger is actually silhouetted by the indelibility of the message. Indeed, since the majority of readers will be lurkers, the apparent act of information exchange is generally not reciprocated: a contributor may expose her or himself to public or private criticism without knowing who the critics are, and without them being similarly exposed. As Brian admitted:

> I don't want to make a fool of myself because I don't know enough about social issues ... I still get the glow of embarrassment if I know I've put something up and someone's contradicted me ... I'm very conscious of my spelling — I never was any good — yes you can erase them [messages] but if you don't know it's a mistake in the first place ...

It is, as Kuper (1989) noted, the equivalent of being the only nude bather on a conventional beach. Moreover, the beach remains conventional only to the extent that the bathers reproduce the network that conjoins partly clothed humans with a delimited territory of sea-shore. To close with the analogy, wheeling a changing machine onto the beach may make changing more private — but it also draws attention to the activity within and reinforces the onlookers' assumptions that the inhabitant of the machine is fundamentally afraid of self-exposure. And if the onlookers were to sabotage the actor network by wheeling the newfangled machine into school....

Conclusion

In this paper I have sought to illustrate some of the problems raised by the experiences of Open University students taking the DT200 course. Although rather grandiose claims have been made for the benefits of CMC the reality is considerably more mundane. Information Technology may embody some significant advantages over conventional communications but these are seldom radical, depend on the interpretive action of actors and often buttress the existing unequal participatory patterns rather than undermine them. Participation also depends upon the strength of the particular actor network and a weak link in the network may be critical in undermining participation. This network is not merely the sum of the parts but is an entity which may be regarded as *sui generis*. For human actors within such a network the level of participation is crucially related to its solidity which, in turn, depends upon the durability of the elements which make up the fusion. Such obduracy, however, does not lie within the artefacts themselves but in the significance allocated to the artefact. In short, the success of CMC as a medium for facilitating participation cannot be adequately explained through any of the three orthodox approaches considered at the beginning. Technological determinism suggests that CMC necessarily operates as an electronic bridge and that the very provision of the bridge coerces people into crossing it; the 'failure' of the vast majority of OU students to comply signals the evaporation of this illusion. Social determinism avers that the technology is irrelevant and what really matters are the social processes at work; since CMC is axiomatically dependent upon the satisfactory operations of a very sophisticated technical system this 'black boxing' of the technical systematically ignores what it cannot analyze. Designer technology fails as a solution too: the CoSy system and the computer conferences were designed for one particular mode of operation but employed by students for different, and sometimes opposite, purposes. Finally, I have argued for the utility of the interpretive actor network approach: CMC is a highly contingent system of human and non-human elements that fuse to generate a phenomenon that is greater than the sum of its parts — but exactly what this sum is depends upon the interpretive processes and actions of the participants, not upon any 'objective' account of the actor network. The solution to the problem of participation does not lie with a technical fix, because the notion of a god from the machine is fundamentally flawed: the *deus ex machina* cannot save its disciples because it is not independent of them — it only exists when they ensure its production and reproduction.

Acknowledgments

I would like to thank Brunel University for funding this project and Steve Woolgar, John Beynon and Hughie Mackay for their constructive criticism.

References

BELL, D. (1960) *The End of Ideology*, Glencoe, Ill., The Free Press.
BELL, D. (1973) *The Coming of Post-Industrial Society*, New York, Basic Books.

BIJKER, W.E., HUGHES, T.P. and PINCH, T. (Eds) (1987) *The Social Construction of Technological Systems*, Cambridge, Mass., MIT Press.

BLAUNER, R. (1964) *Alienation and Freedom*, Chicago, Chicago University Press.

BURNHAM, D. (1983) *The Rise of the Computer State*, London, Weidenfeld and Nicholson.

CALLON, M. (1986) 'The sociology of an Actor Network', in CALLON, M., LAW, J. and RIP, A. (Eds) *Mapping the Dynamics of Science and Technology*, London, Macmillan.

CLARK, J., MCLOUGHLIN, I., ROSE, H. and KING, R. (1988) *The Process of Technological Change in the Workplace*, Cambridge, Cambridge University Press.

CLEGG, S.R. (1989) *Frameworks of Power*, London, Sage.

COCKBURN, C. (1983) *Brothers: Male Dominance and Technological Change*, London, Pluto.

COWAN, R. SCHWARTZ (1983) *More Work for Mother*, New York, Basic Books.

CRITTENDEN, W.J. (1988) 'Individualism reconsidered: political theory and contemporary conceptions of the self', DPhil thesis, Oxford.

DAVIS, L.E. and TAYLOR, J.C. (1976) 'Technology, organization and job structure', in DUBIN, R. (Ed.), *Handbook of Work, Organization and Society*, Chicago, McNally.

DENNIS, A.R., GEORGE, J.F., JESSUP, L.M., NUNAMAKER, J.F. and VOGEL, D.R. (1988) 'Information technology to support electronic meetings', MIS Quarterly, December, pp. 591–618.

DEX, S. (1988) *Women's Attitudes towards Work*, London, Macmillan.

DUTTON, W.H. (1988) 'The automation of bias', in the Open University's *An Introduction to Information Technology: Social and Technological Issues*, Milton Keynes, Open University.

FINNEGAN, R. and HEAP, N. (1988) *Information Technology and its Implications*, Milton Keynes, Open University Press.

FREEMAN, C. (1987) 'The case for technological determinism', in FINNEGAN, R. *et al.* (Eds) *Information Technology: Social Issues*, Milton Keynes, Open University Press.

GALLIE, D. (1978) *In Search of the New Working Class*, Cambridge, Cambridge University Press.

GOLDTHORPE, J.H., LOCKWOOD, D., BECHHOFER, F. and PLATT, J. (1968) *The Affluent Worker: Industrial Attitudes and Behaviour*, London, Cambridge University Press.

GOLDTHORPE, J.H., LOCKWOOD, D., BECHHOFER, F. and PLATT, J. (1969) *The Affluent Worker in the Class Structure*, London, Cambridge University Press.

GRINT, K. (1990) *The Sociology of Work: An Introduction*, Cambridge, Polity Press.

HABERMAS, J. (1971) *Knowledge and Human Interests*, London, Heinemann.

HELD, D. (1987) *Models of Democracy*, Cambridge, Polity Press.

HILZ, S.R. *et al.* (1982) *The Effects of Formal Human Leadership and Computer Generated Decision Aids on Problem Solving via a Computer*, New Jersey Institute of Technology.

HUGHES, T. (1979) 'The electrification of America: the systems builders', *Technology and Culture*, Vol. 20, No. 1, pp. 124–62.

KAYE, A. (1989) 'Computer mediated communication and distance education', in

MASON, R. and KAYE, A. (Eds) *Mindweave: Communication, Computers and Distance Education*, Oxford, Pergamon.

KERR, C., DUNLOP, J.T., HARBISON, F.H. and MYERS, C.A. (1964) *Industrialism and Industrial Man*, London, Oxford University Press.

KIESLER, S. *et al.* (1984) 'Social psychological aspects of computer mediated communications', *American Psychologist*, 39, 10.

KUMAR, K. (1978) *Prophecy and Progress: The Sociology of Industrial and Post-Industrial Society*, London, Penguin.

KUPER, A. (1989) Personal communication.

LATOUR, B. (1988) '*The Prince* for machines as well as for machinations', in ELLIOTT, B. (Ed.) *Technology and Social Process*, Edinburgh, Edinburgh University Press.

LAW, J. (1986) 'On the methods of long distance control: vessels, navigation and the Portuguese route to India', in LAW, J. (Ed.) *Power, Action and Belief: A New Sociology of Knowledge?*, Keele, Sociological Review Monograph.

LAW, J. (1988) 'The anatomy of a socio-technical struggle', in ELLIOTT, B. (Ed.) *Technology and Social Process*, Edinburgh, Edinburgh University Press.

LEAVITT, H.J. and WHISLER, T.L. (1958) 'Management in the 1980s', *Harvard Business Review*, 36, pp. 41–8.

LEWIN, K. (1958) 'Group decision and social change', in MACCOBY, E.E., NEWCOMB, T. and HARTLEY, E.I. (Eds) *Readings in Social Psychology*, New York, Holt, Rinehart and Winston.

LIKERT, R. (1961) *New Patterns of Management*, New York, McGraw-Hill.

McNEIL, M. (Ed.) (1987) *Gender and Expertise*, London, Free Association Books.

MACKENZIE, D. and WAJCMAN, J. (Eds) (1985) *The Social Shaping of Technology*, Milton Keynes, Open University Press.

McLOUGHLIN, I. and CLARK, J. (1988) *Technological Change at Work*, Milton Keynes, Open University Press.

MACPHERSON, C.B. (1966) *The Real World of Democracy*, Oxford, Oxford University Press.

MANSBRIDGE, J.J. (1983) *Beyond Adversary Democracy*, Chicago, Chicago University Press.

MARCUSE, H. (1964) *One Dimensional Man*, Boston, Beacon Press.

MARKUS, M.L. and ROBEY, D. (1988) 'Information Technology and organizational change: causal structure in theory and research', *Management Science*, Vol. 34, No. 5, pp. 583–98.

MASON, R. (1988) 'The use of computer-mediated communication for distance education at the Open University', paper presented at the Computer Mediated Communication in Distance Education conference, Milton Keynes, 7–11 October.

MASON, R. (1989) 'An evaluation of CoSy on an Open University course' in MASON, R. and KAYE, A. (Eds) *Mindweave: Communications, Computers and Distance Education*, Oxford, Pergamon.

MASON, R. and KAYE, A. (Eds) (1989) *Mindweave: Communication, Computers and Distance Education*, Oxford, Pergamon Press.

MILL, J.S. (1982) *On Liberty*, Harmondsworth, Penguin.

NOBLE, D.F. (1979) 'Social choice in machine design: the case of automatically controlled machine tools', in ZIMBALIST, A. (Ed.) *Case Studies on the Labor Process*, New York, Monthly Review Press; reprinted in MACKAY, H., YOUNG, M. and BEYNON, J. (Eds) (1991) *Understanding Technology in Education*, Falmer Press.

PFEFFER, J. (1982) *Organizations and Organization Theory*, Marshfield, Mass., Pitman

POOL, I. DE S. (1983) *Technologies of Freedom*, Cambridge, Mass., Belknap Press.

ROBEY, D. (1977) 'Computers and management structures: some empirical findings re-examined', *Human Relations*, Vol. 30, pp. 963–76.

ROSE, H., MCLOUGHLIN, I., KING, R. and CLARK, J. (1986) 'Opening the black box: the relation between technology and work', *New Technology, Work and Employment*, 1 (1), pp. 18–26.

SILVERMAN, D. (1970) *The Theory of Organizations*, London, Heinemann.

SNIDERMAN, P. (1974) *Democratic Theory and Personality*, University of California Press.

TOFFLER, A. (1980) *The Third Wave*, London, Collins.

TRIST, E.L. and BAMFORTH, K.W. (1951) 'Some social and psychological consequences of the Longwall method of coal getting', *Human Relations*, 4 (1), pp. 3–38.

TRIST, E.L., HIGGIN, G.W., MURRAY, H. and POLLOCK, A.B. (1963) *Organizational Choice*, London, Tavistock.

WEBER, M. (1968) *Economy and Society*, University of California Press.

WILKINSON, B. (1983) *The Shopfloor Politics of New Technology*, London, Heinemann.

WINNER, L. (1977) *Autonomous Technology*, Cambridge, Mass., MIT Press.

WINNER, L. (1985) 'Do artifacts have politics?', in MACKENZIE, D. and WAJCMAN, J. (Eds) *The Social Shaping of Technology*, Milton Keynes, Open University Press.

WOOLGAR, S. (1989) 'Stabilization rituals: steps in the socialization of a new machine', paper presented at the PICT conference, Brunel University, May.

WOOLGAR, S. (1990) 'The turn to technology in social studies of science', unpublished paper, CRICT, Brunel University.

Chapter 8

The Purpose of the Computer in the Classroom

Daniel Chandler

This paper advances the theory that whatever educators may intend to do with the computer in the classroom, the computer projects an ideology which may conflict with their purposes. The elements of this ideology are explored in a discussion of three applications commonly found in schools: data-handling systems, simulations and word-processors. From this exploration emerges a practical basis for the conscious choice of appropriate tools for particular purposes. Finally, a tentative research agenda is offered for those who may be interested in pursuing the implications of the central thesis.

Introduction

Since this paper draws attention to many characteristics of computers in a critical spirit it should perhaps be noted at the outset that it is written from the standpoint not of an 'outsider' to the field but of an educational technologist who has been personally involved in the design, development and use of a great deal of computer software. The introductory catalogue which follows has proved to be a severe test of restraint for some readers who are enthusiastic users of computers (which is a pity, since one would like such people to be more tolerant of others' misgivings). Consequently, it should be noted that the intention of this description of the medium is to draw attention to features which *amplify a particular way of knowing*. It is not a denial of the value of such features to anyone who may find them useful for specific purposes. Rather, it is an attempt to provide a basis for the conscious choice of the computer for some purposes and for its rejection for others, on the assumption that if no such choice is made then one way of knowing may limit the exploration of others.

    The idea that the computer may embody an ideology will seem bizarre to many who are used to hearing it described as a 'general-purpose tool'. And teachers who have consciously avoided 'tutorial' programs and favoured the use of 'content-free tools' (such as word-processors and data-handling systems) may feel that these applications are immune to such a criticism. Those who believe in the 'neutrality' of technology argue that the only legitimate target for criticism is the *use* that is made of it: 'it's a bad worker who blames the tools'. We are also 'reminded' that we are not obliged to use the technology: 'you can always turn it off'.

Such arguments presuppose that the technology does not embody priorities which may run contrary to our purpose or subvert our values and that it allows us to choose how we use it. It is these assumptions which will be questioned in order to expose a neglected aspect of the issue of control. It is contended here that computers can never be 'general-purpose' or 'content-free' tools. Using a computer in any application can transform one's intentions according to an in-built but inexplicit ideology. Reflections of this ideology will be identified in a critical discussion of some of the major computer applications found in schools. Since it is argued that this ideology may transcend specific contexts the focus here is not on the ways in which schools use them but on the nature of the applications themselves. This should not, of course, be taken as a denial of the key role of human mediation in particular social and cultural contexts. Indeed, the discussion of the educational implications of the theory will underline the importance of conscious mediation.

The Great Brain Robbery

One application of computers in primary and secondary schools is the use of data-handling systems (often called information retrieval systems or databases, this latter term being more strictly used to refer to a particular set of data). The basic function of such software is to allow users to record items of data, to sort them into various orders, alphabetic and numeric, to search for data matching specified conditions and to display such data in the form of lists or graphs of various kinds. However, data-handling systems also illustrate the computer redefining information.

The Computer Denies the Human Origin of Information

What one does with computer data-handling systems it often loosely referred to as 'information processing' and the technology itself is often described as 'Information Technology'. It is important to insist that *there is no information in computers* (any more than there is in books).[1] Human beings create information by interpreting the evidence of their senses and through negotiating with other human beings. This is no mere semantic quibble; the language of the computer culture threatens to redefine the world in its own terms. Manuals and users talk of 'storing' information on computers and 'retrieving' it from them. Computers, even more than books, masquerade as 'containers' of information and divorce information from human action and a social context, and thus from meaning. They contain only data, which can be transformed into information only through human interpretation. In a human community interpretations are multifarious, so no one interpretation can be absolute: meaning is negotiated through human dircourse. 'Knowledge is humanly constructed over time in culturally specific ways and continually reconstructed as it is communicated to others'.[2] When we detach the knowers from the known we divorce knowledge from community, from history, from wisdom.

The reductionism of data-handling systems has another dimension. The importance accorded to *data* in thinking, learning and human existence is magnified by its storage in large quantities on computers and by the 'authority' of black box technology. Every time data is stored on a computer the value attached to other sources of information is diminished; in this sense, even more than with printed works of reference, computers take information *away* from people.[3] The prerequisites for retrieval are that users must not only be literate; they must also know how to operate the system (though this, of course, is also true of libraries).

We know more than we can say, still less tabulate in a data-handling system (or codify as rules in an 'expert system'). Much of what we know is acquired informally through lived experience and expressed (often unconsciously) in actions rather than words. Data-handling systems undermine the value of that which they cannot record, which is much of our everyday knowledge. They impose constraints upon the kind of data which can be recorded, filtering out all which fails to conform to their structures. Value is ascribed only to that which can be quantified.[4] In short, data-handling systems *distort* information. Furthermore, they produce users who are prepared to tailor their intentions to the program's rules. In his classic study, *Computer Power and Human Reason*, Joseph Weizenbaum goes further: 'When society legitimates only those "data" that are "in one standard format" and that "can easily be told to the machine", then history, memory itself, is annihilated'.[5]

The Computer Redefines the Nature of Thinking

The spread of the use of computer-based data-handling systems encourages the application of computer metaphors to human cognition. This has the effect of leading many people to define thinking and learning as data processing.

A prominent 'information scientist' declares that

> Man is a machine who stores the information he collects and then utilizes the information to behave in an intelligent way. His senses — eyes, ears, etc. — collect the information in the first place, and in his brain he has what is in effect a vast filing system in which he stores

the information collected, in a complicated cross-indexed fashion. It is like a huge reference library, and in it he is told where to get what information he needs in the outside world.[6]

This is a denial of human creativity. 'Reality', as John Lennon once said, 'leaves a lot to the imagination'. Thought and memory are not data processing but the building and rebuilding of models of the world. Perception and learning are not passive data capture, but the interpretation and elaboration of information according to changing hypotheses. Contemporary reading theory, for example, has helped us to realize that when we read a page we engage in the active *construction* of meaning.[7]

The brain is now commonly described as being like a computer. There has always been a tendency for those studying the brain to employ metaphors from currently fashionable technologies. The Greeks spoke of the brain as being like a catapult; Leibniz described it as a mill. Freud had a steam-engine model of the brain in which urges rushed through it, with dreams acting as a safety valve. Others described it as a telegraph sytem; later it was seen as an automatic telephone exchange. A push-button interpretation of human behaviour dominates behaviourist psychology, and the computer is now an integral part of the imagery of contemporary cognitive psychologists. None of these mechanistic metaphors have done justice to the humanness of being human.[8] A far more positive metaphor is that of the brain as a creative artist.[9] An emphasis on data handling underestimates the importance of ideas: we create ideas; computers can't.[10]

In order to support the needs of the machine we are encouraged to behave like computers ourselves. Data-handling systems promote the collection of 'facts' rather than the generation of ideas. One often hears that computers can take over the 'mechanical' element in a task, 'leaving users free' to concentrate on using their imagination. This is seductive propaganda. One is 'free' only within the framework which the computer legitimates. When one 'interrogates' an existing database, the nature of the system favours hypotheses about patterns in the data rather than about the original choice and formulation of data and the structure into which it has been fitted. At best data-handling systems allow the exercise of the theory-making intellect. There is far more to the human imagination than this.

Data-handling systems *defy interpretation*, since certain kinds of questions are explicitly vetoed. If a question cannot be formed in the language available it will not be answered. These are not questions in any human sense; they are polite requests. Computer professionals may answer this criticism by saying that 'intelligent' systems can handle any question one may choose to ask. Such systems are programmed to accept a wide range of alternative ways of expressing a range of questions. This may make it easier to ask the permitted questions but it can never make possible anything like human discourse. In a data-handling system there is only one answer to any question. Plato stated the fundamental objection (though he was thinking of another

technology — that of written words): 'You might suppose that they understand what they are saying, but if you ask them what they mean by anything
they simply return the same answer over and over again'.[11] These systems
understand nothing: they manipulate data without regard to meaning. The
greatest danger here is that the continuing development of 'natural language
interfaces' may delude us into thinking that a question is truly understood
and that the data 'retrieved' constitutes an adequate answer, when in fact the
question has been imperfectly matched.

A data-handling system offers rewards only for those who agree to play
by its rules and accept its judgments.[12] And as Weizenbaum puts it,

> a computing system that permits the asking of only certain kinds of
> questions, that accepts only certain kinds of 'data', and that cannot
> even in principle be understood by those who rely on it, such a
> computing system has effectively closed many doors that were open
> before it was installed.[13]

The Computer Promotes the Notion of its own Objectivity

All this has the effect of *deifying* data in the computer: the increasing use of
the computer as a medium for storing data and the mystique associated with
its use often leads to the unconscious assumption that it possesses even more
authority than was formerly accorded to the printed word. Each database
tends to convey the impression that it constitutes the best, most comprehensive way of representing available data on that topic. And, as we have seen,
fundamental questioning of such assumptions is not encouraged. The computer culture propagates the phrase, 'garbage in, garbage out', which is to say
that the source of all blame for inadequate data is human. We should do
better to remember that data is *no more reliable* for its storage on a computer,
refusing to subscribe to the subliminal message of 'garbage in, *gospel* out'.

The sources of data are not usually an integral part of a data-handling
system. The lack of emphasis on attribution gives it an air of disinterest, an
impression of neutrality and 'objectivity'.[14] Data is standardized; the hallmark
of the database is an impressive consistency. In fact, this consistency may be
misleading: a result of the tailoring of data to its constraints. A database
conveys the impression that each item is of equal importance and that each
entry was recorded with equal certainty: there is no indication of its author's
perception of its relative status. Unlike a book, it does not usually tell us how
the data was acquired or how it might be verified. It is detached from any
methodology of data collection, from the context of the purposes it was
originally intended to serve, in short from the history of its construction.
Data-handling systems are described as 'general-purpose tools', but we must
remember that all data is collected for a purpose and realize that the purpose
may be subtly embedded in a database. As Goethe put it, 'everything factual

is already theory'. The storage of data in a computer obscures the relativism of the perspective it represents.

Data-handling systems defy challenge. The computer is universal in its scope, absolute in its answers, raising itself above the level of human subjectivity. Phenomena are denatured and data are reified. The computer projects 'objectivity' as *the* way of knowing, and it offers a model of what it requires of us: following repeatable procedures without distraction or involvement. Users must cultivate the practice of deliberate 'distancing'. With a data-handling system we stand back, compare and contrast what it frames. We are not involved. The neutral, impersonal stance requires us to look through dead eyes. Data-handling systems remove the *life* from information.

The Database is Atomistic

Data processing fragments the known. Phenomena are *dis*integrated: broken into discrete bits. In storing data on a computer one engages in deconstruction: splitting things into irreducible categories, defining and labelling them, putting them into boxes. Boxes are for bones: the data they contain are the dead remains of lived experience. Reduced to parts, the meaning of the whole is lost. We are left to regard the phenomenon as *nothing but* what our data-collection has reduced it to: that which can be observed, abstracted, measured and rearranged according to rational rules. In sorting and interrogating a database one specifies, stuctures, dissects and analyzes. And the answers to one's questions are 'ordered' lists and graduated charts abstracted far from the rich stew of human perception. Whatever the limitations of the book, at least data in books is usually embedded: its extrication requires us to be conscious of the context in which it was found, and because the author's purposes may differ from the reader's it may also stimulate serendipitous ideas. In a database data is decontextualized. Data processing prohibits a holistic perspective: databases can only segment, whilst we as humans must *connect*, connecting, as the novelist Ursula LeGuin puts it, 'idea with value, sensation with intuition, cortex with cerebellum'.[15]

Context-Free Living

Computer-based simulation is a technique widely used in curricular applications, although the term is very broad and may include:

(a) scientific simulation, the use of predefined mathematical models of dynamic phenomena in which users may alter specific variables in order to see how this affects the behaviour of the model;

(b) simulation gaming, playing decision-making games within the context of predefined models of social phenomena, allowing players to observe the effects of their decisions on the behaviour of the model;

(c) role-play games, in which the computer acts primarily as a management tool, an application most common in primary schools;

(d) formal modelling, the creation and testing of mathematical models of scientific and social phenomena, a rare application at the school level.

For the sake of simplicity, we shall confine our attention to what is defined here as simulation gaming. Simulation gaming can be found at the upper primary level and, most commonly, in history, geography, English and Social Studies at the secondary level. Computer-based simulation gaming also harbours elements of an ideology.

Computer Simulation Denies the World

A computer-based simulation reduces rich, physical, sensory experiences to cold, abstract visual analogues. It may not be unresponsive to external human intervention, but it remains far removed from the existential context of the human experience it is intended to represent. A computer simulation of life in a slum or ghetto may lead its users to think they 'know' what living in such places is like. Such simulations redefine experience so that human relations become peripheral rather than central; experience is that which is generalizable rather than that which is immediate, local, personal.

Many computer simulations operate in 'real time', which is to say they project an impression of time passing in their own world at the same rate as we measure it in ours, but they are cut off in space as well as time from the known world. Computer-based simulations are self-contained, requiring no reference to an externally observable world. Computer simulations reward users who turn away from the world, joining them in the land of the context-free.

Computer Simulation Mechanizes Experience

Any computer-based simulations of social phenomena is ultimately built upon a mathematical or rule-based model, whether the subject is passenger behaviour in an urban transport system or crossing the USA by covered wagon in 1847.[16] All computer simulations are, at least, built upon the assumption that it is possible to build some kind of formal model of the phenomenon. Since a map cannot be the terrain, simplification is inevitable, but more critically, in a computer simulation the world is viewed as a machine.

The mechanization even extends to those using the computer. Whilst neither knowing nor caring where it is, the computer transforms those using it (and, in the case of group use, relationships) into one of its own mechanisms: social interaction at best consists of intellectual collaboration in abstract technical problem-solving. The only choices users are offered are those legitimized by the machine.

Computer-based simulations do not tell us what is missing. Marcuse tells us:

> The quantification of nature, which led to its explication in terms of mathematical structures, separated reality from all inherent ends, and consequently, separated the true from the good, science from ethics.... And no matter how constitutive may be the role of the subject as point of observation, measurement, and calculation, this subject cannot play its scientific role as ethical or aesthetic or political agent.[17]

Critics may argue that simulations at their best are typically produced by interdisciplinary teams, drawing on expertise in the fields of mathematics, psychology, sociology, business, government and so on. But where are the poets, artists, mystics nad revolutionaries? Whatever the subject, computer simulations can only be asocial, ahistorical, amoral: technological rationalism is imposed on the world of human relations.

Quantification and clear-cut 'rules' of causality enable social life to be portrayed as if it is objective and fixed. This objectivist view of knowledge presents it as data to be transmitted and received. It admits neither to the subjectivist view in which knowledge is a private construct of individual perception nor to the perspectivist view in which 'reality is socially constructed'.[18] Computer simulations cannot be anything more than plausible, subjective and debatable models of the interaction of the chosen variables within the context of the evidence selected by the designers. Such simulations are at the same time based on assumptions which are difficult to question because of their invisibility. Even where the underlying model can be inspected, its complexity may hide assumptions of which even its creators may not have been conscious.[19]

Artificial Writing

The word-processor, of course, allows the typing, editing and printing of text. The print produced is comparable to that produced on a conventional typewriter by a competent typist or to that of a printed book, depending on the type of printer connected to the computer. Word-processors are widely used in both primary and secondary schools. A neglected dimension of the word-processor, however, is that it contains a view of what writing is about.

Word-Processing is Celebration of Form versus Meaning

One of the great attractions of writing with a word-processor is that the writing always looks neat and tidy. The impression of tidiness is so great that a text may look 'finished' before it is. It may look so finished that one does not in fact reread it closely at all. The 'and and' typo is a minor symptom of this phenomenon; lacunae are just as likely. As one perceptive 10-year-old observed, 'the computer makes my writing look better than it is'. There is no indication of the status of the text — whether it is a first draft, a revised draft or a final draft. Whatever stage it represents, the text appears equally neat and finished.

On the other hand, editing is far easier than with pen and paper or a conventional typewriter. It is so easy to change one's words that it is sometimes difficult not to change them: words and sentences can develop an urgent and irresistible itch to be scratched.[20] The habitual use of the word-processor may make users feel that writing must always be polished. Writing done with a word-processor can easily lose any freshness or spontaneity, becoming a 'composition'.[21]

A letter is not written on a word-processor, it is manufactured, constructed. Letters can become lies. It is not just in commercial contexts that the word-processor is used to produce 'tailored' letters: academic and personal circulars are mushrooming, 'personalized' but effectively mechanizing the relationship between senders and recipients. Academic books and papers are not written on a word-processor, they are, all too often, recycled.

Weizenbaum, a professor at MIT, comments on a recent phenomenon in American universities:

> We increasingly receive 'papers' from our students that literally have no author. Various student groups, e.g. fraternities, keep files of all sorts of texts, very roughly classified and indexed, on computers, and students then 'write papers' by invoking programs that patch fragments of texts, selected on the basis of a few keywords, together, format the result neatly and present it as their work.... [This] is then stored as a sourcefile and made to become another fragment.[22]

The screen itself fragments text, offering the writer a limited window through which to view it. As one journalist put it, 'it's difficult to get a shape unless you see it in front of you. There isn't room on the screen for a beginning, a middle and an end'.[23] Although it is true that the whole text can be printed out, doing so each time on wants to review the overall shape of the text in its current form is a major interruption (and a waste of paper). Consequently, for most of the time, the reviewing of text is conducted through the screen. Several pages, continuous or discontinuous, cannot be viewed at once as they can with loose-leaf paper or cards. It is true that many professional systems offer 'windows', which allow users to display several pieces of text at once in framed areas on the same screen. The size and position of these windows can be adjusted, and windows can be overlapped. However, the ultimate limitation is the size of the screen itself (or more strictly the screen resolution: the maximum number of pixels, or light points, which it can display, horizontally and vertically). Spreading pages across a desk or floor in any arrangement is a far more flexible strategy than reviewing text on the screen even with 'windows'.

It is all too easy when using a word-processor to become obsessed with surface features rather than with developing an argument or conveying an experience (a widely observed phenomenon which Allan Collins calls 'downsliding').[24] It is easier to change a word or edit a sentence than to introduce radical structural changes, rearranging large chunks of text. Hence, a spelling may be corrected or a phrase beautified whilst the argument stagnates.[25]

Word-Processing Requires Unambiguous Commitment

The word-processor makes it possible for writers to jump more quickly and easily into print than ever before. This brings to writing the limitations as well as the advantages of the printed word. On the screen editing need never be finished, so it can be frustrating to commit the text to the printed page.

But even on the screen drafting is very different from writing by hand. With pen and paper, one can cross things out without losing them forever. One cannot cross things out in this way on a word-processor. It is a medium intolerant of ambiguity: either one is prepared to commit oneself to that formulation of words or one does not include it. Of course we can print out successive drafts when we use a word processor, but the bigger the document, the longer it takes and the more disincentive there is to do it very often. And there is no easy way to spot the changes which have been made, whereas a handwritten draft retains its crossings out and can easily incorporate arrows and annotations. We can backtrack when we reach an apparent cul-de-sac in our thinking. As I have writen elsewhere, 'Sometimes when we write ... we need a map of the routes we did not choose as well as the one we did. My scribblings are more useful to me as maps than successive drafts on a word-processor. Writing done with a word-processor *obscures its own evolution*'.[26] Whilst it is true that for some writers, for some writing, this might not be a disadvantage, for others it would certainly be an unattractive feature. The poet Philip Larkin developed drafts of his poems in notebooks: in the space of thirty pages or so there might be as many as nine drafts of the same poem and his final version might resurrect lines which had existed in much earlier versions.

Word-Processing Involves the Suppression of the Unconscious and our Sense of Self

Writing with a word-processor is a far more conscious act than writing with a pen. You must switch it on, find a disc (which may need to be formatted), set margins, adjust default settings as necessary, and, while typing, remember all its rules and language for moving around the text, deletion, insertion and copying, formatting, saving, loading and cataloguing.[27] This is inevitably a constraint on individual styles and strategies. A woman on the Pill commented that she felt 'managed' by it: likewise, some of us as writers can feel managed by the word-processor, our rhythms disrupted and reorganized with unknown consequences. When one uses a word-processor, technique can become more important than truth to feeling.

Of course all writing, as opposed to talk, is 'unnatural' in that it has to be deliberately learned. But writing with a word-processor (as with a typewriter) the printing of text, and from the earliest introduction of print this has been *felt* to be 'artificial writing'.[28] The word-processor — like the typewriter — denies the expression of mood by physical manipulation. Handwriting expresses something of ourselves beyond the mere words. It conveys subtle nuances of feeling and changes of mind. A personal letter written (in anything other than a hurried scrawl) by someone with a range of tools to choose from, can also reflect loving care. The word-processor may also threaten an unconscious mode of learning: it is impossible to specify how much of what we have formally learnt has been absorbed through the guiding of the pen by hand. These effects may mean that for those of us to whom handwriting has been important the word-processor may even threaten our sense of self.

Individual style is also threatened by 'spelling checkers' and 'style checkers'. These are increasingly being provided as standard elements of word-processing software. Spelling checkers bring to the attention of the writer any words in the text which are not in the in-built dictionary and offer the writer the options of adding them to the dictionary, correcting them or leaving them as they are. Style checkers attempt to apply guidelines found in manuals of written style and alert the writer to potential errors and infelicities.

A style checker was used to examine an article by Bernard Levin in *The Times* commemorating the Kennedy assassination. In 1300 words, there were supposedly thirty-nine sexist references, twenty-eight confused words, fifteen redundancies, and eighteen passive verbs.

> That extraordinary number of confused words ... turns out not to mean that at all. What the programmers have built in is a loop which finds words capable of *being* confused and flagging them ... Mr Levin is given a hard time for sexist references. One is because the enjoins his readers to remember that John Kennedy 'was a Boston Irishman', which is probably racist and townist as well.... His

article opened with the seemingly impeccable sentence 'We all know where we were when President Kennedy was shot'. *Style Writer* immediately flagged the last two words. 'Was shot,' it said, '— prefer active verbs'. Now that is one theory no one has advanced. Do you know where you were when President Kennedy, the Irish hermaphrodite, shot himself?[29]

Whatever the usefulness of style checkers and spelling checkers to those who may submit their text to them, they represent a celebration of 'correctness' and standardization. Anyone who objects to such facilities may be told that one is not obliged to use them, but their very presence elevates mechanical precision to a primary goal in writing. Style checkers offer judgment without understanding, based on whatever guidelines about style could be easily codified as rules with no regard to meaning. They are crude parodies of bad teachers, a mockery of any serious reflection on style, and a discouragement of the development of individual styles. And yet their presence on the computer gives them authority for many users who have been schooled into self-conscious anxiety regarding their capabilities in writing.[30]

The Elements of an Ideology

It may be objected that all of the examples chosen here are applications, many implementations of which are limited by the state of current technology or design. Programming is not examined here because it is typically learnt for its own sake rather than used by students as a tool in tackling other problems, at least in secondary schools. However, it is often argued that computers can be programmed to behave in whatever way we are able to specify, with the implication that any criticism can be met. This neglects the possibility that programming itself embodies an inescapable ideology. Perhaps at the root of the problem is the fact that computer languages cannot tolerate ambiguity, whilst for human beings, as Bolter puts it, 'there are times when being ambiguous conveys exactly the right sense'.[31]

In attempting to express an idea we often need to sidle up on what we mean. In speech we may make several attempts at shepherding words and listeners towards an area which only we are aware of. In writing we may use similes, metaphors and symbols where plain words do not capture what we are trying to convey. But all this is far from the 'language' of computers, in which there is no place for emotion, intuition, imagination, mystery, the unconscious, humour, sensuality, social interaction, values or meaning.

Let us, however, reflect on the ideological elements which have emerged in the discussion of applications. We have seen from databases that the human origin of information is denied, that thinkng is redefined as data processing, that the computer is put forward as an 'objective' tool, and that the parts are more important than the whole. From simulations we note the denial of the world and the mechanization of experience. And finally, the word-processor reduces human expression to a celebration of form versus meaning, requires our unambiguous commitment, and suppresses the unconscious and our sense of self. It is contended here that all of these messages can be found in any version of the applications which have been examined here, though the precise formulations we may apply to them will differ from observer to observer. It is also suggested that some of them will be found in *any* computer application.

Can these elements be regarded as representing an ideology, neutrally defined as a system of ideas? In that the elements are interrelated and not inconsistent with each other then surely they can. This does not involve a conspiracy thesis: it need not be argued that any group consciously shapes computer applications to promote its ideological ends. Neither is it critical to the argument what we choose to call the ideology, though it should be no surprise that it is entirely consistent with behaviourism. What matters is that it is powerful, invisible and largely unrecognized.

No technology is neutral; the computer is no more neutral than the atomic bomb. Once created we cannot simply 'turn them off'. They shape our purposes. Jacques Ellul's important analysis of 'the technological society' is profoundly pessimistic. 'Technique', for Ellul, includes both mechanical technology and technical values. His view is that technique has reduced man to a mere catalyst. 'Better still, he resembles a slug inserted into a slot machine: he starts the operation without participating in it'.[32] Considering the objection that 'it is not the technique that is wrong, but the use men make of it', he argues that 'technique is a means with a set of rules for the game. It is a "method of being used" which is unique and not open to arbitrary choice. Technique is a use. The individual is faced with an exclusive choice, either to use the technique as it should be used according to the technical rules, or not to use it at all'.[33] If Ellul is not to be proved justified in his pessimism, we must challenge technocratic values and choose only tools and techniques which support our ethical, social and political priorities.

A Convergence of Ideologies

Some of the features of the computer which have been explored here are also characteristic of writing or the book. A key dimension of the computer is the way in which it builds on other technologies of literacy.[34] It intensifies their qualities and elevates their importance. In so doing the danger is that it will further devalue other ways of knowing: in particular, personal experience, oral discourse and the wisdom of the community.[35] This narrowing of knowing is increased by the computer's embodiment of a nineteenth-century emphasis on objective knowledge.[36] These effects have important implications for the way our children learn. Schools have always embraced technologies of literacy, the educational value of which is incontestable. But schooling was responsible for the transformation of knowledge into book-learning, and before the computer takes us one stage further, it is surely timely to reconsider the rich variety of paths to knowledge.

In the context of computer use in education a critical issue is the convergence of the ideologies of the computer and of government educational policies which emphasize 'the Basics', notably in the UK at the present, where a National Curriculum is being imposed on the schools. As Neil Postman has suggested, 'advocates of the "basics" are ... technocrats of the deepest commitment'.[37] 'The Basics' are those subjects which arise from digital symbolism — reading, writing and arithmetic — and as such their mastery is deemed to be quantifiable.[38] By concentrating on the mastery of technical skills we avoid reflection on their purpose or the consideration of other priorities, other ways of knowing.

It is a technocratic goal that everyone should be taught the same thing at the same stage and judged by the same 'precise and objective' measures. The imposition of a national curriculum requires a hierarchical structure of knowledge and the definition of objectives which can be specified in advance, taught to, and then assessed. Grading becomes an end in itself. Indeed it becomes the primary goal: what can be measured dominates what can be taught. Subtlety, ambiguity, imaginative creativity — in short, all that which is most human, which 'does not compute' — is outlawed. Where 'output' is quantified teachers must actively struggle to ensure that learning does not become reduced to data capture, that thinking is not seen as data processing, and that writing and reading — of any kind — is not treated as data storage, transmission and retrieval. A British School inspector commented that he could no longer tell teachers to trust their intuition because now they must follow the National Curriculum. The purpose of education in a national curriculum is defined by the instruments available to quantify learning, and procedure comes to be more important than purpose. Tht is educational technocracy: the rule of the technicians, for whom the computer is an ideal tool. So we should not be surprised that the use of so-called 'Information Technology' has been written into the requirements throughout the National Curriculum in the UK.

Ellul argues that 'technique constructs the kind of world the machine needs'.[39] If this is so and we do not exercise our critical consciousness the computer will shape schools and classrooms into a form which makes its own presence a *sine qua non*. The fact that this technology is supportive of particular techniques does not validate them: *can* should not mean *ought*. But as Jacques Soustelle said of the atomic bomb, 'since it was possible, it was necessary'.[40]

Postman puts it nicely: 'Tests, computers, machines, *and* governments share this propensity. They always end up controlling more ground than one imagines had been given to them'.[41]

Positive Discrimination

The computer is a polarizing technology: in its context we seem destined to be categorized as devotees or luddites, forbidden to be critical without rejecting it outright. There need be no contradiction in being both involved in using technology and at the same time being unwilling to suspend one's critical faculties. We need only remember McLuhan's dictum that 'we are all robots when uncritically involved with our technologies'.[42]

The message of this chapter for classroom teachers is *not* that they should reject the computer as a resource. Indeed, schools have a responsibility to introduce students to a wide range of tools in the context of appropriate purposes. The computer may have a useful role to play in the classroom, including in applications such as those discussed here. Without doubt the computer offers an effective technique for certain clearly-defined tasks, although the issue of 'technological fixes' for deeper problems in education needs separate examination.[43] As Weizenbaum observes, 'the problems facing schools and educators everywhere are personal, political, financial and spiritual. These will not be solved merely by putting more terminals and video screens into the classroom'.[44]

What is vital is that, when using a computer, teachers should consider carefully both their own educational purposes and the underlying ideology of the computer tool they intend to use, in order to determine whether these purposes may be in conflict. A teacher's use of a simulation is an implicit validation of the model for the students. And the more apparently 'content-free' the application, the greater the danger that users will not be conscious of it representing a purpose other than their own, so teachers also need to help students to learn how to make their own well-informed judgments about the suitability of the tool to their purposes.

If you are a teacher try listing some of your own educational ideas relating to the nature and importance of these issues in your teaching:

- information;
- thinking;
- objectivity and subjectivity;
- holism and analysis;
- personal experience;
- values;
- meaning and technique;
- doubt and certainty;
- individual learning styles.

Next turn to the following list which is intended to represent the *inverse* of the elements of the ideology which we have been examining. Consider how this list relates to your own. Whilst it is not intended to suggest that educational priorities can be adequately defined by simply negating the hidden curriculum of the computer, contrary to its ideology classrooms should surely at least be places in which:

- information and meaning should be generated through negotiation rather than collected as data;
- creative ideas should be encouraged;
- there should be an awareness of the subjective nature of ideas and interpretation should be important;
- approaches should be holistic rather than atomistic;
- learning should spring primarily from lived experience;
- ethical, social and political issues should be discussed;
- meaning should be regarded as more important than technique;
- a questioning attitude and an awareness of relativism should be encouraged;
- individual styles and strategies should be supported.

If such priorities flourish in a classroom then the computer may be a tameable resource. The computer is a tool which formalizes and systematizes whatever you choose to do with it. There are special occasions in education when this may be precisely what we want to do. A few of these are considered below.

Data-Handling Systems

In order to illustrate broad educational aims in using data-handling systems we turn to the views of a respected practitioner:

> Information-handling skill are not limited to the technical abilities of using a data-file. The ability to make and test hypotheses about information, to create logical enquiries that will sort and classify information so that a conclusion can be drawn, to recognize that categories are artificial constructs we make to aid our understanding, and not rigid divisions made by others: these are more important skills. They are not skills that can only be learned with a microcomputer; the microcomputer is no more than a sophisticated aid to their acquisition. But with the speed, accuracy and power of a micro and a good data-handling program, much more can be achieved in terms of real learning by children.[45]

Data-handling systems may be handy tools with which students may occasionally choose to pursue their own investigations. With a database it is certainly possible to hypothesize about patterns in the data, which is useful when the quantity of data involved is substantial. As the late John Holt put it, 'it is a good substitute for a card file if, but only if, people want to use that file to get out many different kinds of information, information that fits into many kinds of categories'.[46] Priority must, however, be given to generating ideas rather than collecting and reformulating data. And whilst the computer may be a useful tool in the development of classificatory thinking[47] it should not lead to an overemphasis on such modes of thinking. Students also need to be taught to question the source and authority of computer-based data, be conscious of the specific purpose for which the data was collected, consider the adequacy of the categories used and be conscious of distortion and of what is missing. It is the responsibility of the teacher to ensure that students are aware of the limitations of data-handling systems and choose them only when they are appropriate to their needs.

Here is not the place to explore the characteristics of other resources for exploring information, but we should remember, of course, that they include reference books, card-indexes, filling cabinets, personal maps, charts and diagrams, and, above all, *people*.

Simulations

Regarding the use of computer-based simulations in the Humanities in schools, a publication from the Historical Association comments:

> On advantage of the medium is that it captures attention and arouses interest and enthusiasm. This is at least in part attributable to the fact that the pupil is interested to discover what consequences flow from his own decisions. As had been said, this is particularly attractive where the nuts and bolts of the process are hidden inside the black box. In taking decisions and observing the consequences the student is in fact manipulating the model and discovering its properties — an educationally sound way of learning. The computer provides the unique facility of enabling the simulation designer to hide all or part of the rules in the black box, so that they are only discovered as the game progresses. For example, the promoters of early railways will not know until they will attract from each town. In contrast, it is difficult (though not impossible) to arrange a manual simulation where players do not need to know all the rules in order to play — unless the teacher has to intervene in particular stages, which might involve a considerable burden of supervision.[48]

Computer simulations may sometimes be useful as dynamic illustrations of hypothetical models of social phenomena which cannot readily be under-stood in other ways. It is perphaps both the special usefulness and the fundamental limitation of such simulations that they can give plasticity to theories. A computer-based simulation may be useful in throwing light on the *theory* being presented but it does not illustrate the phenomenon itself. Wherever possible, therefore, students should combine their use of the simulation with direct experience of at least some aspects of the real situation. They might, for instance, use a simulation of an urban bus system, but they should never do so without also being encouraged to draw on their own experience, talking to other passengers and visiting bus companies. It is also essential that the invisible assumptions of the model on which the simulation is built are laid bare and openly questioned: users should always consider what is left out.[49] The ethical and social implications of students' actions within its framework also need to be fully discussed. It is also too easy in a simulation game in which one runs a bus company to ignore the needs of passengers on unprofitable routes, to keep wages low and to fire staff at the touch of a button.[50] These caveats emphasize the importance of the teacher's role when such simulations are used.

We can, of course, use simulation to good effect in the classroom without a computer. Other resources include drama, role-play, active investigation, printed case studies, film and video and board games: each with their own advantages and disadvantages for particular purposes.

Word-Processors

A leading exponent outlines his view of the educational advantages of the word-processor:

> Word processing takes over much of the mechanical operation in-
> volved in the writing process and allows writers to concentrate on the
> thoughts, the semantics, behind the words.... There is a prevalent
> desire among teachers of the language arts to separate the writing
> process from the product. A word processor can encourage this
> distinction, allowing pupils to draft and redraft their work effortlessly
> and then to produce a variety of versions in hard copy for circulation
> and comment.... The neatness of a final draft from a printer
> can be an incentive towards mechanical precision in syntax and
> spelling....[51]

The word-processor may be useful for writers when (and if) they want to formalize and circulate a piece of writing. It may also suit some as a convenient redrafting tool for certain kinds of extended writing. Such writers may well find them helpful in supporting their work on a text over a long period of time, an opportunity from which many students would benefit. Others may consider it useful on those occasions when they are becoming frustrated with being unable to read their own handwriting. It may not be a suitable tool for writers whose style or purpose involves the subordination of technique to the exercise of the unconscious. Many writers feel that it does not suit them — at least in the early stages of drafting — for 'creative writing'.

Once again, the teacher's role is vital in helping writers to choose tools appropriate to their needs and supporting them in using these tools sensitively, with regard to disadvantages as well as to advantages. Students will, of course, use pencils, pens, and notebooks, and hopefully also typewriters, loose-leaf paper and cards, whiteboards or blackboards, overhead projectors, carbon paper, photocopiers and duplicating machines.[52]

These educational uses of the three applications discussed are occasional. However, if the classroom is a room full of computers, as Seymour Papert has argued it should be, how far can we make any real choice or hope for other ideologies to prevail? This is a particularly disturbing thought when one considers that even now in many British secondary schools, students go to 'computer rooms' to use computers.

No Cause for Concern?

We have seen that data-handling systems, simulations and word-processors embody hidden assumptions about such concepts as information, society and writing and that the computer amplifies the importance of 'objectivity' at the expense of that which cannot be measured. However, even those who accept that there may be some truth in this perspective may well feel that no teachers worthy of the name would allow this ideology to subvert their educational values and priorities. Certainly there are many teachers whose use of computers is imaginative and sensitive. Several humane strategies spring to mind:

(a) **Group use** British schools pioneered the use of computer programs with small groups of students, focusing on the value of the *discussion* which takes place

(b) **Restricted role** It is in the primary schools that one is most likely to see the use of software as a springboard for a wide variety of activities *away from the keyboard*.

(c) **Decentralized provision** Some schools have consciously avoided having separate rooms full of computers, which helps to counteract the notion that the computer is 'special'.

Such strategies reflect a genuine desire to keep the computer in its place, but we should still ask whether activities are being *built around* the computer rather than it being chosen when it meets a need, particularly when there is such pressure to 'integrate' the computer into all areas of the curriculum and to extend its usage by the youngest children in our schools. When teachers use computer software and teach 'thinking skills' such as hypothesis testing, inductive reasoning and problem solving, are they doing so because they are the appropriate educational priorities or because they are what the computer software exemplifies (or requires)? On what educational grounds are computers being used by children in infant classes, where informal social and kinaesthetic learning have traditionally been at the heart of education?

At times the computer appears to be, as the saying goes, a solution in search of a problem. Some educators are undoubtedly seduced by the ingenuity of particular applications. Even Papert's *Mindstorms*, which is regarded as advocating liberating uses of computers in education, presents an example of 'computer poetry' which suggests, as Theodore Roszak has recently commented, that 'creating literature is nothing but filtering vocabulary through linguistic formulas'.[53] This is pure behaviourism: it was the psychologist J.B. Watson who wrote in 1925, 'One natural question often raised is, how do we ever get new verbal creations such as a poem or a brilliant essay? The answer is that we get them by manipulating words, shifting them about until a new pattern is hit upon...'.[54] Only a man who saw himself as a machine could have writtren these words. It is true that the computer makes possible some things which are difficult or even impossible to do without it, and we do need to see a variety of applications before we are aware of what these features are. However, we must always make our first priority what is *worth* doing with the computer rather than what it can do.

The subtlety of computer ideology is such that even talented and experienced teachers may not always be aware of it. They cannot fight what they cannot see. How often does one see the kind of perspective explored in this paper reflected elsewhere in print? Teachers are naturally unlikely to find much sign of it in the manuals which accompany the software they use; at least cigarettes carry a health warning. Many well-meaning educators seek to treat the computer as an 'ordinary' tool like a book or a pen. In the sense that it should not be treated as 'better' than other tools this might seem a helpful corrective, but as we have seen, to regard it as a tool like any other is a dangerous delusion. For other teachers, at a time of low morale in schools, it may seem attractive to use computer-based materials which may appear to require minimal teacher intervention.

Only teachers fully aware of the hidden message of the computer can attempt to counteract them. And their task is not easy. It is not merely a question of keeping the computer in its place, choosing it when it is an appropriate tool and using each application critically as well as imaginatively. Teachers must also develop approaches conveying messages at least as potent as those of the computer, to overcome the myth of 'objective knowledge' by stressing the negotiation of meaning, the generation of ideas, the subjective nature of facts, holistic learning, the primacy of experience, the value of everyday knowledge, truth to feeling, the value of ambivalence, and a sense of self. We must subordinate the computer to the rich diversity of human experience rather than allowing its use to amplify only those aspects of experience which conform to its ideology.

The consequential cost of using computers may be too great if they displace other priorities, and if all users are not conscious of at least the potential for hidden messages and able to make real choices when and how to use the technology. The criticisms expressed here cannot be met by designing new tools (although there may be lessons for design) or by simply changing the ways in which they are used. They can be met only if we change the ways in which tools are *chosen*.[55]

A Research Agenda

This paper has offered a theory; it has not attempted to prove it. The central argument inevitably reflects personal values and is not easily susceptible to proof, but it would appear to be rich in potential for further exploration. The argument that the features of the ideology may transcend the context necessitated focusing on several different types of application and their functions rather than on specific programs in use. It would naturally benefit from classroom case studies, but a classroom focus was not possible in a paper of this length. The issues arising from the theory outlined here need to be explored in research focusing in particular on comparative studies of particular examples of the genres in use in the classroom, as a result of which the observations concerning the nature of a transcendent ideology can be validated and refined. Some of the questions which need to be addressed are as follows:

- **Features** What general characteristics do experienced users associate with the computer as a medium, and with particular uses of it as a tool? What strategies does the computer make possible which cannot be employed with other tools? What strategies does it inhibit?
- **Choice** How far are users conscious of such qualities as being advantageous or disadvantageous for specific purposes? Does such awareness help users to make a conscious choice whether or not (and how) to use the computer for particular applications? Do teachers who are responsible for introducing students to the use of the computer as a tool regard it as necessary to teach students to be conscious of constraints as well as advantages? Is it possible to teach users to be conscious of the computer embodying an ideology?
- **Strategies** When does a lack of such awareness result in users adapting their intentions and strategies to the constraints of the tool? What strategies do students employ when they are using the computer as a tool which differ from strategies they might otherwise employ for the same task? Is the technology ever responsible for the transformation of users' learning styles? Are users ever conscious of this, and how do they feel about it?
- **Values and concepts** How far are *social values* and the understanding of key concepts such as *information, thinking, learning* and *the purpose of writing* influenced by students' use of computers over

time? What evidence is there that the technology is promoting technocratic goals in schools? How far do the applications found in schools reflect or subvert the explicit or inexplicit educational philosophies of the classroom teacher and the school? Are the messages of the technology affected by the types of applications used?

Only after such questions have been addressed can we attempt to answer the question of whether it is actually possible to counteract the bias of such a dominant technology. Unless we can, the purpose of the computer in the classroom may not be that which teachers choose for it.

Acknowledgments

Without wishing to imply their complicity in what some will take to be a heretical stance, the author would like to express his thanks to friends and colleagues for their helpful comments on various drafts of this paper, especially Anthony Adams (University of Cambridge), David Butler, Don Clark (Open University), Stephen Clarke (University of Leeds), Geoff Evans (University College of Wales, Aberystwyth), Alan Greenwell (University of Lancaster), Ken Jones, Harry McMahon (University of Ulster), Peter Medway (University of Leeds), Mike Peacock (University of Leeds), Robert Protherough (University of Hull), Brent Robinson (University of Cambridge), Mike Sharples (University of Sussex), Matti Sinko (University of Helsinki), Leslie Stratta (formerly of the University of Birmingham), Ann Tregenza, Steve Westmore, and Joseph Weizenbaum (Massachusetts Institute of Technology). A mere acknowledgement is far from sufficient for the extensive and detailed observations of Stephen Marcus (University of California at Santa Barbara) whose dedication to true academic dialogue is a rare treasure.

Notes

1 See ILLICH, IVAN (1975) *Tools for Conviviality*, Glasgow, Fontana/Collins, p. 101. Note that there is no contradiction between this and the assertion that the computer projects an ideology, since it is argued that the ideology is part of the nature of the medium.
2 BOWERS, C.A. (1988) *The Cultural Dimensions of Educational Computing*, New York, Teachers College Press, p. 43. This book, which came to the author's attention only during late revision of this paper, is thoroughly recommended to the reader as a broad and stimulating treatment of the theme.
3 Jean-Francois Lyotard has argued that the emphasis in the computer culture on 'scientific' information is undermining a traditional narrative form of knowledge in which human relationships are central. See Lyotard, J.-F.

(1984) *The Postmodern Condition: A Report on Knowledge*, Minneapolis, University of Minnesota Press.

4 Stephen Marcus has suggested that databases are characterized here in a way that does not apply to some of them. He instances laser discs filled with still and motion images which have multiple-criteria search functions. These are not dealt with here because they are mixed media systems and would have required too great a digression into other technologies. Dr Marcus provocatively comments that he is not sure to what extent the computer is one medium or many media. It is the author's contention that the features of databases (and of other types of computer application) can clearly be identified even in such visual 'retrieval systems'.

5 WEIZENBAUM, JOSEPH (1976) *Computer Power and Human Reason: From Judgment to Calculation*, San Francisco, W.H. Freeman and Co., p. 238.

6 GEORGE, FRANK (1979) *Man the Machine*, London, Paladin/Granada, p. 184.

7 The brain is presented as a model builder, a creative agent, in the work of Jerome Bruner: 'We now regard perception as a constructive process, in which we build a perceptual world from samplings of the sensory field,' (quoted in MILLER, JONATHAN (1983) *States of Mind*, New York, Pantheon, p. 40). For an accessible introduction to contemporary reading theory based on constructive meaning-making see SMITH, FRANK (1978) *Reading*, Cambridge University Press. See also ISER, W. (1978) *The Act of Reading: A Theory of Aesthetic Response*, London, Routledge and Kegan Paul.

8 For a very readable philosophical refutation of the view of the mind as a computer program see SEARLE, JOHN (1984) *Minds, Brains and Science*, Harmondsworth, Penguin, Chapter 2, 'Can Computers Think?'.

9 See SMITH, FRANK (1983) *Essays into Literacy*, London, Heinemann, p. 119. Brian Sutton-Smith has argued that mind is a narrative concern revolving around interpretation and consensus. See SUTTON-SMITH, BRIAN (1983) 'The origins of fiction and the fictions of origin', in BRUNER E. (Ed.) *Story, Play, Text*, Washington, D.C., Proceedings of the American Ethnological Association. See also note 3 above.

10 Theodore Roszak comments on the work of creative artists: 'If their work ... could be computerized — and there are those who see this as a sensible project — it would overlook the elemental fact that in the making of these glorious things, these images, these utterances, these gestures, there was a supreme joy, and that the achievement of that joy was the purpose of their work.... The technical mind that by-passes the making in favour of the made has already missed the entire meaning of this thing we call 'creativity''.' See ROSZAK, THEODORE (1969) *The Making of a Counter Culture*, New York, Anchor/Doubleday, p. 234.

11 PLATO, *Phaedrus*, section 275, in Walter Hamilton's (1973) translation: PLATO, *Phaedrus & Letters VII and VIII*, Harmondsworth, Penguin, p. 97.

12 This is not to suggest, of course, that the rewards in using a database may not be real, as many academics who have used online bibliographic databases will testify.

13 Weizenbaum, *Computer Power and Human Reason*, p. 38.

14 As the scientist and philosopher Michael Polanyi has argued, there is no such thing as 'objectivity'. See POLANYI, MICHAEL (1959) *Personal Knowledge: Towards a Post-Critical Philosophy*, Chicago, University of Chicago Press.

15 LeGuin, Ursula (1982) in Wood, Susan (Ed.) *The Language of the Night*, New York, Berkeley, p. 68.

16 The allusion here (and in the later section on 'positive discrimination') to simulations of passenger behaviour in urban transport systems reflects the author's critical stance on the use of one of his own programs (developed with Steve Westmore) — THE BUS GAME — published as part of 'Technology and Design, Part 2' (BBC Soft, 1988), although no criticism of the formal model developed by the Transport and Road Research Laboratory is intended.

17 Marcuse, Herbert (1968) *One-Dimensional Man*, London, Sphere, p. 122.

18 Berger, Peter L. and Luckmann, Thomas (1967) *The Social Construction of Reality: A Treatise in the Sociology of Knowledge*, Anchor, p. v.

19 'The programmer acts within a context of language, culture, and previous understanding, both shared and personal. The program is forever limited to working within the world determined by the programmer's explicit articulation of possible objects, properties, and relations among them. It therefore embodies the blindness that goes with this articulation' (Winograd, Terry and Flores, Fernando (1986) *Understanding Computers and Cognition*, Norwood, N.J., Ablex, p. 97).

20 Gould's research at IBM suggested that even very experienced users of word-processors tended to tinker with their text even after they had stopped improving its quality. See Gould, John G. (1981) 'Composing letters with computer-based text editors', *Human Factors*, 23 (5).

21 As Mike Peacock has pointed out, 'good literature' may not necessarily be fresh and spontaneous: James Joyce and Flaubert, for instance, both made extensive use of redrafting. The point here is that with the word-processor there is a danger that one way of writing may be encouraged at the expense of another.

22 Joseph Weizenbaum, personal communication, 22 June 1988.

23 Banks-Martin, Nancy, quoted in Berman, Caroline (1988) 'Hands-on Types', *The Guardian*, 18 February, p. 25.

24 See Collins, Allan and Gentner, D. (1980) 'A framework for a cognition theory of writing', in Gregg, L.W. and Steinberg, E. (Eds) *Cognitive Processes in Writing*, New Jersey, Lawrence Erlbaum Associates, pp. 51–72.

25 It would be interesting to discover whether the amount of use a word-processor function receives is directly related to the effort it takes to use it.

26 Chandler, Daniel (1986) 'Writing in the third person, *The Times Educational Supplement*, 24 October. For further comments by the author on the word-processor as a writing tool, see his *Young Learners and the Micro-computer* (1984), Milton Keynes, Open University Press, Chapter 3, 'Words which dance in light', reprinted also in Scanlon, Eileen and O'Shea, Tim (1987) *Educational Computing*, Chichester, John Wiley.

27 Word-processors contain 'default' settings which one must either conform to or consciously change. For instance, the word-processor used for this paper defaults to right-justified text, that is, every time one uses it for writing one must turn off that function unless one wants all one's text automatically spaced across the page and aligned to both margins as in a printed book. As it happens, this writer usually prefers text with a ragged right-hand margin (since it provides more cues for the reader).

28 The term 'artificial writing' (*ars artificialiter scribendi*) comes from a description of an early form of printing in a document dated 1444 (quoted in FEBVRE, LUCIEN and MARTIN, HENRI-JEAN (1984) *The Coming of the Book: The Impact of Printing 1450–1800*, London, Verso, p. 52).

29 JACKSON, HAROLD (1988) 'Prose and cons', *The Guardian*, 8 December, p. 33.

30 Reflecting on the preceding observations on the distinctive character of writing with a word-processor, Stephen Marcus has suggested that there may be scope for a literary version of the Turing Test of Machine Intelligence: 'Do you think a group of judges could distinguish between (the published versions of) two short stories, one written with a computer (word processor) and one without?'. Readers may find it entertaining to review the academic offerings currently before them with the same question in mind.

31 BOLTER, J. DAVID (1986) *Turing's Man: Western Culture in the Computer Age*, Harmondsworth, Penguin, p. 131. It has been objected that an element of ambiguity is allowed in certain computer languages, such as POP-11, in which the symbol → means different things in different contexts, and that referential ambiguity can exist in data structures. However, such examples pertain only to the deliberate specification of explicit alternatives: they are quite alien to the creative human use of ambiguity. For instance, (contrary to what some critics might lead us to believe) symbols in art and poetry are not ciphers which it is possible to 'translate' into unambiguous words: the symbols themselves are the only possible way of saying what they say. See ROSZAK, THEODORE (1973) *Where the Wasteland Ends*, New York, Anchor/Doubleday, pp. 127–30.

32 ELLUL, JACQUES (1964) *The Technological Society*, New York, Vintage/Random House, p. 135.

33 Ibid., p. 98.

34 See ONG, WALTER (1982) *Orality and Literacy: The Technologizing of the Word*, Methuen, Chapter 4.

35 See GOODY, JACK (1987) *The Interface between the Written and the Oral*, Cambridge, Cambridge University Press, especially Chapter 7.

36 See BOWERS, C.A. (1987) 'Teaching a 19th century mode of thinking through a 20th century machine', in *Proceedings of the National Educational Computer Conference*, Oregon, International Council on Computers for Education, pp. 114–18.

37 POSTMAN, NEIL (1979) *Teaching as a Conserving Activity*, New York, Dell, p. 48.

38 Significantly, many courses about computers are presented as 'computer literacy' courses.

39 Ellul, *The Technological Society*, p. 5.

40 Ibid., p. 99.

41 Postman, *Teaching as a Conserving Activity*, p. 96.

42 McLUHAN, MARSHALL and FIORE, QUENTIN (1968) *War and Peace in the Global Village*, New York, Bantam, p. 18.

43 The issue of the computer as a 'technological fix' is explored in relation to writing in schools in an article by the author (see note 26).

44 Joseph Weizenbaum, quoted in LONG, MARION (1985) 'Turncoat of the computer revolution', *New Age Journal*, December, p. 49.

45 Ross, Alastair, in Jones, Ron (1984) *Micros in the Primary Classroom*, London, Edward Arnold, p. 43. Note that this passage and the other commentaries on educational aims were selected not as targets for implied criticism but as brief passages from accessible sources representative of typical advocacy of the educational aims of particular applications. They have been taken out of contexts in which their purpose was inevitably different.

46 John Holt, personal communication, 22 December 1983.

47 See, for instance, Underwood, Jean (1986) 'The role of the computer in developing children's classificatory abilities', *Computer Education*, Vol. 10, No. 1, pp. 175–80.

48 Historical Association, *Computers in Secondary School History Teaching*, quoted in Adams, Anthony and Jones, Esmor (1983) *Teaching Humanities in the Microelectronic Age*, Milton Keynes, Open University Press. See also note 45.

49 See Bowers' analysis of cultural bias in the VOYAGEUR program in his book mentioned in note 2.

50 See note 16.

51 Robinson, Brent (1985) *Microcomputers and the Language Arts*, Milton Keynes, Open University Press, pp. 84–5. See also note 45.

52 A useful table of features for various writing media (together with a valuable outline of a variety of writers' approaches to writing) can be found in Sharples, Mike and Pemberton, Lyn (1988) 'Representing writing: an account of the writing process with regard to the writer's external representations', Brighton, School of Cognitive Sciences, University of Sussex.

53 Papert, Seymour (1980) *Mindstorms: Children, Computers and Powerful Ideas*, Brighton, Harvester Press, pp. 48–50; Roszak, Theodore (1986) *The Cult of Information*, Cambridge, Lutterworth, p. 81.

54 Watson, J.B. (1925) *Behaviourism* (reprinted 1970, New York and London, W.W. Norton) quoted in Koestler, Arthur (1967) *The Ghost in the Machine*, London, Pan, p. 28.

55 The author would like to point out that he does not claim to be immune to manipulation by computer-based tools, despite his efforts to be alert to the danger.

Notes on Contributors

Michael Apple, one of America's most distinguished Sociologists of Education, teaches at the University of Wisconsin, Madison. He is the author of a large number of publications which address threats to democracy and education, most notably *Education and Power* (1982) and *Teachers and Texts* (1986) from which the paper in this volume is taken.

Michael Barnett is Reader in Physics and Research Coordinator for Remote Sensing at Imperial College, London. He is at present Visiting Fellow, Post-16 Education Centre, University of London Institute of Education.

John Beynon is Reader in Communication Studies in the Polytechnic of Wales. A former journalist, he became first an English and Social Studies teacher in London area comprehensive schools and then a teacher trainer. He has published widely in the ethnography of schooling (most notably *Initial Encounters*, Falmer Press, 1985) and is currently completing a book on masculinity and education to be published by Routledge in 1991.

Richard Capel worked in special education for twelve years in both compulsory and post-16 education. Since completing an MA in 1983 he has had a strong research interest in Information Technology in education. He has recently been involved in a European COMET project concerning human-centred computer integrated manufacture and has written extensively on special needs in further education.

Daniel Chandler lectures on the Masters degree in Educational Technology at the University College of Wales, Aberystwyth. He is the author of several books on educational computing, including *Young Learners and the Micro-Computer*, Open University Press, 1984. He is currently engaged in research on writers, writing and the word-processor.

Keith Grint has taught sociology at Brunel University since 1986. Prior to that he was Research Fellow at Nuffield College, Oxford. He has diverse research interests and is currently concerned with the social aspects of computer networks and racism within trade unions. His book, *The Sociology of Work: An Introduction*, was published by the Polity Press in 1990.

Hughie Mackay lectures on social aspects of technology at the Polytechnic of Wales. He holds dual postgraduate qualifications both as a technologist and a sociologist. Between 1981 and 1985 he carried out field-based research on school management for the Open University, most notably *Headteachers at Work* (with Valerie Hall and Colin Morgan, Open University Press, 1986). His recent research had been into the sociology of technology and he is the editor (with Michael Young and John Beynon) of the companion volumes, *Understanding Technology in Education* and *Computers into Classrooms* (Falmer Press, 1991). He is currently developing with colleagues a taught M.Sc. in Innovation, Culture and Technology to start in the Autumn of 1991.

Peter Medway taught English and Humanities for many years in secondary schools. On joining the School of Education at Leeds University he led the team which carried out the national evaluation of the TVEI curriculum, participating in a special study of technology education, an interest he has since maintained in lecturing and writing. He has a particular concern with language-related aspects of technological activity; with technology as an aspect of practical capability more generally; and with technology as a component of post-compulsory vocational and academic curricula. He now lectures in the Department of Linguistics, Carleton University, Ottawa.

Index